Perspectives on Indian Education

Perspectives on Indian Education

Kavita A. Sharma

GYAN

ISBN : 978-81-212-1313-4

Price : ₹ 890

First Published, 2017

Published by

Gyan Publishing House
5, Ansari Road
Daryaganj, New Delhi-110002
Phone: 9811692060
E-mail: books@gyanbooks.com

Printed at: G. Print Process, Delhi.

Cataloging in Publication Data—DK
Courtesy: D.K. Agencies (P) Ltd. <docinfo@dkagencies.com>

Sharma, Kavita A., author.
Perspectives on Indian education / Kavita A. Sharma.
pages cm
Includes bibliographical references.
ISBN 9788121213134

1. Education, Higher—India. I. Title.

LA1153.S53 2016 DDC 378.54 23

Contents

Dedicated to
My husband Amb. J.C. Sharma and the future,
our grandchildren Maya, Trayi and Viraat

Foreword

The saga of education in India is complex and varied. It is also central to the development of the nation, especially as it plays an ever-increasing role in the global knowledge economy. This book provides an analysis of a range of central issues, from contemporary higher education themes to the role of Swami Vivekananda's views on education.

The complexities discussed in this book include differing philosophies of education that have competed for attention in India over time, the divisiveness of affirmative action and reservations, education and religious minorities, the internationalisation of higher education, and others.

Significant attention is paid to affirmative action and reservations. Here, the Indian experience, both the successes and failures, can be useful to other countries, since India is not the only country affected by deep and embedded inequalities in access and success in education. Indeed, India probably has the most stringent set of policies relating to affirmative action for a range of populations in the world. A significant part of this book is focused on analyses of aspects of this theme.

Kavita Sharma brings a lifetime of concern with education and scholarship and analysis of key educational issues to this book. Her insights will assist in understanding a range of still perplexing problems.

Philip G. Altbach
Center for International Higher Education
Boston College, USA

Acknowledgement

This book is a collection of articles written over several years. These also form a part of my journey in trying to understand and grapple with Education and in particular with Higher Education. Many institutions and people have been a part of my journey and I would like to acknowledge all of them. While it is impossible to name all, I would like to thank among institutions, Indian Council of Philosophical Research, Centre for Policy Research, University Grants Commission, National University of Educational Planning and Administration, Fulbright New Century Scholars Program, Sharada Mission, North Gujarat University and Banaras Hindu University. Of course, the most important is Hindu College, Delhi University where I have spent the major part of my life and which has provided incentives in more ways than one to make me write.

Dr Subhash Kashyap, Dr Amrik Singh, Dr Arun Nigvekar, Dr K.B. Powar, Dr Ved Prakash, Dr Pratap Bhanu Mehta, Dr Govinda, Dr Kirit Joshi and many other colleagues and seniors have played a part in the writing of these essays, stimulating thought, discussing and giving me insights that were invaluable.

Thanks are due to Ms Rajesh Sharma, Ms Nirmala Hari and Ms Vardhani for providing patient and untiring secretarial assistance. Ms Indu Ramchandani has been all through with me painstakingly editing each one of these articles. I am also grateful to Pankaj Kumar for copy-editing these articles.

Finally, I would like to thank my husband Amb. J.C. Sharma who had been with me in my journey of life till, January 2014. Without his unstinting support, my writing could never have materialised.

Kavita A. Sharma

Preface

When Shri Amit Garg of Gyan Publishing House came to me with the proposal that he wanted to bring out a volume of my writing on education, I was surprised, humbled, and even a little amused, all at once. I didn't think I had done that much work, nor did I think that anyone would be interested in what I had written. When he persisted, I tried to collect my scattered pieces on education and the outcome is this book—a collection of essays that have been written for different occasions and different publications, over a long period of time. I have of course, left out several essays as I have tried to create some order in the volume.

In the first section, beginning with independent India, we have the Constitution and the journey, which made education a fundamental right from a directive principle. The section, then, deals with some institutions that have shaped the evolution and growth of education in India such as, the University Grants Commission, the Association of Indian Universities, and the National University of Educational, Planning and Administration. The second section deals with contemporary issues such as, globalisation and its impact on the education system of India together with the emergence of the private sector. The issues pertaining to affirmative action, education of religious minorities and vocational education occupy a sizeable space as they are such vital preoccupations in our mental landscape. The place of research and its relevance to society, the internationalisation of education and education as a soft power have been seen from my eyes as a socially concerned educator.

The final section is more philosophical as it tries to connect education to the spiritual strand that has been a part of educational thought in India and to some visions and aspirations of a national education during the independence struggle. It ends with the contribution of Pandit Madan Mohan Malviya in setting up a major university, the Banaras Hindu University, in which he brought together the strands of Indian knowledge, traditions, and a contemporary scientific outlook.

This collection is by no means exhaustive in the issues that I have touched upon. It is only an attempt to share with my readers as I tried to grapple with some of my thought processes that resonated in me over the years, and which may concern them as well.

I'm grateful to various organisations that gave me an opportunity to think, study and learn. Some of these are the Centre for Studies in Civilisations, the University Grants Commission, the Association of Indian Universities, the Fulbright Scholar Programmes of the United States Department of State Bureau of Educational and Cultural Affairs, Hindu College, Delhi, Ministry of External Affairs, the Centre for Policy Research, the Gnostic Centre and others. Similarly, I have received guidance and affection from so many people that it would be impossible to name all those to whom I owe a debt of gratitude. However, I would like to acknowledge that I learnt some vital things in my life from Dr Bharat Ram, Dr Kapila Vatsyayan and Professor Amrik Singh. My parents Professor L.P. Agarwal and Dr Savitri Agarwal, both eminent doctors, taught me to strive continuously, which made me continue to write in spite of heavy administrative and family responsibilities. This book would not have been possible without my dear friend Ms Indu Ramachandani, who not only always encourages me and puts things in perspective but also painstakingly reads and edits everything I write. Finally, I want to thank my husband Ambassador J.C. Sharma, who is no more with me physically but with whom I always walked hand-in-hand and continue to do so, in spirit.

Kavita A. Sharma

Part - I

1

Education as a Constitutional Right*

In November 2002, education from the age of 6 to 14 years became a fundamental right. As it has been realised, the right to education has to be correlated with human rights—without education, other human rights cannot be achieved either. In the Indian context, the power of education was realised both by the colonial rulers and the nationalist leaders, although for different reasons. Hence, education became a contested site and formed an integral part of the independence movement. It was accorded the highest priority in the Constituent Assembly. However, the country did not have resources to provide education for all. Therefore, it was made a Directive Principle of State Policy rather than a Fundamental Right. But its significance is evident from the fact that Article 45 of the Constitution was the only one that prescribed a deadline —ten years from the date of coming into force of the Constitution —for the universalisation of education up to the age of 14 years. Since then this deadline had to be extended, ten years at a time, up to 2002 when education became a fundamental right.

The issue of compulsory education moved centrestage with the Supreme Court verdict in the *Mohini Jain* case in 1992 when it said that Directive Principles were fundamental to the governance of the country and could not be read separately from Fundamental Rights. It saw the right to education as an integral part of the right to life guaranteed under Article 21. In 1993, the Supreme Court reiterated this in the *Unnikrishnan* case making it incumbent upon the State to provide basic education to all citizens during their childhood. By the 1990s, there was worldwide increased attention on education and India was staking its claim in the international community

* A much longer version of this article was published in Kashyap, Subhash, C. (ed.). 2014. *Constitutional History of India: Federalism, Elections, Government and Rule of Law*, History of Science, Philosophy and Culture in Indian Civilisation, Vol. XIV, Part 5B, Gen. Editor, D.P. Chattopadhyaya, New Delhi: Centre for Studies in Civilisations.

as a major player. So, it could not afford to lag behind in the social indices of growth. Ideas such as the human development indices had already gained currency in the minds of policy makers. Ultimately, on the recommendation of a Committee headed by Muhi Ram Saikia, it was decided to make education up to 14 years of age a fundamental right through a constitutional amendment.

The effectiveness of legislation as an instrument of empowerment, however, can only be gauged from the qualitative difference it makes to both individuals and groups who are entitled to it. Children from marginalised families still cannot access schooling and even when able to, many drop out only to get absorbed into the workforce in the informal sector. The task ahead is daunting. The issue is not just of access to schooling but also that of reforming the entire teaching and learning process, and revamping the obsolete administrative apparatus that hinders more than it serves.

The 86th Amendment to the Indian Constitution that made education a Fundamental Right from the age of 6 to 14 years was inserted as Article 21(A) making it possible for any citizen to seek enforcement of the right by way of resorting to writ jurisdiction under Article 32. A corresponding duty was imposed upon the parents to send their children to school by Article 51(A) making it their Fundamental Duty to do so. Article 45 was amended to make the state "endeavour to provide early childhood care and education for all children until they complete six years of age." Thus, a long process that started in 1996 was completed six years later.

Directive Principle versus Fundamental Right

Several questions arise. Education for children from 6 to 14 years of age was already a Directive Principle under Article 45, so what was the need to make it a Fundamental Right? What is a Directive Principle and what is its importance? How did the Executive view its obligation to provide universal elementary education and what steps did it take to achieve it? Why was it not achieved in ten years as had been mandated in Article 45? Was it because the state saw it as only one social goal out of many and hence did not accord it the priority that was needed? Did the state not do this because it felt that the economy would not be able to absorb so many educated youth and unemployment would create social unrest? What view did the judiciary take of this constitutional directive to the state? What difference would it make to move the provision of universal elementary education from Directive Principles to Fundamental Rights? That is, what are the implications of education as a Fundamental Right and how would it be enforced? Against whom would it be enforced? Why was it necessary to impose a duty on parents and guardians to educate their children?

Leaders with political authority and moral influence both in pre-independence and post-independence India had recognised the pivotal role of education but somehow this recognition had not translated into effective implementation. Gopal Krishna Gokhale, for instance, was a strong advocate of the promotion of basic education and as soon as the Indian Councils Act of 1909 made it possible for Indians to propose legislative reform. He formulated the pioneering Elementary Education Bill to empower local authorities to introduce compulsory education.

Mohandas Karamchand Gandhi placed a moral premium on education. He rightly did not identify literacy with education. Literacy was neither the end of education nor even the beginning. Education for Gandhi was something that visibly distinguished man from beast. Real education was one that enabled one to discriminate between good and bad. It involved training of the mind, will and control of desires. Gandhi wanted it to be so revolutionised as to answer the wants of the poorest villager and develop each individual to his highest potential. It would not only mould the new generation, but would also reflect a society's fundamental assumptions about itself. In true Indian tradition, the function of *Nayee-Talim* was not to teach an occupation, but through it to develop the whole person.

Gandhi rejected colonial education and put forward a radical alternative. His proposal intended to turn the education system on its head and change the established structure of access to educational opportunities. He knew that democracy could be made functional not just by the assimilation of facts, but by right education. He asserted that only that education could be truly national, which reflected the national conditions. He saw spinning and weaving, therefore, as an essential part of any national system of education. The idea was not simply to introduce handicrafts as a compulsory school subject, but to make the learning of a craft the centrepiece of the entire teaching programme. It implied a radical restructuring of the sociology of school knowledge in India where productive handicrafts had been associated with the lowest groups in the hierarchy of the caste system. The aim of university education, according to Gandhi, was to turn out true servants of the people who would live and die for the country's freedom. Gandhi was equally concerned with equity and accessibility of education to all and to that extent he recommended the establishment of *Vidyapeeth*s in the villages.

Dr B.R. Ambedkar too regarded education as vital for the liberation of the oppressed castes. Education was also of paramount concern to social reformers and political figures, such as Ram Mohan Roy, Maharshi Karve, Pandita Ramabai, Swami Vivekananda, Sri Aurobindo, Jyotiba Phule, and Rabindranath Tagore of pre-independent India. The founding fathers of modern India and the framers of the Constitution were, therefore, fully conscious of the importance of education in making India a strong nation, but they faced a daunting task. Nevertheless, they took measures to make it an integral part of the Constitution by placing it in the Directive Principles. Dr S. Radhakrishnan, the first Vice President, Pandit Jawaharlal Nehru, the first Prime Minister, and Maulana Abul Kalam Azad, the first Education Minister, all had a deep love for learning and were convinced that without education there could neither be free and enlightened citizens nor could the much-needed skill and talent be developed in the country. They not only emphasised the vital role of education, but also dreamt of quality education.

Azad thought education was the birthright of every individual, the means by which he could develop all facets of his personality. Education gave a person access to the world of knowledge and helped him to live harmoniously with his environment. At a practical level, it enabled him to acquire the skills needed to earn his livelihood but the real object of education was to make students useful members of the community. Therefore, he felt it was imperative for the government to put into place a liberal and humanitarian system of education. Nehru saw the improvement of the individual as the main aim of education and was convinced that without it social progress was not possible. India, he said, had decided to give the highest priority to education so that people could imbibe the values of reason and tolerance. Education, for Nehru, was not merely a matter of acquiring the skills of reading and writing. Essentially, it had to develop minds so that they had the flexibility to accept new ideas and values. Simultaneously, it had to train people in manual craft and make them useful to society.[1] For Radhakrishnan, education, apart from its individual and social values, developed ethical and spiritual values that were necessary for both the individual and society. A philosopher and teacher, he headed the First Education Commission on universities of independent India.

International Recognition of Fundamental Rights

By the twentieth century, Fundamental Rights were recognised and incorporated in the constitutions of all civilised states. Sweden had taken the lead and they gradually became a part of the law of nearly all European states spreading in time to the rest of the world. Many states enumerated social and economic matters in their constitutions, but they tried to distinguish between rights, those that were inalienable and those, being social in nature, that depended on state laws for their implementation. In this context, the constitutions of the Principality of Liechtenstein of October 5, 1921 and that of the Spanish Republic of December 9, 1931 were significant.

The Constitution of the Principality of Liechtenstein, for the first time, devoted a separate chapter guaranteeing economic and social rights to its citizens. The phraseology used indicates that the economic and social provisions were more or less directives to the state and not as binding in character as those relating to individual rights. However, the separate chapter on social and economic matters in this Constitution did not have much influence on the framing of subsequent constitutions because Liechtenstein was a very small principality in Europe.

A decade later, the Constitution of the Spanish Republic of 1931 made a similar separation of economic and social rights from political and personal rights. Two separate chapters were provided in Part III of the Constitution. One dealt with fundamental rights, entitled, "Rights and Duties of Spaniards: Individual and Political Guarantees." The other was concerned with social and economic rights and was called, "Family, Economic Conditions and Culture." Again the phraseology indicated that the social and economic rights were in the nature of 'Directives' to the state although this was not explicitly stated. The Spanish directives were wider in scope than those of the Principality of Liechtenstein because they included family and cultural matters apart from social and economic ones. Both, however, suffered from serious defects. They went into too many details that should normally have been left to administration and legislation. Both countries being predominantly Roman Catholic, the impact of religion was evident and that made it difficult for non-Catholic and secular countries to completely emulate.[2]

The Constitution of Ireland, which came into force on December 29, 1937, made a clear distinction between "Fundamental Rights" relating to personal rights and others pertaining to family, education, private property, religion, and social and economic matters that were placed under "Directive Principles of State Policy."[3] This not only served to indicate their importance, as they were made a part of the Constitution, but there was also an awareness that it was difficult to provide for them. They nevertheless represented a significant advance as for the first time a clear distinction was made between justiciable and non-justiciable rights within a constitutional document. Apart from the Irish Constitution, a similar distinction was recognised by Dr Lauterpacht in the *International Bill of the Rights of Man*. The substantial provisions of the Bill were in two parts. Part I dealt with rights to be enforced by ordinary courts and Part II incorporated those that were incapable of or unsuitable for such enforcement.

Fundamental Rights in the Indian Constitution

As the Indian Constitution was being drafted, the question arose about incorporating justiciable fundamental rights. At the same time, there were socialist ideals of economic and social equity that could not be made judicially enforceable because by their very nature they depended on societal factors and resources available and were therefore not matters of simple enforcement by the courts. Yet, the thought was that they were so vital and significant in laying down the roadmap for the future of India that they should also be a part of the Constitution.

Sir B.N. Rau, the Constitutional Advisor to the Constituent Assembly, who had studied the other constitutions, was instrumental in separating the Fundamental Rights from the Directive Principles. He was familiar with the Constitutions of Principality of Liechtenstein, of Spain and Ireland as well as with the *International Bill of the Rights of Man*. Following their example, Sir B.N. Rau explained that there were two broad classes of rights. One required the State to abstain from taking prejudicial action. The second required it to take positive action. The former could be easily enforced, but the latter could only be guaranteed in so far as it was practicable. For example, the State could not guarantee the right to work beyond making a policy that gave citizens opportunities to find occupations through which they could earn a livelihood. Other factors, such as economic development came into play for this right to become a reality. The State, on the other hand, could on its own ensure that nobody was deprived of his liberty without the due process of law.[4] Thus, Sir B.N. Rau said that one kind of right was not suitable for enforcement by legal action while the courts could enforce the other. However, he noticed that in some constitutions like former USSR and Germany, both classes of rights had been placed together probably because, "Neither was intended to be enforced by legal action."[5] It was only in the Irish Constitution in 1937 that a distinction had been made between the enforceable Fundamental Rights and the non-enforceable Directive Principles of Social Policy. Thus, both Fundamental Rights and Fundamental Principles of State Policy or Directive Principles were incorporated into the Indian Constitution; the former relating to personal and political rights enforceable by the courts and the latter relating to social, economic and other matters unenforceable by the courts.

The Directives had to be implemented by the legislature and the executive as they were fundamental to governance. They differed from fundamental rights in as much as the electorate could not demand their enforcement through the court as a matter of right. Ultimately a bifurcation was made in the Constitution between civil and political rights, and social and economic because the latter, it was felt, could not be made enforceable until appropriate actions were taken by the State to bring about changes in the economy.

The Directives embody the ideals and aspirations of the people. They elaborate on the proclamation made in the Preamble and are the goals of a welfare state. But since their realisation is dependent on finances and time factors, it is difficult to subject them to judicial scrutiny. If a chapter on "Fundamental Rights" is essential for a modern democratic State with a written Constitution, it is equally important to incorporate a chapter on Directive Principles of State Policy for a welfare state. It has been considered more important to implement the Directives than even the Fundamental Rights if a choice had to be made between the two. The First and Fourth Amendments were done to give effect to the Directives. Nehru observed while moving for consideration of the Lok Sabha, the Constitution (First Amendment) Bill on 16 May 1951:

> The whole conception of the Fundamental Rights is the protection of individual liberty and freedom....That might be said to be the dominating idea of the nineteenth century and it was continued and it is a matter of fundamental importance. Nevertheless, as the nineteenth century marched into the twentieth century and as the twentieth century went ahead, other additional ideas came into the field, which are represented by the Directive Principles of State Policy.[6]

Since the Indian leaders were convinced that education was the key to nation building and that every individual had a right to get education, they gave the States the responsibility of providing free compulsory education up to the age of 14. Although this provision was made a part of Directive Principles, which are not justiciable in a court of law rather than as part of enforceable Fundamental Rights, its importance had been consistently emphasised.

The Courts had been gradually emphasising that it was necessary and important to implement the Directive Principles, but the rise of Public Interest Litigation in the 1970s was a major initiative on the part of the Supreme Court to reach out easily to the people. It was recognition of the fact that the majority of the population was unable to access the judicial system because of social, economic and other liabilities. The judiciary tried to infuse the spirit of social justice into the constitutional provisions.

In particular, the ambit of Article 21 dealing with life and liberty kept expanding to include even the right to a passport as it encompassed the right to travel.

Once the Court took a broader view of the scope and content of the fundamental right to life and liberty, Article 21 was interpreted to include what really were economic, social and cultural rights and which had been enshrined mainly in the Directive Principles. In *Francis Coralie Mullin*, the Court declared:

> The right to life includes the right to live with human dignity and all that goes with it, namely, the bare necessities of life such as adequate nutrition, clothing and shelter and facilities for reading, writing and expressing oneself in diverse forms, freely moving about and mixing and commingling with fellow human beings. The magnitude and components of these rights would depend upon the extent of economic development of the country, but it must, in any view of the matter, include the bare necessities of life and also the right to carry on such functions and activities as constitute the bare minimum expression of the human soul.[7]

The real breakthrough in the field of education came with *Mohini Jain vs State of Karnataka.*[8] The question was whether private medical and engineering colleges could charge capitation fee as a consideration for admission to non-meritorious students. Mohini Jain from Meerut was admitted to Sri Medical College in the State of Karnataka in February/March 1991 and asked to deposit of Rs 60,000 as the tuition fee for the first year. This was according to the differential fee structure put in place by the medical college. The candidates admitted under "Government Seats" were to pay Rs 2,000, the Karnataka students not admitted against Government Seats had to pay Rs 25,000 and those from outside Karnataka Rs 60,000 per annum. Mohini Jain's father wrote to the Management that he could not afford to pay Rs 60,000 and so she was denied admission.

The question that arose was whether there was a "right to education" guaranteed to the people of India under the Constitution. Taking into consideration Articles 21, 38, 39 (a) and (f), 41 and 45, the Supreme Court said:

> It is no doubt correct that 'right to education' as such has not been guaranteed as a Fundamental Right under Part III of the Constitution, but reading the above quoted provisions cumulatively, it becomes clear that the framers of the Constitution made it obligatory for the state to provide education for its citizens. The preamble promises to secure justice "social, economic and political" for the citizens. A peculiar

> feature of the Indian Constitution is that it combines social and economic rights along with political and justiciable legal rights. The preamble embodies the goal which the State has to achieve in order to establish social justice and to make the masses free in the positive sense. The securing of social justice has been specifically enjoined an object of the State under Article 38 of the Constitution. Can the objective which has been so prominently pronounced in the preamble and Article 38 of the Constitution be achieved without providing education to the large majority of citizens who are illiterate? The objectives flowing from the preamble cannot be achieved and shall remain on paper unless the people in his country are educated. ...[A]n individual cannot be assured of human dignity unless his personality is developed and the only way to do that is to educate him.[9]

The Court cited Dr Ambedkar:

> In enacting this Part of the Constitution, the Assembly is giving certain directions to the future legislature and the future executive to show in what manner they are to exercise the legislative and the executive power they will have. Surely, it is not the intention to introduce in this Part these principles as mere pious declarations. It is the intention of the Assembly that in future both the legislature and the executive should not merely pay lip service to these principles but that they should be made the basis of all legislative and executive action that they may be taking hereafter in the matter of the governance of the country.[10]

From this, the Court concluded, "The Directive Principles which are fundamental in the governance of the country cannot be isolated from the Fundamental Rights guaranteed under Part III" and:

> The Fundamental Rights guaranteed under Part III of the Constitution of India including the right to freedom of speech and expression and other rights under Article 19 cannot be appreciated and fully enjoyed unless a citizen is educated and is conscious of his individualistic dignity. The "right to education", therefore, is concomitant to the Fundamental Rights enshrined under Part III of the Constitutional mandate to provide educational institutions at all levels for the benefit of the citizens.[11]

A larger bench of five judges in *K.P. Unnikrishnan vs State of Andhra Pradesh* examined the correctness of this decision. The Court refused to accept the non-enforceability of the Directive Principles. It asked:

> It is noteworthy that among the several articles in Part IV, only Article 45 speaks of a time-limit; no other article does. Has it no significance? Is it a mere pious wish, even after 44 years of the

> Constitution? Can the State flout the said direction even after 44 years on the ground that the Article merely calls upon it to endeavour to provide the same and on the further ground that the said article is not enforceable by virtue of the declaration in Article 37? Does not the passage of 44 years–more than four times the period stipulated in Article 45–convert the obligation created by the Article into an enforceable right? In this context, we feel constrained to say that allocation of available funds to different sectors of education in India discloses an inversion of priorities indicated by the Constitution...It is relevant to notice that Article 45 does not speak of the "limits of its economic capacity and development" as does Article 41, which *inter alia* speaks of right to education. What has actually happened is more money is spent and more attention is directed to higher education than to—and at the cost of—primary education. (By primary education, we mean the education, which a normal child receives by the time he completes 14 years of age.)...We clarify, we are not seeking to lay down the priorities for the government—we are only emphasising the constitutional policy as disclosed by Articles 45, 46 and 41. Surely the wisdom of these constitutional provisions is beyond question.[12]

The Court then proceeded to examine how this right would be enforceable and to what extent. It clarified the issue thus:

> The right to education further means that a citizen has a right to call upon the State to provide educational facilities to him within the limits of its economic capacity and development. By saying so, we are not transferring Article 41 from Part IV to Part III—we are merely relying upon Article 41 to illustrate the content of the right to education flowing from Article 21. We cannot believe that any State would say that it need not provide education to its people even within the limits of its economic capacity and development.[13]

The Department of Education, Ministry of Human Resource Development (HRD), initiated consultations in 1996 at various levels including consultations with political organisations and education experts. The proposal was discussed at the Conference of Chief Ministers on July 4-5, 1996 and again in a Conference of State Education Ministers and State Education Secretaries on August 9-10, 1996. The educational experts discussed the proposal at a conference chaired by Shri S.R. Bommai, the then Union Minister for HRD, on August 16, 1996. The administrative, legal and academic implications of the proposal of making education a justiciable Fundamental Right needed to be seriously considered. It was recommended that a committee of State Education Ministers be constituted to go into the matter in depth. Accordingly, the Ministry of HRD constituted a committee chaired by Shri Muhi Ram Saikia, the then Union Minister of State for HRD (Education), in August 1996.

The Saikia Committee

The Saikia Committee was to examine and consider the legal, academic, administrative, and financial implications of the proposal to amend the Constitution to make free and compulsory education a Fundamental Right. It was to suggest the statutory measures required for its implementation and to indicate guidelines for facilities that had to be provided, the lack of which would be justiciable.

The Committee finalised its report in a meeting held on January 10, 1997 in Cochin. It reviewed the status of free and compulsory education in India including the existing Constitutional, legal and policy framework.[14] Article 45 had directed the State to provide free and compulsory education up to the age of 14 years within ten years of the commencement of the Constitution. The National Policy on Education, both in 1986 and as modified in 1992 had also provided for free and compulsory education up to the age of 14 years before the beginning of the twenty first century. The Programme of Action (1992) to give effect to the National Policy too had outlined various strategies for achieving this goal.

The Committee found that while there was no central legislation making elementary education compulsory in the country, 14 states and four union territories had passed laws to make primary education obligatory. These statutes normally had three parts: the State Government had the power to notify areas in which the Act would be implemented; penalties were prescribed for not sending children to school; and an authority that could grant exemption from this legislation had been provided for. Tamil Nadu took a step forward in 1994. Instead of providing for gradual notification of areas to be covered by compulsory education, it enacted the Tamil Nadu Elementary Education Act 1994 that extended the legislation to the whole state rather than to notified pockets.[15]

The Committee also took into account the impetus given by the Supreme Court judgement in the Unnikrishnan case in 1993 in which it had unequivocally stated that the citizens of the country had a Fundamental Right to education and that this Right flowed from Article 21 of the Constitution. This was an enlargement of the scope of what constituted the right to life and liberty under Article 21.

Various state governments had already taken several measures, such as abolishing tuition fees up to upper primary schools in government schools.

Education in schools run by local bodies and private-aided institutions was also mostly free. But other related costs of education, such as textbooks and uniforms had to be borne by the parents. In the case of Scheduled Castes/Scheduled Tribes (SCs/STs) and girls, state governments had even provided for free textbooks, uniforms and other expenses at the primary level.

The Committee acknowledged that; even in States and Union Territories with the appropriate legislation, compulsory education remained largely unenforced because of various socio-economic and cultural factors together with administrative and financial constraints. The Central Government had not enacted a central legislation because it read Article 45 as binding on States rather than on parents. It had, therefore, advocated a consensual approach to motivate parents and children, the key elements of which were: community involvement; decentralisation of planning and management of school education; motivating children to attend school regularly; improving infrastructure and facilities in schools; developing locally relevant curricula; improving the quality of textbooks; teacher training; child-centred learning; and adopting minimum levels of learning.[16]

In order to universalise elementary education, both the Centre and the States emphasised three aspects: (i) Universal access to enrollment; (ii) Universal retention of children up to the age of 14 years; and (iii) Ensure substantial improvement in the quality of education to enable all children to achieve essential levels of learning.

The Committee noted that all these efforts had resulted in considerable gains. The number of primary schools had gone up to 5,90,421 and upper primary up to 1,71,216 in 1995–96 compared to 2,10,000 primary and 13,000 upper primary in 1980–81. This had resulted in massive expansion in student enrollment, especially in rural and semi-urban areas. According to the Fifth All India Education Survey, 94.6 per cent of rural habitations had a primary school within one km and 85.4 per cent had upper primary school within three km. But severe disparities still remained because of gender, regional, sectional, and caste factors. Only two-third of the number enrolled completed primary schooling and half, the upper primary. Even their achievement levels were very low. A large number of eligible children were out of school and a significant proportion dropped out, not only because of socio-economic and cultural factors, but also because of lack of infrastructure — low levels of learning, shortage of teachers, non-availability of teaching and learning materials and textbooks, and a curriculum that did not fulfil local needs. Thus, not only was there no central legislation to provide for free and compulsory education up to the age of 14 years, even states that had provided for it had been unable to implement it. About 6.3 crore children in the age group between 6 and 14 years were still out of school in India.[17]

The Committee felt that making compulsory and free elementary education a Fundamental Right could help in removing obstacles in the way of the universalisation of elementary education and operationalising it in a practical framework. However, it was an enormous task that involved administrative, academic and financial challenges in which the states, the Planning Commission and the Ministry of Finance would all have to co-operate. The States and Union Territories were asked to give the financial estimates of the costs involved including those of the administrative machinery required for implementation. The Union Law Secretary felt that while there would be administrative and legal difficulties in implementing the proposal, it would also have several beneficial fallouts. The constitutional amendment would help to build societal efforts to promote education. It would demonstrate that India had the necessary political will and administrative resolve to universalise education up to age 14. It would also send the right signals to the international community and donors that India was serious about achieving education for all by 2000. Further, both the government and non-government sectors would be galvanised into taking the necessary measures to provide education for all. It would put the required pressure on the central and state governments so that they felt the need to fulfil their commitment to provide six per cent of GDP for education, out of which 50 per cent would be spent on primary education. It was thought that the revitalisation of Panchayati Raj because of the 73rd Amendment had provided the necessary machinery for decentralisation and implementation of universal education at the ground level. There would be other beneficial spin-offs like it would help in the eradication of child labour. It would also positively impact other social indicators like population growth, health and women's development. It would also enhance economic productivity and reduce unemployment.[18]

Expert Group

The Saikia Committee was concerned about the possibility of large-scale litigation if elementary education became a fundamental right and the massive mobilisation of resources required for its implementation could not be found. Hence, an Expert Group was set up in 1998 to look into the financial resources that would be required for implementing universal elementary education.[19]

The Group pointed out that granting elementary education as a Fundamental Right to all citizens up to the age of 14 years implied that all children, including those who had so far been denied the opportunity of schooling would also have an equal entitlement to a period of formal and normal schooling to be provided by the State. The Group looked at innovative, alternative schooling forms but found that they were not less costly and hence advocating them on account of shortage of resources was not tenable.[20]

The Group noted that the judgement in the Unnikrishnan case was significant because education could no longer be regarded as just an incremental developmental goal. It had become a justiciable entitlement of every Indian child in the age group of 6 to 14 years, which could not be deferred by the State at its convenience. So far, universal elementary education had competed with other desirable social goals in the allocation of available resources, but a justiciable Fundamental Right meant that the State had to immediately make resources available for it superseding other important claims. Fortunately, education as a fundamental right had the support of all political parties. However, mammoth resources were required and there was a simultaneous need to monitor the spending to strictly guard against all forms of waste and corruption.

The Group spelt out how it would be possible to pay for universal elementary education out of normal budget allocations assuming a reasonable rate of growth of the GNP of about five per cent annually in real terms, a reasonable rate of increase in tax/GDP ratio from 16 to 18 per cent by 2007–08, and the gradual increase in the allocation of the Central and the State budgetary expenditure on education to reach about six per cent of the GDP by 2006–07. The Group estimated an additional requirement of Rs 1,36,822 crore with Rs 1,06,350 crore recurring and Rs 30,572 non-recurring expenditure over a period of ten years, between 1998–99 and 2007–08. This was higher than the estimate of Rs 40,000 crore made earlier by the Saikia Committee.

The Saikia Committee had also deliberated on whether compulsory education should only be a Fundamental Right or whether it should also be a Fundamental Duty so that every parent could be compelled to send the child to school. While a Fundamental Right would make it obligatory for the State to provide the necessary infrastructure and facilities for elementary education and the lack of which could be challenged in a court of law, making it a Fundamental Duty would also enable the State to penalise parents for not sending their children to school. Some members thought that considering the huge financial outlay involved, only primary education could initially be made a Fundamental Right. This could be reviewed after three to five years and after that the Fundamental Right could be extended to the upper primary levels. However, it was finally decided that since the commitment to free and compulsory education up to 14 years of age had been made within the Constitution, it was not possible to renege on it. Besides, the Supreme Court had also ruled along the same lines. Some members suggested that even Secondary Education could be made a Fundamental Right but the idea was dropped because the implications would be enormous.

Recommendations of the Saikia Committee

The Committee made some recommendations that would be required to make education both free and compulsory up to the age of 14 years a Fundamental Right after considering the necessary financial, academic and administrative measures:

1. The Constitution of India be amended to make education up to 14 years of age a Fundamental Right.
2. Simultaneously, an explicit provision in the Constitution to make education a Fundamental Duty of every citizen who is a parent or guardian to provide opportunities for elementary education to all children up to 14 years of age.
3. It was not necessary to enact a central legislation to make elementary education compulsory. States should either amend their existing laws or enact fresh legislation to give effect to the proposed constitutional amendments.
4. The Central Government to provide broad guidelines for its enactment in consultation with the States and the Union Territories.[21]
5. Fresh state legislation should:
   (i) allow the state governments and the local bodies to enforce the law selectively in a phased manner;
   (ii) provide grounds for exemption from compulsory school attendance;
   (iii) provide for imposing punishment on defaulting parents of which the minimum and maximum should be laid down;
   (iv) provide for establishing primary schools within a distance of 1–1.5 km from rural habitation provided there was a population of 250 in the catchments area;
   (v) provide for the establishment of upper primary schools within a distance of three km from rural habitation provided there was a population of 500 in the catchment areas; and

(vi) allow state governments to relax the last two norms in case of hill, desert, tribal, and inaccessible areas so that the proposed schools were viable but the existing state norms should not be flouted.[22]

6. The states should decide what they mean by free education according to their local requirements and constraints. But to ensure uniformity, free elementary education should include the following:

   (i) Exemption from tuition fee.

   (ii) Provision of free textbooks and stationery for all primary school children and girls up to the upper primary level.

   (iii) Mid-day meal programmes be continued.

   (iv) State governments may provide other incentives, such as free school uniforms, cash or scholarships, and other facilities, according to their economic capacities and priorities.

   (v) The delivery system of incentives be streamlined so that the benefits actually reached the eligible children. For this, the administrative machinery of supervision, inspection, monitoring and evaluation of elementary education had to be augmented and strengthened.[23]

The Committee contended that while making financial and administrative arrangements for the implementation of free and compulsory education up to 14 years of age, it was important to keep the qualitative aspects of education in mind. For this, arrangement had to be made for free and in-service training of teachers and for the requisite number of textbooks. Supplementary teaching materials had also to be provided for both teachers and students.

Basic Minimum Facilities

The Committee outlined certain basic minimum facilities that were needed and which had to be made justiciable. It recommended that the facilities envisaged in Operation Blackboard for all primary and upper primary schools should be the minimum infrastructure that had to be put in place. For primary schools it meant at least two large rooms, a veranda, and separate toilet facilities for boys and girls. When the enrollment was more than hundred, there had to be at least three rooms. Two teachers of whom at least one should be a woman, if possible, was the minimum teaching staff required. In case of enrollment of over hundred, at least three teachers were needed. Essential teaching materials like blackboards, charts, a small library, toys and games and some equipment of not more than Rs 10,000 per school were also essential.

In case of upper primary schools, the Committee recommended at least one room for each class and, where there was more than one section, one room for each section. Together with classrooms, one Headmaster's Office, necessary toilet facilities, contingency grant of Rs 1000 per annum, library grant of Rs 40,000 per annum going up to Rs 50,000 in case of schools in tribal areas, and at least one teacher for each classroom were the essential requirements. The burden of resources had to be shared between the central and state governments according to the existing pattern. However, these norms would not be applicable to alternative schooling facilities.[24]

Primary Responsibility

The Committee felt that the primary responsibility of promoting elementary education should remain with the state governments who should consider measures to enable local bodies in urban and rural areas to raise resources for the improvement of facilities in schools. An 'education cess' was one of the recommendations. Central support was also needed especially for schemes dealing with the education of girls, SCs and STs. Central and state governments should allocate 50 per cent of budgetary allocations for education to elementary education and ensure that funds meant for this were not diverted elsewhere.[25]

The Committee recommended that the medium of instruction at the primary level should be the regional language; and where the regional language was not the mother tongue, arrangements should be made to provide education in the mother tongue. In order to effectively implement the programmes of universal elementary education, it was necessary to mobilise public opinion in its favour, build up social support and involve the communities themselves in a big way. The non-governmental organisations should be assisted in their efforts to promote universal elementary education and made more focused as should be the Panchayats. The government had to simultaneously continue its efforts to motivate parents and children for elementary education.

Apart from factors such as, judicial activism, the work of non-governmental organisations, and greater awareness in the people, building up in India, a rights-based approach to education had also been developing globally, when India made education a Fundamental Right. India is a signatory to several of these international instruments.

The Present-day Scenario

According to a recent assessment, the country has achieved near universal enrollment as indicated by the GER (Gross Enrollment Ratio). However, examined against the participation of age-specific population, there is still a sizeable gap in the NER (Net Enrollment Ratio). Some states, such as, Bihar, Jammu and Kashmir, Nagaland, Rajasthan, Uttar Pradesh, and West Bengal seem to face serious problem demanding immediate attention. Although female enrollment has shown a significant increase during the last few years, gender disparity does not seem to have reduced. Figures show that there are at least as many girls outside school as there are inside in the age group of 6 to 14 years. Measures to improve access and enrollment have to be coupled with suitable measures to retain children in school long enough for them to complete the full cycle of primary education. While the inability to retain them has been a problem, there has been a significant decline in dropout rates between 1991 and 1999. This is particularly pronounced in the case of girls.

Recognising the problem of regional and gender disparities, the central and state governments have initiated several special measures to ensure that no one is deprived of access to basic education. Modifying traditional distance and population size norms, and establishing primary education facilities in smaller habitations have yielded positive results. Another major effort is of participatory school mapping and micro-planning as demonstrated by the *Lok Jumbish* project in Rajasthan. This is being implemented in many parts of the country under the District Primary Education Programme (DPEP) as well as other Education For All (EFA) projects. Orchestrating the local demand for schooling through established local community structures such as village education committees, mother-teacher associations, local core teams and women's groups has helped in mobilising the demand for schooling and reducing the apparent distance between the community and the school. District-specific approach has been adopted as more centralised planning is often unable to respond to local needs.

Further, it has been recognised that children who are not enrolled for schooling at a primary stage are a more difficult group in terms of their socio-economic and cultural background. This is especially true for the girl child and the problem is more acute and complex at the upper-primary stage, as is clearly indicated by the combined GER for the stage. These complexities demand more innovative methods for providing primary education through formal and non-formal channels. With this in view, alternative schools, residential camps, and schools for adolescent girls have been organised both in government and non-government sectors with encouraging results. It has also been recognised that the educational development of children cannot take place without adequate attention to their health and nutritional status. It is in view of this that the government of Tamil Nadu initiated a programme of nutritious meals for all school-age children more than a decade ago. Following the significant impact the scheme made on the participation of children in school, the Government of India in all the states is implementing a national programme of mid-day meals since 1995. Special scholarships have been provided for girls in several states. In some states, education for girls is free at all levels, including university education. Also, the procedure for recruiting teachers in almost all the states envisages that at least women teachers fill 50 per cent positions. Another problem area is the educational deprivation of the SCs and STs as education is a critical factor in their economic betterment. Special provisions have been made for this purpose.

A novel experiment called *Shiksha Karmi* project was tried out in Rajasthan. Successful during the initial years, the project has expanded to cover a large number of habitations in the state. Apart from this, the government has tried to provide second track educational facilities such as *Shramik Vidyapeeths*, *Mahila Shikshan Kendras*, *Jan Shikshan Kendras*, *Mahila Samakhya* and other kinds of non-formal education centres. Some of these measures are certainly useful but what is really required is an effectively functioning primary school in every village.

A problem closely related to universal elementary education is that of out-of-school children, many of whom end up as working children or child labourers. According to the 1991 census, there were 11.28 million child workers (6.18 million boys and 5.10 million girls) in the age group 5–14. The figure stands at around 20 million in the 2010 census if children in the age group of 15-19 years are counted, as the census does. About 91 per cent of these children continue to be concentrated in rural areas. The Government of India and several state governments have been running Non-Formal Education (NFE) centres for nearly two decades to meet the immediate requirements of these children.

There are other areas of concern such as the education of children with special needs. Inclusive education has become a common theme of all discourses on basic education the world over. The 1989 UN Convention on the Rights of the Child, to which India is a signatory, states that, "disabled children have the right to participate in the community and their education should lead to their fullest possible social integration and educational development." India has incorporated a number of policy documents, legislation and programme strategies. The Rehabilitation Council of India (RCI) Act was adopted in 1992 and the Persons with Disabilities (Equal Opportunities, Protection of Rights and Full Participation) Act was passed on December 22, 1995. With this, the necessary legal instruments have been created but much ground needs to be covered.

It is difficult today to carry on any discourse in education without referring to the emerging partnership between the government and NGOs, particularly in the field of basic education. In fact, NGO coalitions have emerged as major actors even at a global level through their intensive advocacy campaigns and focused field-level action programme in developing countries. There is a general perception that NGOs represent the organised front of civil society at large and the local community where they work in particular. While this general perception cannot be contested, the relationship between the government and NGOs may not always present a picture of perfect collaboration and synergistic partnership in achieving the goal of universal elementary education.

However, the overall picture shows that the increase in literacy rates during the 1990s has been significantly higher than in the previous decades. As per the 2001 census, the literacy rate for the seven-plus age group is 65.38 per cent. Although gender disparity remains pronounced, a converging trend is emerging for the first time. The male-female literacy gap, which was about 25 per cent in 1991, has been reduced to around 20 per cent in 2001. According to the NSSO survey report released in June 2015, literacy rate in rural areas is 71 per cent and 86 per cent in urban areas. In the age group of seven years and above, the male literacy rate was 33 per cent while female literacy rate was 67 per cent. Hence the male-female literacy gap seems to have reduced further.

While literacy has improved, the worrying part is that learning outcomes remain dismal. If these don't improve, children will continue to be forced into labour or will be exploited. This is detrimental not only to the Indian economy which will see a demographic disaster rather than benefit from its demographic dividend, but to the country as a whole as well. India will not realise its leadership potential because education and healthy childhood are fundamental.

References

1. For views of Azad, Nehru and Radhakrishnan, refer to Prem Kripal and Raba Shome, (eds.). 1989. *Foundations of Education for Free India: Towards a New Quality of Life*, New Delhi: Allied Publishers.
2. See K.C. Markandan, 1980. *Directive Principles of State Policy in the Indian Constitution*, pp. 9-29. New Delhi: ABS Publications.

3. *Ibid.*
4. Constitutional Precedents Third Series, 1947, Fundamental Rights (I), p. 18. This also appeared as B.N. Rao, ed. B. Shiva Rao, 1960. *India's Constitution in the Making*, Chapter 13, Calcutta: Orient Longman.
5. *Ibid.*
6. Lok Sabha Debates Part II May 16, 1951.
7. Francis Coralie Mullin vs. Administrator, Union Territory of Delhi, AIR 1981 SC 746.
8. Mohini Jain vs. State of Karnataka (1992) 3 SCC, 666. See also K.P. Unnikrishnan vs. State of Andhra Pradesh (1993) 1 SCC 645. See also AIIMS Students Union vs. AIIMS (2002) SCC 428. Also refer to D.N. Chanchala vs. State of Mysore (1971). 2 SCC 293.
9. *Ibid.*
10. *Ibid.*
11. *Ibid.*
12. K.P. Unnikrishnan vs. State of Andhra Pradesh (1993) 1 SCC 645. See also N. Kurshichekku Hajl vs. State of Kerala (1995) Supp. 2 SCC 382.
13. *Ibid.*
14. Report of the Committee of State Education Ministers on Implications of the proposal to make Elementary Education a Fundamental Right, New Delhi: Government of India, Ministry of Human Resource Development, Department of Education, 15 January 1987.
15. *Ibid.*
16. *Ibid.*
17. *Ibid.*
18. *Ibid.*
19. Report of the Group of Experts on Financial Resource Requirements for Making Elementary Education a Fundamental Right, New Delhi: Government of India, Ministry of Human Resource Development, Department of Education, New Delhi, 1998.
20. *Ibid.*
21. Report of the Committee of State Education Ministers on the Implications of the Proposal to make Elementary Education a Fundamental Right, New Delhi: Government of India, Ministry of Human Resource Development, Department of Education, 15 January, 1997.
22. *Ibid.*
23. *Ibid.*
24. *Ibid.*
25. *Ibid.*

2

Association of Indian Universities: The Precursor to UGC*

The Background

Modern higher education in India can be said to have started in 1854 with Wood's Despatch, which wanted the government to create a properly articulated system of education from the primary school to the university, and which also recommended instituting universities at Calcutta, Madras and Bombay modelled after London University. The preliminary spadework was considerable and naturally took some time, but in as early as 1857, the Government of India passed Acts of Incorporation of all three universities. Mirroring, as it were, London University, they were purely examining and affiliating bodies and undertook no research or teaching. The actual teaching was done in colleges, but the university laid down the syllabi and conducted the examinations.

Indian Universities Act, 1860

The Acts of Incorporation of the Universities mentioned the degrees by name that the university might confer. It was afterwards found desirable to add others to the list and therefore, in 1860, the Indian Universities (Degrees) Act was passed, empowering the universities to confer such diplomas or degrees as had been or might be approved by the bye-laws or regulations.

Following the Indian Universities Act of 1860, it was proposed to establish a university in Punjab, especially for oriental learning and instruction through the medium of the vernacular language of the province. It was eventually established in 1882 by a special Act of Incorporation.

* This article is based on S.S. Bhandarkar, *Association of Indian Universities: A Short History 1925-85*, 1985. New Delhi: Association of Indian Universities.

A university college was established at Lahore in 1869 and it achieved university status in 1882. The Mohammedan Anglo-Oriental College at Aligarh was established in 1875. This institution started with a few school classes, but later developed into Aligarh Muslim University. The Government of North-Western provinces submitted proposals for establishing a Central College at Allahabad that would form the nucleus of a university for resident undergraduates in 1869 and then in 1879. It was finally established by a special Act of Incorporation in 1887.

Indian Education Commission, 1882

The Government of India appointed an Indian Education Commission in 1882, but did not give it the right "to enquire into the general working of Indian universities." The Commission, therefore, contented itself with making only a few observations in connection with the improvement of affiliated colleges. While drawing the attention of the local government to the need for "providing or extending the means of collegiate education" at several places, it recommended, "the rate of aid to each college be determined by the strength of the staff, the expenditure on its maintenance, the efficiency of the institution and the wants of the locality." Special grants were also to be made, "whenever necessary, for the supply and renewal of buildings, furniture, libraries and other apparatus of instruction."

The recommendations of the Indian Education Commission of 1882 were of minor importance. Nothing was said about the relation of the collegiate courses of study to the practical needs of the students and of the community. The benefits of properly organised residential facilities were mentioned, but no suggestions were made for their expansion. While recognising the value of the "system of instruction becoming more thorough and more scientific," the Commission had no concrete proposal to offer. Its recommendations however, led to a rapid multiplication of high schools with regard to secondary education. As a consequence, there was a great increase in the number of students appearing at the entrance examinations of the different universities and subsequently seeking admission to colleges for higher education.

Inter-University Board (IUB)

By 1925, there were 14 universities. On March 23, 1925, representatives of 11 universities met in the library of the University of Bombay and formed themselves into the Inter-University Board (IUB). Sir Chimanlal H. Setalvad, the Vice-Chancellor of the host university welcomed the delegates. Although the IUB itself had been formed in 1925, its genesis can be traced to a much earlier date, to 1919. The first three universities of Bombay,

Calcutta and Madras that had been founded in 1857, they necessarily had vast jurisdictions as they were required to cover the entire India. However, by 1925, the number of universities had risen to 14 and so each served smaller areas, generally province-wise. Each was governed by its own independent Act or charters which were essentially similar but there was no mechanism of coordination between them or of mutual recognition of degrees. Hence, student mobility became a problem as did the recognition of degrees and diplomas especially for these students going to the UK for further study.

The urgent need for a coordinating body among universities was pointed out by the Calcutta University Commission, popularly known as the Sadler Commission in 1919. The Second Congress of the Universities of the Empire, a body that had been established in 1912, also passed a resolution on July 6, 1921, recommending and emphasising to the Indian Universities, the need for an association of Indian universities that could look after matters of mutual interest. The Lytton Committee on Indian students studying in the United Kingdom also expressed a hope that an inter-university body would soon be established to coordinate the course being taught in Indian universities and arrange for their recognition in foreign universities.

A Conference of Indian Universities had been held in Shimla in May 1924. Lord Reading, the then Viceroy of India, made some important points in his inaugural address. He pointed out: "With a multiplication of institutions, with alterations in type, with changes in internal systems and with financial stringency affecting the complete execution of projects, there is no small risk of some deviation from the right road to educational efficiency...it is a time for mutual help and for cooperation between universities. A united front must be shown. There must be a joint effort to develop higher education in India to the highest standards. There must be a combination to meet reasonable criticism and to remedy defects."

The Conference actively recommended a coordinating agency, the IUB, and a committee consisting of Dr H.S. Gour, Dr C.V. Raman, Dr J.C. Ghosh, Diwan Bahadur M. Ramachandran, Mr Manohar Lal, Professor P.S. Burrell, Professor P. Seshadri, Mr F.P. Herne, Mr Rass Masood, Dr L.K. Hyder and Mr L.G. Owen, was formed to pilot the proposal. At the Conference, a lively discussion took place on whether the advisory character of the Board should be specifically mentioned in the constitution, whether the larger universities should have more than one member, and whether the headquarters of the Board should be Delhi or Allahabad. It was finally agreed that there was no need to spell out the advisory character of the organisation in its constitution, each university should be represented by one representative and the Board opted for its headquarters to be in Delhi.

Mr Littlehailer, the Officiating Educational Commissioner assured the newly created Board that the Government "did not have the slightest intention of controlling directly or indirectly the Board or of interfering in its deliberations." He then withdrew and Rev. E.M. Macphail, the Vice-Chancellor of Madras University was elected the first Chairman of the Inter-University Board. He contributed significantly to the shaping of the character of the Board in the early years.

The subjects discussed at this meeting related to the conditions of service of university teachers with special reference to the rules of leave and pay together with equivalence of examinations. One of the important concerns pertained to bogus degrees. The Board resolved that all possible measures should be adopted to prevent the sale of bogus degrees and to do this, it should consult the Board of Education, Washington, on what steps it had taken to deal with a similar issue in the USA. Also, the constituent universities were recommended to record the degrees and other academic distinctions of their teachers working in constituent and affiliated colleges and the academic institutions from which these had been conferred.

In the first two years of its inception, the Board worked from a room in Maharaja's College, Mysore made available to it by its Principal, Mr N.S. Subba Rao who was also the Secretary of the Board. No permanent appointments were made and the routine work was carried out by the Secretary. Mr A. Hydari took over from Rev. Macphail and was the next Chairman of IUB. The universities increasingly began using the Board and so it was suggested the services being given by it should be made into its permanent feature. The Secretary was requested to visit the university centres to take the consent of university bodies to renew the term of IUB for another two years.

At the end of five years, the Board held a conference of the universities that considerably "strengthened its position and enhanced its usefulness and importance in the estimate of the Universities." Apart from the services that the Board rendered to the universities, it also undertook several publications. Bulletins of the Inter-University Board were published as well, pamphlets giving information regarding the standardisation of legal education in India, facilities for Oriental Research and facilities for Scientific Research in Indian universities. The Board published the yearly *Handbook of Indian Universities* to which was added a historical account of the origin and development of Indian universities. Another significant publication which the Board undertook since 1935 was the *Bibliography of Doctoral Dissertations*.

The Board obviously did very good work and received favourable press for it both at home and abroad. In October 1930, the London Times devoted a whole article to it in its educational supplement in which was pointed out, "increasingly useful place the IUB had filled in the past five years." "It has", it observed, "brought the universities into constant touch with each other and in many important directions has been the instrument of cooperative action."

By 1945, not only had the number of universities increased but also their activities and problems. This could not be completed in one annual meeting and hence it was suggested that a Standing Committee should be created that would ensure a business-like administration of the Board, prepare the agenda, budget, and financial estimates for the annual meetings and also be responsible for the day-to-day inter-university problems.

Recommendations for a University Grants Commission (UGC)

In 1950, a conference of vice-chancellors was called in Madras (now Chennai) by which time the IUB had established itself as the authentic voice of the universities. The Conference was to consider the proposed Government of India Bill to establish a Central Council of University Education to ensure the coordination and determination of academic standards in institutions of higher education. Having considered this proposal in all its aspects, the Conference unanimously rejected the proposed Central Council of University Education and requested the government to set up a University Grants Committee instead "on the lines on which such a committee is functioning in Great Britain." The resolution continues – "While not interfering with the autonomy of the universities which are statutory bodies with special duties and responsibilities devolving upon the university authorities constituted under the various university Acts, the view of the IUB should be taken into consideration when large questions of policy are concerned and it should be the endeavour of the universities to implement those views. This Conference is further of opinion that where any question arises as to the propriety or otherwise of any action taken by a university, or where a government (Central or State) feels it desirable that any question pertaining to universities in general should be considered, such questions be referred to the IUB and the IUB should make enquiries and report thereon to the universities and the government concerned." The Conference further said that the IUB which consisted of the vice-chancellors of Indian universities should henceforth function in a more intensified manner so as to enable the universities to appreciate fully the problems of universities in general and of individual universities in particular.

It was in 1966 that the insignia and the Memorandum of Association were adopted by the IUB. The idea of giving the Board a legal identity came originally from Dr C.D. Deshmukh and Dr B.D. Laroia, the then Secretary of the Board. However, it was later implemented by Amrik Singh, the Secretary of the Board. Dr Deshmukh also gave the Board its motto.

Registration and Rechristening as AIU

The Board was registered as a Society under the Societies Registration Act, 1860, on September 29, 1967 through the efforts of Amrik Singh whose tenure, of 17 years beginning in 1963, saw the active growth and development of the organisation. It was renamed the Association of Indian Universities (AIU) in 1973 during his tenure. He was deeply involved in not only the registration of the Inter-University Board as a society and in getting its name changed, but also in its finances, organisation, finding space for its office and activities and eventually building its present premises. He expanded the organisation both qualitatively and quantitatively and established or strengthened three important divisions in it: Library and Documentation (1964); Publications and Sales (1966); and Research (1975).

A perusal of the documents shows Amrik Singh struggling and taking active steps to get possession of the land allotted to the Association for constructing its own buildings. He had to make constant efforts to hire space for the Association as an interim arrangement to enable the Association of Indian Universities to fulfil both its administrative and academic functions at a reasonable price as resources were small and had to be optimally utilised. The allotment of land was also part of his Golden Jubilee agenda so that the foundation stone for the AIU building could be laid at that time.

During Amrik Singh's tenure, the Association of Indian Universities was active, dynamic and played a significant role in the evolution of higher education in India. There were two abiding themes that played themselves out in varying forms during his time with his active encouragement and involvement as he was deeply committed to both. One was the autonomy and independence of the university and the other was the pivotal role of the teacher and the accountability that must necessarily go with it. For example, when the pay and allowances were revised according to the recommendations of the Sen Committee, a code of conduct for teachers was to be drawn up. This did not happen except in a few universities. The AIU kept pushing for teacher accountability although with a degree of pragmatism. For instance, the periodical assessment of the work of every teacher was recommended and it was also suggested that no professor should be appointed on a permanent basis but on contract to be renewed every five years. The combination of idealism and pragmatism could also be seen while talking of examination reforms. The AIU was clear that teaching, learning and examination were part of an integrated process and so recommended that no extra payment need be given to teachers for the marking of scripts. But when this recommendation led to rather unhappy consequences, the AIU revised its opinion and left the decision to individual universities.

The AIU took up other issues like raising fees that had remained stationary for over forty years. While fees certainly needed to be revised there was consciousness that poor students, especially those coming from backward communities, would have to be provided scholarships to avoid hardship. The AIU strongly supported sports and extra-curricular activities. However, it was clear that no extra credit need be given to students to pursue these extra-curricular activities. So great was the involvement of AIU in inter-institutional sports activity which was also a part of its mandate that Amrik Singh himself went as a member of the Indian official delegation to the Moscow Olympic Games and spent a little over a fortnight there in this connection.

There were some ongoing issues like examination reforms, financing, terms and conditions of service of teachers and their accountability. Apart from these, the AIU took up the issue of foreign students as far back as 1980 and the implications of increasing the number of foreign students studying in India. It took up the issue of language —the medium of instruction and availability of textbooks in various languages other than English. Professor S.C. Dube and Professor Amrik Singh prepared a detailed note on the subject for the Ministry. There were other important issues that AIU dealt with like the implications of education being made a concurrent subject, and the change to the 10+2+3 system.

Over and over again, the issue of autonomy of universities came up. Reports were produced on the academic standards in universities and the autonomy of universities. One onerous but extremely significant work that the AIU took upon itself was to ensure that universities were given help when they were put under pressure by governments to take uncalled-for and less than desirable decisions. For example, in 1980, Amrik Singh as the Secretary of AIU wrote forcefully to the then Governor of Bihar about the relationship between a vice-chancellor and the state government. He pointed out that Uttar Pradesh and Bihar were the only two states where the vice-chancellor was appointed at the pleasure of the chancellor.

It had been done in Andhra Pradesh in the mid-sixties and the AIU had strictly opposed it submitting a memorandum to the Prime Minister in March 1966 where it was stated:

> Conditions of service for vice-chancellors should not be made humiliating or unattractive in any manner so that suitable people may not feel deterred from accepting the post of vice-chancellorship.

This memorandum was then endorsed to the Education Commission. The pivotal issue was that no vice-chancellor could function effectively without the positive and consistent support by the state government. There could be situations of temporary breakdowns of communication between the vice-chancellor and the state government, but these could only be a passing phase. Hence, there was no reason to insert a clause in terms of appointment of the vice-chancellor that he serve at the pleasure of the chancellor, as it compromised his dignity and hurt the interest of the university system as a whole. When a vice-chancellor did not enjoy the confidence of the state government, he had no choice but to leave. The Prime Minister was urged to intervene and get the clause deleted.

Allied to it was the question of choosing the right persons to serve as vice-chancellors. In his memorandum, Amrik Singh pointed out that over the years, the office of the vice-chancellor had got considerably politicised. A number of reasons had contributed to this situation. One of them was the keenness of some state governments to appoint persons who were politically close to them. This had led to unavoidable consequences. When a particular Chief Minister or Education Minister went out of office, the vice-chancellor appointed by him ceased to be acceptable to the new Minister and hence he wanted a person acceptable to him appointed in his place. Such a situation could arise without a change in the ruling party. Just the change of Minister or Chief Minister could bring about this situation. It created an uncertainty in the tenure of the vice-chancellor causing inescapable damage to administrative continuity and stability and so was detrimental to the university system. Hence, said the Memorandum, only such a person should be selected as a vice-chancellor who was free from political affiliations. This, in other words, meant only a person academic in outlook and background should be appointed to this office and such a person would also be more likely to be acceptable to the academic community.

Amrik Singh was again seen taking up the cause of the Vice-Chancellor of Berhampur University in the same year in no uncertain terms. Following an agitation by the university employees, the Vice-Chancellor Professor T. Ratho's term was abruptly terminated. Amrik Singh, taking up his cause, pointed out that the agitation was fading out, the examinations were going on according to schedule, and the summer vacation had started. Therefore, there was no urgency to abruptly end Professor Ratho's tenure. It might have been more appropriate to let him go at the end of his tenure which was after the vacations. The way the matter had been dealt with, he stated, had hurt the prestige of the University. He urged on behalf of AIU that the decision on the vice-chancellor be reconsidered especially because the university was only a decade and a half years old and no vice-chancellor had been able to serve out his full term. He followed this up with another letter, pointing out that injustice had not only been done to Professor Ratho, but to the University itself.

Amrik Singh's deep involvement with AIU shows itself in his planning its Golden Jubilee celebrations. He presented a detailed note to the Board in which he proposed, among other things, that the history of the Board be written by June 1974; and a three-day international seminar on higher education be arranged to which inter-university organisations of various countries be invited to send delegations, the IUB providing local hospitality only. It had earlier been suggested that the member universities be asked to contribute Rs 1 lakh each towards the Endowment Fund of AIU, but Amrik Singh realised that the financial position of the universities was such that it might not allow them to do so. However, he felt that they make efforts to get as near the figure as possible. If sufficient resources could be put into the Endowment Fund, Amrik Singh proposed that a Golden Jubilee Fellowship in Higher Education be instituted. He also wanted a commemorative volume to be brought out for which ten to fifteen distinguished persons could be asked to contribute their articles. He wanted an exhibition of books on higher education. The Association had always been active in sports and had organised several inter-college and inter-university sports meets. Hence, it was only appropriate for Amrik Singh to propose a significant sports activity, but it showed his far-sightedness when he suggested that it should be a Joint Sports Meet of neighbouring countries—Bangladesh, Burma (now Myanmar), Nepal, Afghanistan, Pakistan, and Sri Lanka.

Research and academic publishing were two other areas of keen interest for Amrik Singh. He not only researched and published himself, but also he tried his best to encourage these activities in AIU and attempted to create systems for both. Several studies in his time were done on issues that still remain significant and vital like the semester system and practical examinations. He himself put forward several ideas in this area that seem radical even today. For instance, he asked why examinations for the same semester or year could not be held several times to enable students to appear in them at their own pace. Dates could be announced well in advance so that students could decide whether they wanted to appear for the first examination or at any other time. Another suggestion he made was that more than one question paper might be set to prevent leakage.

Significant issues were studied and documented for future reference and for providing policy inputs. Some examples are, "Enrollment in Higher Education: A Trend Analysis," "Resource Allocation on Education: An Inter, Intra-Country and Inter-Temporal Pattern Analysis," "Socio-Economic Background of Delhi University Students," and "Effects of 10+2+3." Two major studies were "Problems of Under Populated Colleges" and "Problems of First Generation Learners." The AIU studied the different aspects of university finance as a statistical analysis and conducted several researches on the economics of education.

As far as academic publication was concerned, Amrik Singh accepted that no serious steps had been taken by AIU up to 1980 in this direction. Addressing a two-day workshop on academic publishing organised at the behest of AIU, he remarked that it was a curious time to be discussing this subject as the outlay on higher education had been scaled down and the result was that grants for laboratories and libraries had been reduced. The unintended consequence was that Indian publishing had received a serious setback as libraries were the biggest buyers of books and purchased about 90 per cent of all books sold. When library grants are cut, book buying is bound to be affected and that is precisely what had happened.

To remedy the matter of academic publishing and to bring it to the consciousness of the universities, a questionnaire was circulated to get an idea of what was the state of university publication. What emerged was that only about half the universities in the country had their own printing set up, but it was important, emphasised Amrik Singh, that every university should have its own printing unit however small. At the same time, he was pragmatic enough to recommend that each of these units needed to be run as business enterprises. All the inputs whether it be the site or the building or the cost of machinery, had to be accounted for as part of capital investment for which the press had to eventually become self-sufficient enough to pay.

The distinction between printing and publishing needed to be understood. Printing preceded publishing but was not the same as publishing. Publishing, strictly speaking, was to bring out a book for sale to booksellers and others interested in it. Its main focus of activity was to plan the book, produce it, and eventually sell it. Hence, every publishing unit had to have three important sub-units: an editorial department to deal with the author and be part of the preparation of the manuscript for the press; the production department of highly trained persons who could produce each book according to its nature and this was a fairly technical job; and personnel to market books, which was slightly different from marketing other goods.

Again, Amrik Singh's realism comes in when he accepted that academic publishing was only possible when textbooks are also printed as these provided the money for the former. Textbook printing could be called the "bread-and-butter" for academic publishing. The basic point about a university press, he pointed out, was its essential commitment to scholarship. Scholarly books had to be written and published. If other publishing houses were willing to do so, it was good, but if not, it was the duty of the university press to bring out such publications regardless of whether it was economical. The fruits of scholarship had to be made available to other scholars even when the costs were high because a large expense was incurred in funding the kind of scholarship in a university. If the outcomes of that scholarship were not made available to other scholars, the earlier investment on research would go waste. In any case, scholarship was expensive only in the short run. In the long run it not only paid for itself, it also generated much more than what was invested on it. This had been the experience of those countries that had invested in scholarship and the experience in India would be no different if the country chose to spend on research and its dissemination. The only thing necessary was to ensure that the scholarship was genuine.

Amrik Singh was well aware of the practical difficulties encountered in publishing in Indian universities. An Indian university had no system of publishing and therefore, often books got published because somebody canvassed or the author was able to influence those in the decision-making positions. This led to mediocrity. To avoid this, it was important to ensure standards by getting the manuscripts referred by peers before publication. After giving a detailed outline for university publishing, Amrik Singh proposed the establishment of an Inter-University Press along the lines of a university press. This was because he realised that a single university might not have the requisite resources for a university press, but if the resources of universities were pooled, it would be possible to establish quality university publishing.

Obviously, in spite of the limited funds available to it, the AIU was taking the lead in significant issues pertaining to universities in particular and higher education as a system together with its role and relevance. Once the UGC got established, there was necessarily some strain between the two organisations because both dealt with some areas in higher education. The AIU was the only body whose members were the universities of the country represented either by the vice-chancellors or their nominees.

Its mandate was to represent the universities of India; act as a bureau of information and facilitate communication; promote coordination and mutual consultation amongst universities; liaise between universities and governments, both central and state; cooperate with other universities or bodies, national or international, in matters of common interest; promote and undertake programmes that would help improve standards of instruction, examination, research, textbooks, scholarly publications, library organisation and others that contribute to the growth and propagation of knowledge; help universities to maintain their autonomous character; facilitate student mobility and exchange of members of the teaching and research staff, sharing of infrastructure, joint-research projects and publications between universities in the country or with the counterparts abroad; promote publication; undertake research and organise seminars, conferences and others. Its mandate also included acting as a National Sports Promotion Organisation for promoting sports and welfare activities for teachers and students.

Enhancing the Relevance of AIU

Areas of overlap between the mandate of the AIU and that of the UGC were evident. Obviously there were some tensions and Amrik Singh put the matter into perspective. He pointed out, that the AIU had helped shape the very inception of UGC. In a note with regard to the future of AIU, he emphasised that if AIU seemed to be losing ground to UGC it was because of its own difficulties. To remain relevant, AIU needed to take itself seriously. Amrik Singh did some plain speaking. One criticism that its members made was that they heard about it approximately once a year and that too on the occasion of the annual meeting. The meeting itself was attended by not more than two-third of the vice-chancellors. The discussions were not rigorous or thorough. Quite often even the agenda was rushed through. Some retrieval of the situation had been attempted by holding a seminar along with the annual meeting, but the dominant feeling was that it was not well-organised and gave the impression of being perfunctory.

To remedy the situation, Amrik Singh made two suggestions. One was that in addition to the Standing Committee, the AIU have three committees to deal with different areas of its functioning:

- Committee 'A' to deal with mainstream universities usually of the affiliating nature and which received funding from the UGC and the state governments;
- Committee 'B' to deal with agricultural universities, which received funding from ICAR and the state governments; and

- Committee 'C' which may deal with IITs and other technical universities. Some universities had strong faculties of technology and these may also wish to be represented in Committee 'C'.

In addition, the Standing Committee needed to be reorganised to deal with matters like finance, equivalence of degrees, research projects, dealings with foreign countries and other such matters. In order to cope with the increasing tempo of work, funds were needed. It was therefore proposed that the Ministry of Education be asked to increase the funding.

Amrik Singh emphasised upon the members of AIU that it was the AIU that had assisted in establishing organisations such as the CSIR, the Indian Medical Council (IMC) and the UGC itself. In a letter to M.C. Chagla, the then Education Minister, Amrik Singh had written of his disagreement with the amending provisions in the UGC Bill that excluded the vice-chancellors and heads of institutions, which could receive grants from the UGC by being its members. He accepted that the UGC in Great Britain did not have vice-chancellors as its members, but that was because its principal function was to make grants to universities. In India, the UGC was not merely a grant-giving body but was also charged with the duty of coordination and maintenance of standards of higher education, which was essentially an academic function. The exclusion of vice-chancellors from the membership of the UGC would weaken its academic character and capability. Of course, this could be remedied to some extent by appointing university persons to the Commission but, as he said, it would be difficult to find many individuals of the right calibre and experience for this purpose. Therefore, the government would necessarily have to turn to retired vice-chancellors. Of course, a distinction could be made between a serving and a retired vice-chancellor, but its significance was not material enough to justify altogether excluding serving vice-chancellors from becoming members of the Commission. On the contrary, said Amrik Singh, the IUB was convinced that the UGC had definitely benefited by the presence and participation of its vice-chancellor-members in its deliberations and owed its successful functioning to them. Hence for a few negatives that may be there in their inclusion, it was not correct to overlook their many positive contributions.

However, it was necessary to maintain close and effective liaison between the IUB and the UGC and both needed at least one member from the other body sitting on their respective councils. For some time, the IUB and the UGC worked in close coordination as was seen during the Fourth Five-Year Plan. The Standing Committee of the IUB in 1966 recognised the importance of consultation and collaboration between the IUB and the UGC. The Committee felt that it was necessary to build certain conventions, and evolve a method for the close collaboration and exchange of information on as wide a scale as possible between the two bodies. The Secretary was asked to make the minutes of the meetings of the Committee available to the UGC for information. Also, periodical meetings between chairmen and secretaries of the two bodies needed to be arranged for the exchange of information and the evolving of a common approach. Joint meetings needed to be arranged at least once a year and a suitable agenda worked out between the secretaries of the respective bodies.

Amrik Singh pointed out that the IUB was a democratic and representative body of all the universities in India; and universities were the representatives of all their colleges; both constituents and affiliated. Hence, the Board needed to be regarded as the supreme body for the consideration of problems of university education and given that status by both the government and the UGC. The Board, in its turn, had to take appropriate steps to interact with appropriate bodies to gather both professional academic opinion and the government's opinion on matters relating to university education before making major recommendations to their member-universities. Universities were the preservers of academic standards, and therefore had to remain and function as autonomous bodies. Keeping this is mind, the IUB as the representative of universities, naturally had to have the final responsibility for the maintenance and improvement of academic standards. Of course, it had to work closely with the UGC—the body entrusted by the Parliament with the coordination of standards in university education. But there was no getting away, according to the analysis presented by Amrik Singh, from the fact that the IUB had the ultimate responsibility for the coordination of standards in higher education, not only because its members alone were the implementers, but also because they were self-governing bodies. Once this principle was recognised, concrete arrangements for the promotion of mutual cooperation and collaboration between the UGC and IUB in all the academic matters could be easily worked out. Therefore, he suggested that the annual reports of the UGC be placed for discussion not only before Parliament, but also before the IUB. This was even more imperative as by an amendment, the University Grants Commission Act had excluded serving vice-chancellors from its membership.

Obviously much water has flown under the bridge since the days when Amrik Singh was the Secretary of the AIU. However, many of the issues raised way back in the late 1960s are still alive although their form and tenor may have changed.

3

Establishment of the University Grants Commission*

The University Grants Commission (UGC) came into existence through an Act of Parliament in November, 1956. However, the idea of creating the UGC to regulate the standards of higher education can be traced to the University Education Commission (Radhakrishnan Commission, 1948), better known as the First Education Commission, which in its report had initially recommended its establishment. To a certain extent, the efforts towards expansion of higher education in the colonial period also pointed in that direction. The system of higher education in independent India as well as its regulatory mechanism evolved in a way as a continuation of the colonial system. Hence, the challenges of the higher educational system that the UGC had to confront, as it began its work, have to be viewed in the context of the colonial set up.

The idea of establishing a University Grants Committee was first conceived in England for its institutions of higher education. It was to be responsible for estimating grants from the government to the universities to supplement their income from tuition fees and other sources. Several *ad hoc* committees of a similar nature had been formed in England for this limited purpose in as far back as 1831, till a permanent body came into existence in 1919. The President of the Board of Education held a conference of the representatives of the British universities immediately after the First World War and promised aid to them. Consequently, a Standing Committee of the Treasury was appointed, "to enquire into the financial needs of university education in the United Kingdom and to advise the government as to the application of any grants that may be made by Parliament towards meeting them."[1] Thus, a University Grants Committee was created to enable Parliament to make an informed decision on the allocations needed for

* This article is based on the author's book: *Sixty Years of University Grants Commission: Establishment, Growth and Evolution.* New Delhi: University Grants Commission.

higher education and to distribute the available grants to the various universities.

Dr Amarnath Jha first mooted the proposal for such an institution in India in a resolution at a meeting of the Inter-University Board in 1936. However, he did not really think of a national body but rather a grant-giving body for each province or region. Nothing came of the proposal, however, because the university representatives who were present at the meeting could not evolve a consensus amongst themselves. In 1943, the Central Advisory Board of Education drew up a national plan for the post-war development of education, popularly knows as the Sargent Plan. Through it, the Inter-University Board once again revived the idea of a "Central Grants Committee." It was also realised that a national plan of development of education could not be implemented without central financial aid. The Board, however, was at the same time anxious that the Government of India should not exercise any powers of "control and inspection." The Sargent Report observed that there had been "a general lack of planning in University education," and that, "both the Central and Provincial Governments had yielded to popular pressure in bringing universities into existence without providing the necessary resources to enable them to function on sound lines."

Further, there appeared to be a need for an authority to coordinate university education in the interest of the country as a whole. Accordingly, it suggested that such a body be created somewhat on the lines of the University Grants Committee in Britain. The idea was to set up the Indian University Grants Committee as a statutory body consisting of a few eminent individuals, which would neither directly connect with the government, whether central or provincial, nor with any particular university. However, they were to be eminent people preferably with considerable experience of university administration. The main function of the proposed Indian University Grants Committee was supervision over the allocation of grants to universities from public funds and to ensure that they had enough resources to meet the demands that might be made on them. It was envisaged that such financial assistance would be given as block grants for a certain number of years, to enable the universities to plan ahead. Also, all grants to universities for new developments would be made by the central government through the Grants Committee.

The Report further recommended that in addition to its main functions, the proposed Grants Committee should also be empowered to encourage private benefactions; coordinate university activities so as to avoid overlapping, and to adjust, as far as possible, the output of the universities to the economic needs of the country; prevent undesirable competition among them; ensure periodic visits to the universities in order to ascertain their needs; establish cultural contacts; remove all international barriers and arrange for the exchange of teachers and students with foreign countries.

The Government of India appointed a University Grants Committee in 1945, vide the Department of Education, Health and Lands Resolution dated June 4, 1945 consisting of four part-time members to advise the government on the grants to be given to the Central Universities. The Constitution of the Committee was amended and its scope enlarged by the Department of Education Resolution dated July 27, 1946, and the Ministry of Education Resolution dated December 16, 1947. It was also empowered to deal with other universities. Neither the Committee's chairman nor its members were full-time and its functions were restricted to being basically advisory. It functioned as an intermediary body between the government and the universities. Its job was to advise the government on the allocation of grants from public funds to the central universities and to any other universities whose case for such grants the government might refer to it. It was also supposed to advise universities with respect to any question or matter that might be referred to them by the government. However, the Committee could not be very effective and was kept in abeyance till 1950, once the Government of India accepted the recommendations of the University Education Commission.

There were several reasons for the inadequate performance of the University Grants Committee: (a) its personnel and powers were limited; (b) since neither its chairman nor its members were full-time, they found it difficult to find the time that the Committee's effective functioning required; (c) their resources were limited and it was hard for them to familiarise themselves in detail with all the universities requiring their assistance. Even with regard to allocation of funds to universities, the Committee had no funds of its own and could only make recommendations to the Ministry of Education, which, in turn, forwarded them to the Finance Ministry.

Here lay the genesis for the future UGC. From the functioning of the first Committee, the advantages were seen and the need was felt, for a body that could itself allocate both recurrent and central grants to universities from the Centre. However, it was also thought that States should retain the responsibility for undergraduate courses and even bear fifty per cent cost of postgraduate courses and research. One idea was that such a Committee or Commission should be a large body in which all subjects should be represented. On the other hand, it was realised that this would make it very unwieldy and so it might be better for the Commission to be a small body but have a panel of experts in each subject or a group of cognate subjects who could, then, visit the universities and report to the Commission. These experts should work in an honorary capacity, being only paid their expenses for visiting universities or attending meetings. For the Commission to be able to command respect, it was necessary for it to have people of high reputation both for wisdom and integrity.

The Radhakrishnan Commission

After India's independence, a University Education Commission was set up in 1948 under the chairmanship of Dr Sarvepalli Radhakrishnan. Its mandate was to report on university education and suggest improvements and extensions that were desirable both for the present and for the future requirements of the country. The University Education Commission recommended in its Report (1948–1949) the setting up of a Central University Grants Commission/ Committee which, working through the Ministry of Education, would allocate sums made available by the central government in accordance with the special needs and merits of each university. It also considered it absolutely necessary to establish a greater coordination between the Central and State governments.

Traditionally, education in India had been a provincial concern, but Article 246 of the Constitution of India gave the central government the responsibility of coordination and determination of standards in institutions for higher education or research including scientific and technical institutions. The Radhakrishnan Commission felt that while good governance of institutions for higher learning was possible only if wide powers were given to the State governments, the initiative in public education needed to be taken by both the provincial and the central government. However, coordination had to lie with the Centre to ensure that all States and Union Territories acted within certain limits and observed certain minimum standards. It was also necessary to ensure that gradually a coherent national policy would emerge on education. Joint planning by the Centre, States, and the Union Territories was needed in several areas.

Therefore, it suggested that education should be placed in the concurrent list in the Constitution. Coordination was not only needed between the Centre and the States but also among the universities themselves. Since research and advanced teaching had become extremely expensive, all universities could not specialise in every field. The only solution was to give the recommended University Grants Commission the task of coordination along with the sanction of giving or withholding grants.

Further, national laboratories, had to be established and scientific surveys carried out. These, it was felt, should be coordinated with the corresponding departments of the universities to prevent wasteful duplication of efforts. The Radhakrishnan Commission also recommended a two-way recruitment —that is, from the universities to laboratories and other research institutions and vice versa. The UGC was given the function of securing the cooperation of various agencies for this purpose by either sanctioning or withholding grants.

Following the publication of the report for establishing the University Education Commission, the Government of India proceeded to adopt more systematic measures for the coordination and determination of standards in universities. However, it took no immediate action to establish the recommended University Grants Commission. The existing University Grants Committee, too, was allowed to fade away. Instead of constituting a regulatory body, after the adoption of the Constitution of India, the government tried to regulate the universities through a Universities (Regulation of Standards) Bill (1951). The Bill provided for setting up the Central Council of University Education for the coordination and determination of academic standards in institutions of higher education in India. It was felt that neither coordination of institutions nor determination of their standards, which under the Constitution (entry 66 of List I) lay within the exclusive authority of Parliament, was possible unless the central government had some control over establishing new universities, the definition of their territorial jurisdiction, and the determination of the standards of teaching and examinations in universities, both old and new. The problem had become more acute on account of the tendency to multiply universities.

Significantly, the Central Council of University Education envisaged in the Draft Bill was not to be given any financial responsibility in respect of the universities. Its only concern was with matters relating to coordination and maintenance of standards in the sphere of university education. The Draft Bill was circulated to the State governments as well as to the universities for their opinion. As Humayun Kabir stated at a conference of vice-chancellors and representatives of universities in India held in September 1952 (approximately one year after the Bill was circulated), no State government except for one, had opposed it. However, universities were strongly and persistently against the Bill. They had three main objections:

- It was for the universities themselves to regulate, maintain and coordinate their own academic standards.

- If an outside agency undertook this job, it would amount to violating the university autonomy.
- Standards were low because of lack of funds and once adequate funds were made available, there would hardly be any problems.

The Ministry of Education, however, did not immediately agree to drop the Bill. Perhaps the government had a two-fold anxiety that while the Constitution had made education a 'State' subject, it had placed the responsibility of coordination and determination of standards in higher education on the Centre. The Centre therefore, could not carry out its responsibility without some kind of legal machinery. This was the purpose of the proposed Council. After another conference of Vice-Chancellors and State Education Ministers, in April 1953, the central government agreed to set up a UGC, which would have some of the powers that had been envisaged for the Council in the earlier Bill together with grant-giving functions. The body was to be called a 'Commission' rather than a 'Committee' to indicate that it had more autonomy than a committee would have. Thus, after a series of conferences and consultations, the idea of setting up a Central Council of Education was abandoned and it was agreed to set up a University Grants Commission as had been prescribed by the University Education Commission, presided over by Dr S. Radhakrishnan.

The Government of India set up an interim UGC by a resolution to advise it on the allocation of grants-in-aid from public funds to the central and other universities. It was also to advise the government on the allocation of grants-in-aid to other universities and institutions of higher learning whose case for such grants might be referred to the Commission by the government. It was to advise universities and other institutions of higher learning in respect of any questions referred to it by the government. The UGC was inaugurated by Maulana Abul Kalam Azad, the then Education Minister, and began to function from the last week of December 1953 with the noted scientist Dr Shanti Swarup Bhatnagar as its Chairman, together with eight other members. Samuel Mathai, Secretary of the Inter-University Board, was appointed as Secretary of the Commission.

The newly appointed UGC held its first meeting on December 28, 1953. Addressing the Commission, Maulana Azad gave an assurance that the government would treat its recommendations as binding and would be guided by its advice. He said that as the budget for the year had already been approved, the Chairman would be informed of the amount available for university education and the Commission would be free to allocate amounts among the universities. At its inaugural meeting, its first Chairman, Dr S.S. Bhatnagar, said that the success of the Commission would depend entirely on the autonomy it enjoyed and on the effect its advice had not only in university circles but also on those who were actively involved in the university and educational activities.

Prime Minister Jawaharlal Nehru inaugurated the Commission. His wide-ranging address covered almost all the issues that confronted higher education at that time. Addressing the meeting in Urdu, he said that establishing the Commission marked a revolutionary step in the field of higher education in the country. He urged the Commission to keep pace with the changing times and to suggest major policy decisions that would catalyse progress in the educational field. He said that he had given anxious thought not only to the establishment of the Commission, but also to the developments leading to its formation. A Grants Commission with the powers that had been given to the new body should have been set up years ago, he added. The older generation could then have kept in touch with the problems of the young in universities and could have also observed how men of their own generation were running educational institutions.

New factors had swept aside the old order. Jawaharlal Nehru expressed the hope that the UGC would evolve a policy that would bring about a complete reorientation of university education. India's independence had released forces that had revolutionised the thinking of young men in particular. There was a keen demand for education from all over the country even in its distant and interior parts. The villagers were even prepared to construct school buildings provided the government was willing to run them. That showed how earnest they were about learning. On the other hand, a question had also arisen, whether there was any use of opening more schools when the utility of the present educational system itself was in doubt.

Referring to the numerous colleges and the overcrowding of students in classes, Pandit Nehru wondered whether students learnt anything at all in such conditions. They might be better off with private tuitions and learning. He affirmed that in a changing world, decisions taken today became outdated after two or three years. But basic education alone seems to stay as the fundamental article of faith in the education system. Of course, it has to be modified to suit the circumstances. It was heartening he felt, that the Government of India had finally woken up to the responsibility given to it under the Constitution and had set up an independent Commission to act both as guide and guardian to the universities. He praised Maulana Azad for having assured the Commission at the very outset of non-interference by the government. Unhampered by day-to-day official control and certain in the knowledge that its recommendations would be binding on the government, the Commission could do a great deal to help universities to revive and reform themselves.

Focusing on a vision for the universities, the Prime Minister said that they needed proper direction and fresh funds. They needed to cut out waste and duplication and each institution had to have a character of its own instead of being a mere manufacturer of degree holders, as many had become. The running of such institutions had to be placed in the hands of those who understood the meaning and aim of education and not of careerists using universities for fulfilling their own ambitions. The Commission, in this context, had an immensely important and responsible role to play. With the purse strings in its hands, it would be the final arbiter in educational matters. Not expecting quick results, the Commission would at least improve the educational atmosphere so that universities would no longer be in a state of chaos or perpetual crisis.

Early Years

Entrusted with these awesome responsibilities and daunting tasks, the Commission started its work with surprisingly few resources, facilities and infrastructure. To begin with, accommodation for the Commission and the first group of office staff had to be found. A retired former Assistant Secretary in the Department of Education was appointed as the Assistant Secretary of the Commission. The Ministry of Education was very cooperative and gave the services of a few officers. The first office of the Commission was in Mandi House and later some rooms were built for it on the top floor of the building of the Council of Scientific and Industrial Research (CSIR) at what was then called the Old Mill Road. Later, the Commission constructed its own building and moved into it in 1963.

The Chairman, Dr S.S. Bhatnagar died at the beginning of 1955. He had very little time to devote to the Commission in the few months in office. He had continued to hold the office of the Secretary of the Ministry of Natural Resources and Scientific Research and also that of the Director General of the CSIR. The other first members of the Commission were also very distinguished people. Apart from K.G. Saiyidain and K.R.K. Menon who were Secretaries in the Ministry of Education and Finance, respectively, the other members were Dr A.L. Mudaliar (Vice-Chancellor, Madras University), Acharya Narendra Dev (Vice-Chancellor, Banaras Hindu University), Nevroji J. Wadia (Vice-Chancellor, Bombay University), Dr J.C. Ghosh (Vice-Chancellor, Calcutta University), Dr Zakir Husain (Vice-Chancellor, Aligarh Muslim University) and Pandit H.N. Kunzru, MP. The Commission, therefore, began its life prestigiously, but no one seemed to have a clear idea of what they were supposed to do. There was also no clear indication of the funds that would be available.

Before the first meeting of the Members of the Commission, Dr Bhatnagar wanted to do something 'dramatic' that would catch the attention of the universities. So it was considered that, to begin with, the salaries of the teachers should be raised by twenty-five per cent immediately. However, the Commission had not been allocated any funds yet and the then Finance Minister, C.D. Deshmukh, strongly opposed the proposal on the grounds that it would lead to limitless increase in expenditure. Nevertheless, the measure was implemented and became the first step in what was to become one of the major activities of the Commission–the periodic revision of salary scales of university and college teachers.

The Commission began its life in the middle of the First Five-Year Plan, and in the first year of its existence, its main concerns were really to secure adequate funds, recruit staff, establish contacts with universities, and identify their urgent needs for development. It had several meetings with the Planning Commission for determining the funds that should be made available. This was a rather difficult exercise since there was as yet no clear enunciation of either the principles according to which funds would be allocated for the purposes for which funds would be needed.

The Planning Commission tended to think in terms of "targets" to be achieved during a plan period and only "allocated" funds for them. The development of education, the raising of standards, the improvement of quality of teaching and the encouragement of research, could not always be expressed in financial terms or quantitative targets. The situation was not made easier by the procedural arrangements by which the funds allocated for the UGC were doled out in instalments by the Ministry of Education. Although the Commission was expected to operate in Five-Year Plan periods, it could never be sure that the 'plan funds' would in actual fact be available to it. This led to some difficulty and dissatisfaction later on, as all grants of the UGC to the universities for 'development' purposes had to be limited to one Plan Period and no guarantee could be given that the grant would continue into the next Plan Period.

For a year or so after Dr Bhatnagar's death, the Commission did not have a full-time Chairman. Humayun Kabir, Secretary, Ministry of Education, succeeded Dr Bhatnagar as Chairman and discharged those duties in addition to his own duties in the Education Ministry from January 2, 1955 until he resigned on February 22, 1956. H.N. Kunzru, who was a member, then took over as Chairman between February 23 and August 28, 1956. C.D. Deshmukh succeeded him as Chairman on August 29, 1956.

The Ministry of Education had been working on a Bill for setting up the UGC as a statutory body. There were some discussions in the Commission on the provisions of the draft Bill. The Commission's main anxiety was that the Act should not make the UGC a purely advisory body and that it should have autonomous powers to determine and disburse the grants that could be paid to the universities. While the UGC was to be modelled on the British University Grants Committee, care needed to be taken so that the universities in India did not lose their autonomy. The Chairman of the University Grants Committee in England, Sir Edward Hales, had seen a copy of the draft Bill of the Indian UGC and commented that appointing three vice-chancellors as members was "a cardinal blunder." This issue also arose in Parliament later during the course of the discussion on the Bill.

The UGC Bill in Parliament

Dr M.M. Das, Parliamentary Secretary to the Minister of Education, introduced a Bill in Parliament on September 30, 1954 to make provision for the coordination and determination of standards in universities and for that purpose, to establish a UGC as a statutory body. Earlier Maulana Azad introduced the statement of object and reason on September 24, 1954, which read as follows:

> The Constitution of India vests Parliament with exclusive authority in regard to coordination and determination of the standard in institution for higher education or research and scientific and technical institutions. It is obvious that neither coordination nor determination of standards is possible unless the central government has some voice in the determination of standards of teaching and examination in universities, both old and new. It is also necessary to ensure that the available resources are used to the best possible effect. The problem has become very acute recently on account of the tendency to multiply universities. The need for a properly constituted commission for determining and allocating top universities funds made available by the central government has also become more urgent on this account. It is, therefore, proposed to establish a University Grants Commission as a corporate body, which will enquire into the financial needs of universities for any general or specific purpose. The Commission will also have the power to recommend to any university the measures necessary for the reform and improvement of university education and to advise the university concerned on the action to be taken for the purpose of implanting such recommendations. The Commission will act as an expert body to advise the central government on problems

connected with the coordination of facilities and maintenance of standards in universities. The Commission in consultation with the university concerned will also have the power to cause an inspection or an enquiry to be made of any university established by law in India and to advise the university on any matter, which has been the subject of an enquiry or inspection. The Commission shall also advise, whenever such advice is sought, on the establishment of new universities.

The Bill also seeks to restrict the use of the word 'University' or the power to confer degrees, etc., to institutions as such by law in India or to institutions, empowered to do so by an Act of Parliament and provides a penalty for contravention of these provisions by an individual or a corporate body.

While the provisions of the Bill do not apply to institutions of higher education which are not universities, power is vested in the central government to declare any institution for higher education to be a university for the purposes of this Bill by issuing a notification in the Official Gazette.

The motion for the reference of the Bill to a joint committee of the Houses was moved by Dr M.M. Das on December 18, 1954, and was discussed the same day in the House, as well as on February 22 and 28, 1955. It was adopted on February 28, 1955. The Rajya Sabha discussed the motion on March 15, 16 and 21, 1955, and concurred in the said motion on March 21, 1955. The message from Rajya Sabha was read out to the Lok Sabha on March 22, 1955.

A lively debate ensued on the motion of referring the Bill to the Joint Committee that lasted for about six hours. Not only the broad principles, but also the objects and the reasons of the Bill were debated, and each and every provision of the Bill was subjected to a detailed scrutiny by several Members of Parliament. The first sitting of the Committee was held on April 2, 1955, to draw up a programme of work. At this sitting, the Committee also had a general discussion on the provisions of the Bill, which was continued at the second sitting held on April 18, 1955. The Committee took up clause-by-clause consideration for the Bill on April 19, 1955, which was continued at further sittings on April 21, as well as July 4, 5, 6 and 7, 1955 and concluded on July 9, 1955. The Committee sat in Poona from July 4 to July 9, 1955 and held five sittings with the permission of the Speaker. A motion for extension of time up to July 30, 1955 for presenting the report of the Committee was moved in Lok Sabha on April 29, 1955 and adopted. The Committee considered and adopted the report on July 26, 1955.

The majority of members, who took part in the debate before the Bill, referred it to the Joint Committee, cutting across party affiliations, as they expressed great concern about academic independence and firmly emphasised that the autonomous character of the universities must be maintained. Many expressed the fear that the UGC would be nothing more than an appendage of the central government.The central government would exert undue influence upon the universities through the UGC, thereby endangering their autonomy. Keeping this in view, Dr M.M. Das took care to inform the Lok Sabha, that the keynotes or the guiding principles of the Committee were the maintenance of academic independence and autonomy of the universities.

The Committee was of the opinion that:

> University education is a State subject and the States should be responsible for the maintenance of the universities, their constituent and affiliate colleges. The Centre should not take upon itself any responsibilities in the matter. The UGC will give grants where it thinks, that is helping a university in achieving its raison d'être, the advancing of the bounds of knowledge. University autonomy is basic to democracy in education and education for democracy. The concept of educational planning and engineering is also essential in a modern society. Therefore, any agencies set up for educational planning must be democratically constituted so that the criterion for determining such planning will be the claims of individual and academic freedom communicate with the needs of society rather than the policies of the government administrations.

The Committee was fully conscious of the great importance of the proposed measure and its far-reaching consequences. There was continual awareness that they were dealing with universities, the supreme and highest educational organisations of the country upon the well-being of which depended the future of India. It was careful, not even by a word or a phrase, to include any provision that could be construed to give either the central government or the Commission any authority over the universities. So much so that the Committee, according to Dr M.M. Das, had reduced the University Grants Commission to a mere Advisory and Consultative Body having no power to enforce its recommendations. The only authority that the Commission had, if a university did not agree or refused to carry out its recommendations, was to withhold its grant. The Commission could not impose any other punishment. The Bill was vigorously debated in both Houses of Parliament. Issues ranged from the very necessity of establishing a University Grants Commission to what was meant by the determination of standards and coordination, women's education, sports, rural universities, the examination system and the reforms required in it, the question of overcrowding and student absenteeism, the status of institutions that were neither universities nor colleges, the need to help and look after affiliated colleges where most of the teaching and learning took place, the funding of educational institutions and its implications, university autonomy and the demands of planning, national purposes to be achieved and a host of other issues.

Dr K.L. Shrimali made a comprehensive statement with regard to all the points raised pertaining to the Bill on December 6, 1955. He explained that a kind of partnership had to be created between the government and the universities. Both had a social purpose and universities worked for the realisation of the purpose as much as the government did. However, when planning was being done for national life, some kind of planning for universities was also inevitable. Universities could not be given absolute autonomy. In fact, no social institution could have such autonomy, since all of them had to work within a certain societal framework. The universities, too, had to realise that they had to adjust to major social needs and be responsive to the changes that were taking place in society. If they did not do so, they would defeat the very purpose of their existence.

While the government was anxious to maintain the autonomy of the universities, he said it was also crucial for it ensure that their development should be responsive to the national needs. The government could not be completely indifferent to what was happening in the universities and was aware that there were all kinds of factions, groups and intrigues. In such circumstances, the government could not ignore the ground realities and so some kind of planning was necessary. In a planned society, while the freedom of the universities had to be assured, harmony had also to be ensured between the two. The broad objectives of the Constitution had to be realised and the universities, needed to do their bit in this endeavour.

The government could not be indifferent to these broad objectives and national purposes while being very conscious of the fact that within this framework, the autonomy of universities needed to be respected and they had to be allowed to develop in their own way. A healthy relationship between the government and the universities was necessary. There should be no day-to-day interference of the government in the functioning of the universities. It was hoped that the setting up of the UGC would bring about such a harmonious relationship.

After this general statement, Dr Shrimali went through the Bill, clause by clause, incorporating amendments wherever required. Finally, both Houses of Parliament passed the Bill on March 3, 1956. In November 1956, the government published the required notification and the University Grants Commission became a statutory body with effect from November 5, 1956.

The UGC Act

Two important provisions of the 1951 Bill, which gave teeth to the proposed UGC, had been deleted. The 1951 Bill vested the central government with the power of approving or not approving a university established by a State Legislature. In the 1956 Act, this provision was altogether deleted and it was open to the State Legislature to establish any university without reference to the UGC. The second important change made in the new Act as compared to the 1951 Bill was that in the earlier Bill, it was open to the central government to de-recognise any degree conferred by a university provided the said university failed to carry out any directions given to it. This de-recognition would be for the purpose of employment under the central government or for any other purpose. Now, this provision too was deleted.

The University Grants Commission Act, as finally passed gave the UGC the responsibility for the allocation of funds, placed at its disposal, to universities, for the maintenance and development to central universities, and for the development to State universities —as a means to achieve the objectives of, "The promotion and coordination of university education and for the determination and maintenance of standards of teaching, examination and research." The authority of the Commission to improve standards got diluted and remained merely advisory and, in the situation prevailing in the country at the time, largely ineffective. Although the body as it emerged did not have the power to create new institutions or disaffiliate existing ones, it still shaped itself into a unique body, different from its model in the U.K., of combining in itself both functions of giving grants and of coordinating and maintaining standards.

The Commission was meant to be a corporate body consisting of nine members, to be appointed by the central government. The members were to be chosen as follows:

- Not more than three members from among the Vice-Chancellors of universities.

- Two members from among the officers of the Central Government to represent the government.
- The remaining members from among those who were educationists of repute or had achieved high academic distinction.

The one condition was that not less than half of the total members so chosen could be from among persons who were not officers of the central government or any of the State governments.

The Central Government was to nominate a member of the Commission as the Chairman; one who was neither an officer of the Central Government nor of any State government. Every member was to hold office for a term of six years. The Commission could associate with anyone whose assistance or advice it desired in carrying out its functions. The general duty of the Commission was to take, in consultation with universities and other bodies concerned, all such measures as it considered fit for the promotion and coordination of university education and for the determination and maintenance of standards of teaching, examination and research in universities.

The Act set forth the power and functions of the Commission under Article 12 as follows:

> It shall be the general duty of the Commission to take, in consultation with the universities or other bodies concerned, all such steps as it may think fit for the promotion and coordination of university education and for the determination and maintenance of standards of teaching, examination and research in universities, and for the purpose of performing its functions under this Act, the Commission may:
>
> (i) Inquire into the financial needs of the universities.
>
> (ii) Allocate and disburse grants to universities established or incorporated by or under a Central Act for the maintenance and development of such universities or for any other general or specified purpose.
>
> (iii) Allocate and disburse such grants to universities for development purpose.
>
> (iv) Recommend to any university the measures necessary for the improvement of university education.
>
> (v) Advise the Central and State governments to allocate grants to universities for any general or specified purpose out of the Consolidated Fund of India or the State, as the case may be.

(vi) Advise any authority, it required, on the establishment of a new university or the expansion of the activities of any university.

(vii) Advise the Central or any State government or university on any question, which may be referred to the Commission by the Central, or the State government or the university, as the case may be.

(viii) Collect information on all such matters relating to university education in India and abroad.

(ix) Require a university to furnish it with such information as the case may be needed relating to the financial position of the university or the studies in the various branches of learning undertaken in that university; and perform such other functions as may be prescribed or as may be deemed necessary by the Commission for advancing the causes of higher education in India.

The UGC Act of 1956 has been amended from time to time as situations have demanded by Parliament by Act No. 27 of 1970 (No. 33 of 1972). The Act was further amended by the UGC Act, 1984 (No. 59 of 1984) and the UGC (amendment) Act, 1985 (No. 70 of 1985).

The UGC Today

As it functions today, the principal concerns of the UGC are coordination and maintenance of standards; allocation and disbursement of grants; and interface with institutions that receive advice and grants from it. Much of the UGC's infrastructure is deployed in these three areas.

When the UGC came into being as a statutory body, it consisted of nine members including the Chairman whose office was a full-time salaried one. According to the Act, all members, including the Chairman, were to be appointed by the central government. Apart from the ex-officio members, the rest were to be educationists or those who had obtained high academic distinction. The Commission was assisted in its work by a full-time paid Secretary, an Assistant Secretary and some staff. It was empowered to associate itself with others whose assistance or advice it might need from time to time.

As amended in 1972, the University Grants Commission consists of a Chairman, a Vice-Chairman and ten other members. The Chairman and the Vice-Chairman are full-time members, while the others are part-time. The Commission in addition has a non-member secretary. While the

Commission itself decides on policy issues, the implementation of it is left to the secretariat of the UGC.

Two members are chosen from among the officers of the Central Government to represent the government. Not less than four are to be chosen from among those who are teachers of universities at the time when they are so chosen and the rest from among:

(i) those with knowledge of, or experience in, agriculture, commerce or industry;

(ii) members of the engineering, legal, medical or any other learned profession;

(iii) Vice-Chancellors of universities or who, not being teachers of universities, are, in the opinion of the central government, educationists of repute or have achieved high academic distinctions.

However, not less than half of the members chosen under (iii) should be from among those who are not officers of the Central or any State government.

While the original Act provided that no more than three members to be appointed from among Vice-Chancellors of universities, the amended Act of 1972 provided that not less than four members be chosen from among the teachers of universities. In the originally constituted UGC, teachers of universities had no place as such. In the amended Act, they were given representation to the extent of at least one-third of the total membership. The Vice-Chancellors of universities were also now included in one of the three categories from which the remaining four, or less than four, members were to be chosen. This was a significant change in the Constitution because it gave due recognition to the views of university teachers in shaping policies and determining the activities of the UGC. This was appropriate as it was the universities that had to implement them and ensure that the objects of higher education were being truly served.

With the expansion of higher education and in pursuance of the National Policy on Education (1986), the UGC decentralised its function by opening six regional offices from 1994 to 1999, and two additional bureaus. The regional centres set up are the Southern Eastern Regional Office (SERO) in Hyderabad; the Western Regional Office (WRO) in Pune; the Central Regional Office (CRO) in Bhopal; the North Eastern Regional Office (NERO) in Guwahati; the Eastern Regional Office (ERO) in Kolkata; and the South-Western Regional Office (SWRO) in Bangalore. The two bureaus are the Northern Regional College Bureau in Delhi that function from Feroze Shah Road and Delhi University South Campus. The aim is to enable the

UGC to respond to the needs of the growing number of colleges throughout the country.

According to a UGC report, "Higher Education at a Glance", presenting vital statistics pertaining to higher education from 1950 to 2013, there are 700 degree-awarding institutions in the country. Of these 44 per cent, that is, 306 are State universities; followed by 129 or 18 per cent deemed universities, central universities and institutes of national importance are 6 per cent and 10 per cent, respectively. There are only 154 private universities accounting for 22 per cent share.

This shows the tremendous growth of higher education. Out of these, the UGC funds 39 central universities, 153 State universities, 24 deemed universities and 5,420 colleges. In 1950, the total number of universities was 30, mostly government-run or funded, and the number of colleges was 695, giving an average of 23 colleges per university. In 2011, the number of universities grew 30 times to stand at 634, while there were 33,023 colleges, averaging about 52 colleges to each university. In actual fact, the pressure of colleges on universities is much more than it appears because many are either private or unitary universities.

The student strength in higher education, too, has also obviously risen manifold. It was 3,97,000 in 1950 growing steadily to 83,99,000 in 2001. After this, the next ten years saw an unprecedented surge in enrollment rising to 1,69,75,000 in 2010–2011.

This shows that the UGC has come a long way from 1956 when C.D. Deshmukh took over as its first full-time Chairman. He came to this post after he resigned as the Finance Minister. A highly erudite and learned person, he quickly acquainted himself with the major challenges of higher education in India. His early experience of administration and financial management proved very valuable to the UGC and his personal eminence helped in establishing its authority in the country.

The expenditure on higher education was 7.92 per cent of the total public expenditure, which was 0.64 per cent of GDP. In 2009, it stood at 16.36 per cent of total public expenditure, that is, 3.77 per cent of GDP of which higher education got 32.3 per cent. The UGC funds universities and colleges, apart from the individual schemes in which funding is given to research scholars and teachers. It achieves these objectives through various schemes launched periodically.

While undoubtedly the UGC has grown with the education system and has become not only a grant-giving but also a policy-making body, it has not always been able to emphatically shape and implement policy.

The retreat of the Central Government under pressure from States and universities from the stand it had taken in the draft Universities (Regulation of Standards) Bill, 1951 and acceptance of a radically diluted UGC Act, 1956, was a crucial event in the history of higher education in India. It resulted in the laissez-faire growth of universities and colleges whose proliferation led the UGC to concentrate primarily on infrastructural facilities such as buildings, equipment, libraries and adequately qualified staff.

Growth and Development

Although it started functioning on December 28, 1953, UGC became a statutory body only in 1956. Established on the recommendation of the First Education Commission chaired by Dr Radhakrishnan, its principal concerns were the coordination and maintenance of standards; and the allocation and disbursement of grants. Therefore, it had a direct relationship with educational institutions that it advised and financed. Since its very inception, the UGC was given wide-ranging responsibilities. It continues to regulate fees and prohibit the acceptance of donations. It inspects universities and withholds grants where it considers fit. Since it is the main statutory body that has been given responsibility for higher education, its evolution is naturally connected to the way universities expand and grow; the problems and challenges that they face; and how these challenges are to be met both at the policy level and at their implementation. The issues are several: expansion and the resources that can be made available, their optimum utilisation, the medium of instruction, starting of new courses, needs of infrastructure and staff, student welfare, skill development, use of ICT for promoting access, equity, and research, open and distance learning, diversification and interaction with the community and extension activities.

As the higher education system has grown, so has the UGC. The 1950s and 1960s saw an explosion of student enrollment that increased by as much as 11–14 per cent. While the UGC had to cope with the increased financial demands of universities, it was faced with the classic dilemma of quantity and quality. The Kothari Commission confronted the situation and recommended wide-ranging reforms pertaining to welfare measures for students, the examination and evolution system, and reduction of regional disparities. The UGC, recognising the need for quality and excellence in higher education, took steps to promote certain departments where commendable work was being done as Centres of Advanced Study. It also emphasised scientific and technical education while it developed Area Studies for research on countries of particular interest to India.

Expansion and Autonomy

As the Commission grappled with the problem of numbers, it realised that while they were overwhelming yet in the relevant age group, the access to higher education was hardly adequate. Limited resources enjoined caution against reckless expansion, yet expansion could not and would not be denied. It also had to be equitable as education was a tool for upward mobility for the weaker sections of society. In the 1970s and 1980s, while the usual measures such as, examination reforms, strengthening of infrastructure, student welfare and others took place, steps were taken to consolidate the gains made while moving towards new areas for development. Efforts were made to attract and retain talent in the teaching profession by revising salaries to bring them more or less at level with the All India Services. At the same time, efforts were made to lay down the essential qualifications necessary while recruiting teachers and to recommend promotional avenues. The Sen Committee, appointed in 1973, made recommendations to that end.

Attempts were also made to give greater academic freedom to educational institutions and organisations. The idea of autonomous colleges came up in 1967–68. Not only for colleges, autonomy was recommended even for university departments. Women's education began to be foregrounded at the same time as it was acknowledged as a critical input in societal transformation. At the same time, the Commission began to turn its attention to the educational problems of the marginalised and underprivileged sections of society, the Scheduled Castes and Scheduled Tribes.

While the UGC grappled with the problem of numbers, it could not abandon its responsibility towards quality. While it tried its best to provide facilities and in-service programmes for teachers, it also decided to bring in accountability and deny grants to colleges and institutions that did not follow the guidelines issued by it. It also identified new areas for measures to be taken to provide access and opportunities while simultaneously introducing measures that would streamline and strengthen higher education. The Mehrotra Committee reviewed the pay scales of teachers. The recommendations had some specific objectives: make the teaching profession attractive for the talented; ensure accountability and in-service training, and increase the general awareness of the teachers. The UGC tried to fulfil its responsibilities by setting up Academic Staff Colleges and Orientation programmes. The National Policy on Education (1986) also had made far-reaching recommendations that needed to be actualised. The Commission identified some major spheres of work for itself, such as autonomous colleges, redesigning courses, establishing State Councils of Higher Education and Accreditation and Assessment Councils, Alternative Models of Management in Universities, National Qualifying Test for recruitment of teachers, broad-based research and development, training and orientation of teachers, improvement of efficiency, and education for the Minorities, Scheduled Castes, Scheduled Tribes, the physically challenged, and women. As it went about its assigned tasks, the UGC tried its best not to impose decisions from above but to facilitate them through dialogues with universities, State governments, teachers and students.

Struggling with numbers, and with issues of general development that required access to all sections of society while maintaining quality, the UGC tried to harness technology and media to reach out where classrooms could not physically go. Rapid global changes also highlighted alternative management modes. If an efficient delivery system had to be established, the approach had to be decentralised and participatory, for only then effective implementation was possible. At the same time, issues of funding and resource mobilisation had to be confronted as well. While it was absolutely clear that the State had to accept the main responsibility for higher education, the possibilities of private funding were explored.

As the twentieth century drew to a close, fresh challenges were accepted. The main among them was globalisation. National boundaries were getting blurred and the means of communication had become rapid, almost instantaneous, making knowledge increasingly available through information technology. The UGC had to adjust and to adapt. Internationalisation of education, the creation of virtual classrooms, use of television channels for the dissemination of knowledge, distance education, development of vocational skills, interdisciplinary research, sophisticated science centres, area studies of different countries, as well as pursuit of excellence through different means like Centres of Advanced Study were all efforts to satisfy diverse and often contradictory needs and requirements of higher education.

The Golden Jubilee year 2002 was also the watershed in the life of the UGC. Issues pertaining to higher education were widely discussed and disseminated throughout the country through public lectures and national and regional seminars organised by the UGC. This prepared the ground for widespread debate and discussion on higher education. The challenges became a concern in the public domain giving rise to a continuing discourse to the extent that was not commonplace earlier. It was then not merely coincidental that the decade after the Golden Jubilee period was one of intense activity.

In its journey of 60 years, UGC has played a key role in the expansion of higher education and the creation of skilled human resource that has helped the country to grow and develop. In addition, this human resource has gone out of India and made a mark in different countries giving India the identity of a knowledge-based society. Hence, much has been achieved but of course, far more needs to be done. If we look back from 1953, when UGC was first established as a committee, to the present, it has come a long way indeed. It has evolved from a grant-giving advisory body to one that shapes policy and its implementation.

Obviously the future path of the UGC is going to be radically different and expanded from the one traversed so far. As the only statutory body in the country that is mandated to coordinate and maintain standards of higher education in the country, the UGC will have to shoulder much greater responsibilities for which it will have to prepare itself. To begin with, it will have to improve its physical infrastructure.

If the UGC has to shoulder all the new responsibilities, it has to restructure and expand its domain of action to prevent fragmentation and contradiction. For this, it will have to evolve from a Grants Commission to an Education Commission and accept all post-secondary education as its province in one integrated ecosystem of knowledge.

Reference

1. Owen, Tom. 1980. *Oxford Review of Education*, Vol. 6, No. 3, pp. 255-278. The University Grants Committee.

4

NUEPA—From Regional Centre to University*

The National University of Educational Planning and Administration (NUEPA) began life as the Regional Centre for the training of educational planners, administrators and supervisors in Asia at New Delhi in February 1962, under an agreement between the United Nations Educational, Scientific and Cultural Organisation (UNESCO) and the Government of India. Establishment of the Centre was a logical result of the importance attached by UNESCO to the training of planners and administrators who were seen as essential for the proper planning and development of education. The involvement of UNESCO in setting up of such an institute was of immense significance considering that the state of education in Asia was poor. Resources were scant and regional cooperation was necessary for the spread of education in this region. UNESCO was the only organisation that could provide a framework for regional cooperation in education. The vision statement of the institute, "To become a centre of excellence in educational policy, planning and management by promoting advanced level teaching, research and capacity building in national and global contexts," clearly reflected this.

The Centre began with the aim of preparing key personnel needed for implementing the Karachi Plan, formulated in 1959–1960 at a meeting held in Karachi, under the auspices of UNESCO, to look into the educational challenges in its Asian member states. The first director was Shri A.V. Pai. The Centre was re-designated the Asian Institute of Educational Planning and Administration (AIEPA) in April 1965. This Institute began its journey

---

* This article has been extracted and summarised from the author's book: *National University of Educational Planning and Administration and Transformational Journey.* Published by NUEPA, 2015.

without any infrastructure of its own. Pending the construction of its buildings and hostel, it was temporarily located in one of the buildings of the Indian Institute of Public Administration, New Delhi, with the fellows being accommodated in a government hotel. It shifted to its own premises in 1973. On August 26, 1970 a new agreement was signed between UNESCO and the Government of India, the nomenclature of the Asian Institute was changed to National Institute of Educational Planning and Administration (NIEPA). The evolutionary journey of the institution culminated with its becoming a university in 2006, the only university in the country today for educational planning and administration.

Why UNESCO?

The two World Wars, with their increasing scale of destruction and human loss, brought to the fore, with a sense of considerable urgency, the need to form an organisation that could promote world peace. That the path to it would be through culture and education was realised in the early 1920s as is manifest in the statement of the French philosopher Paul Valery, "A society of minds is the prerequisite for a society of nations." This became a source of inspiration to both thinkers and politicians. It led to the establishment of a unit known as "The Committee on Intellectual Cooperation" in 1922 within the framework of the League of Nations. It was initially composed of 12 individuals, including well-known scientists and scholars such as Albert Einstein, Madame Curie and Sir Jagdish Chandra Bose.

The League of Nations could not prevent the Second World War. The United Nations (UN) was then established in 1945 with the purpose of maintaining international peace and security, developing friendly relations among nations on the principle of equal rights and self-determination and encouraging international cooperation in solving international economic, social, cultural and humanitarian problems. UNESCO, a specialised agency of the United Nations, was created in 1946 to contribute to world peace by promoting international collaboration in education, science and culture.

At the preparatory conference in London in November 1945, sponsored by Britain and France, the French representative declared that the aim of the proposed organisation was, "to create the spirit of peace throughout the world." His counterpart from Britain concurred saying, "Our watchword is education that the minds of the people shall be attuned to peace."

The Constitution of UNESCO came into effect from November 16, 1945. It indicated the possibility of a world where, "Through the wide diffusion of culture and the education of humanity for justice and liberty, lasting peace would be established on the intellectual and moral solidarity of mankind." Julian Huxley's famous formulation was adopted in the Preamble to the Constitution. "Since wars begin in the minds of men, it is in the minds of men that the defences of peace must be constructed." These words recognised the need to banish war following the horrible destruction and loss of life in the Second World War. The Preamble and Act I of the Constitution developed this postulate and declared, in unequivocal terms, that the denial of the democratic principles of dignity, equality and mutual respect could lead to conflicts and wars. A peace built only on political and economic arrangements of governments could not be a lasting one. "The peace must therefore be founded, if it is not to fail, upon the intellectual and moral solidarity of mankind." The objective of UNESCO was to build an international environment of peace with collaboration among nations through education, cultural exchanges, development of science and technology, communication and related fields to further universal respect for justice, rule of law, human rights and fundamental freedoms without distinction of race, colour, sex and religion. It was also realised then that Asia needed urgent help both for promoting education and for finding the resources to do so. India played an important role.

The Karachi Plan

In the Asia-Pacific region, the Karachi Plan worked according to the three fundamental characteristics of the region: its immensity, diversity and unity. The attempt was to develop a capacity in the region to muster resources for cooperation, including funds, from other agencies of the UN, bilateral assistance and foundations.

UNESCO convened a Regional Conference on Free and Compulsory Primary Education in South Asia and the Pacific in Bombay (Mumbai) in 1952 with two objectives. The first was to identify the major needs and problems of the region in the provision of compulsory primary education. The second was to mobilise resources for member states both from within and from outside through international agencies.

After eight years, it was necessary to review the progress so as to plan a more comprehensive and well-coordinated drive for promoting primary education in the area. The General Conference of UNESCO, therefore, in its tenth session in Paris, in 1958, made a financial provision for "preliminary studies in 1959–1960 with a view to initiating a major project for the extension of compulsory primary education in Asian countries."

It was expected that the situation in the region would be frankly assessed and certain definite goals would be agreed upon taking into account the available national resources, both financial and of technical personnel and the international and foreign assistance that might be available. Possible solutions to the problems would be outlined, together with the means required to implement them, actions would have to be taken both in the short- and long-term. The most important challenge was to evolve a working plan for providing universal, compulsory and free primary education in the region.

In pursuance of this Resolution, the Secretariat reviewed all the relevant documents pertaining to Asian member states and conducted a survey for which it sent a questionnaire to the states, seeking more recent information. This was studied and supplemented by the findings of four consultants: Professor J.P. Naik and Dr E.A. Pires from India; Mr M.S. Huq from Pakistan and Mr M. Junsai from Thailand. Each of them made on-the-spot studies of the three or four countries assigned to them to ascertain actual problems and needs in connection with primary and compulsory education. The entire material generated in the process was collected and placed before a Working Party consisting of the four consultants and a Secretariat Staff Member, Mr M.K. Rahman from Pakistan, who was the Programme Specialist in Primary Education.

The Working Party prepared a document giving detailed findings of the survey. It identified both qualitative and quantitative problems and needs of the region that called for urgent attention if primary education had to be made universal. The results of the survey were placed before the Regional Meeting of Representatives of Asian member states on Primary and Compulsory Education held in Karachi from December 28, 1959 to January 9, 1960. The meeting was attended by delegates from 17 member states, representatives of the United Nations (UN), International Labour Office (ILO) and United Nations Children's Fund (UNICEF), now known as the United Nations Children's Education Fund and observers from the World Confederation of Organisations of the Teaching Profession (WCOTP), All Pakistan Women's Association, Ford Foundation and Asia Foundation. The purpose was to plan concerted action within the region, discuss whether the resources for the measures to be taken would come from the national budgets of the member states concerned or would assistance on a bilateral or multilateral basis be required from UNESCO or other agencies operating in the region.

The meeting concentrated on drawing up a Working Plan for the region in the field of primary education to facilitate concerted action by member states, international organisations, in particular UNESCO, and other agencies working on bilateral and multilateral bases. After examining in detail the problems that required urgent attention, it adopted a set of recommendations for action at national levels, indicating measures required to be taken and the help needed from UNESCO and other agencies. The recommendations also included the projects in Primary Education that could be undertaken for the Eleventh Session of the General Conference in November 1960 (implementable in 1961–1962).

The Plan assumed that the total population of the area would rise from 750 million in 1950 to 1100 million in 1980. It proposed to expand schooling facilities, which catered to 35 million (5.7 per cent of the total population) in 1950, to 65 million (8.4 per cent of the total population) in 1960; to 90 million (11 per cent of the total population) in 1965, to 125 million (17 per cent of the total population) in 1970; to 107 million (17 per cent of the total population) in 1975; and 220 million (20 per cent of the total population) in 1980. This was considered modest and realistic as it would attain, after 20 years, a target that had already been achieved by some of the countries like Japan and Sri Lanka, while it was considerably lower than the prevailing position in the advanced countries. It assumed a teacher-pupil ratio of 1:35, which was the international average, a substantial increase in the salaries of teachers, training facilities for them in good training institutions, provision of school buildings and equipment on a moderate scale, textbooks, teaching aids and residences for teachers. The Plan assumed that the average recurring cost per pupil would rise from about six dollars in 1960 to $10 in 1965, $12 in 1970, $16 in 1975 and $20 in 1980. These estimates were very modest compared to the expenditure in more favourably situated areas in the world.

However, expenditure was not the only challenge. A more serious and huge issue was that of personnel. For implementing the programme, 8.5 million teachers would be needed in the entire period, i.e. about 407,000 per annum on an average. The annual need of teachers would rise from 242,000 between 1960 and 1965 to about 580,000 between 1965 and 1970. This would necessitate a rise in teacher educators from the existing strength of 19,000 to 110,000 in 1980, i.e. about 1,700 per annum on an average.

The material requirements of the Plan were also formidable. For an additional enrollment of 156 million children, 5.5 million classrooms would be needed, with four million residences for teachers besides furniture, teaching aids, textbooks and reading materials. Obviously, these goals would generate tremendous activity requiring immense resources in manpower and funds beyond just the requirements of teachers, teacher educators and educational administrators.

The Plan showed that the total cost of implication of even this modest plan would be to the tune of $65 billion per annum. This translated to only $3.5 per annum per head that might rise to five dollars per head by 1980; this actually was a very small amount by Western Standards. The US was already spending 56 dollars per head (of its population) per annum. Very limited finances, however, were available in Asia at this time and therefore the requirements for this modest programme could not be met from internal resources. The average per capita income in many regions of this area was about $60 and the governments could not afford to spend more than four or five dollars per head per annum. It was clear that the progress of primary education could not be left to internal resources only. The only feasible solution lay in external financial assistance of a high magnitude, primarily from the more favourably placed countries and agencies such as the UNESCO, for the following 5 to 20 years. UNESCO would need to use its good offices to make this materialise.

The next important issue was that of the major needs and problems of primary education in this region and how they could be solved. On examining the existing position of primary education in the States of the region, it was found that schooling facilities were inadequate and 87 million out of 152 million children were not enrolled in any school. Administrative machinery for planning and implementing programmes of primary education was inadequate. The teachers were very poorly paid. The facilities for teacher training were inadequate and unsatisfactory. There was a great shortage of classrooms and equipment. Textbooks, reading materials and even paper were in short supply. Teaching methodology was inefficient. All these factors contributed, *inter alia*, to huge wastage and stagnation.

In an effort to solve these problems, each member state was asked to prepare a National Plan for universal, compulsory and free primary education in its area. These plans could broadly be based on the Working Plan adopted by the meeting and indicate the goals proposed to be reached, the period required, the total expenditure involved, the internal resources available, and the type and extent of the external assistance required. Such national plans would be useful both for the mobilisation of internal resources and for seeking external assistance.

The meeting emphasised the pivotal role and importance of educational planning, development, and finance in becoming an integral part of balanced economic and social development. Hence, the meeting recommended to member states that each of them should place their educational plan and the Working Plan for further examination and analysis before their respective Ministries of Education, Economic Affairs, or Finance or any other appropriate national planning body, if possible, by June 1960. This would enable the educational plan to become part of the national development plan, so as to ensure its continuous implementation. It was also recommended that UNESCO should consult the Economic Commission for Asia and the Far East (ECAFE) and other appropriate specialised agencies for undertaking joint UNESCO and ECAFE studies for educational planning and financing as part of balanced economic development in Asia.

The meeting further recommended strengthening the machinery for primary education by staffing it with competent officers. The planning, statistics and finance sections, in particular, were weak and needed special attention. Getting better teachers was next in the order of priority because improved teachers was recognised as the most effective way of raising standards of primary education. This meant revising pay scales in areas where they were low; improving conditions of service, providing security of tenure and for old age. Increased and better facilities for teacher training were required together with training teacher-educators. Larger number of school buildings, adequate equipment and teaching aids also required attention. Finally, assistance and incentives in the form of mid-day meals, health services, free textbooks and educational materials would have to be given to children to attend school. In short, an intensive drive, both quantitative and qualitative, would have to be launched and continuously maintained for 20 years.

Finally, the meeting had to make recommendations on the exact scope and nature of the UNESCO programme for primary education in the Asian Region during 1961–62. It felt that three types of programmes could be organised:

1. Assist programmes at the national level to establish essential organisations for preparing and implementing programmes of compulsory primary education such as units for demographics studies, statistics, research and evaluation, educational finance, school buildings research; and research on textbooks and teaching aids. UNESCO should assist establishing such units by providing expert guidance, facilities for training officials including award of scholarships and fellowships, and monetary grants.
2. The second programme would entail proposals involving more than one state and implemented through bilateral and multilateral arrangements. Projects in this sphere would include research in teaching languages which was a special problem in the Asian region; acquiring curricular and supplementary reading materials and preparing textbooks; education of girls and tribal children.

3. The third programme would propose schemes in which all or most states of the region would be involved. This would mean establishing centres for training teacher-educators, educational supervisors and administrators; research in the design and construction of school buildings; and establishing an Educational Bureau, which would function as a coordinating agency and clearing house in the region for the programme. These projects would be financed mostly through the funds of UNESCO and other agencies of international cooperation.

While the entire plan was welcomed at the meeting, there was acute realisation that the funds available for it were very inadequate. Hence, it requested the Director General to recommend to the General Conference, at its eleventh session to be held in Paris in November 1960, a substantial increase in the allocation of funds and for continuing of the programme for 20 years.

In conclusion, the meeting drew the attention of the advanced countries, UNESCO and other bilateral and multilateral agencies of international cooperation to the magnitude of effort required to provide compulsory and free primary education to the 220 million children of Asia over a period of 20 years. It emphasised the urgency and significance of the successful implementation of this effort because on it depended not only the future welfare of the region, but also the peace and prosperity of the entire world.

To assist member states in developing the various elements of the Plan, UNESCO set up in Bangkok, three regional institutions for teachers' training, school buildings and planning, and a regional office responsible for documentation and coordination. The meeting of the Ministers of Education of the Asian member states —the first of a long series—held in Tokyo reviewed the Karachi Plan in the context of economic and social development and established an inter-governmental framework for regional cooperation. Japan offered its support as an industrialised country.

Establishing the Regional Centre

The General Conference of UNESCO, at its eleventh session, considered the Karachi Plan and authorised the Director-General to initiate work in educational planning and regional activities pertaining to education in Asia. Thus, was born the Regional Centre in February 1962, which was re-designated as the AIEPA on April 1, 1965. The services of the Institute were to be made available to the following participating member states of UNESCO in Asia: Afghanistan, Burma, (Myanmar), Cambodia, Ceylon (Sri Lanka), Republic of China, India, Indonesia, Iran, Japan, Republic of

Korea, Laos, Malaysia, Mongolia, Nepal, Philippines, Singapore, Thailand and Republic of Vietnam.

The main functions of the Institute were to provide short in-service training courses for the officers of the various Ministries or Departments of Education (DoE) of participating Asian member states; undertake and promote research in the techniques of educational planning and administration; place the results at the disposal of such member states; and assist such states, on their request, in organising educational planning services and holding national training courses.

The general supervision of the Institute was vested in a Steering Committee consisting of the Secretary to the Ministry of Education, Government of India, who was to be its Chairperson; the Director of the UNESCO Regional Office for Education in Asia, Bangkok; and the Chief of the UNESCO Mission in India. The Director of the Institute was to be the Secretary of the Committee. The first full-time Director was Dr K.S. Saiyidain who joined in April 1966.

UNESCO assumed the responsibility of meeting the salaries of the full-time staff members and honoraria for part-time lecturers. It would also provide equipment, books and other publications that were not available locally. Under the agreement, UNESCO's assistance was to cease after a 10-year period ending in 1972. The Government of India, on its part, was to provide teaching and residential accommodation, with necessary furniture and fittings, and the administrative and ancillary staff. It was also to meet the cost of internal travel of the staff and of the fellows. The Institute could invite experts and specialists to deliver lectures and to participate in its programmes in the different fields covered by the courses conducted by it.

The first full-time Director of the Institute was Dr K.S. Saiyidain. He joined in April 1966. Author of several books, he had been Education Secretary to the Government of India and a Member of the Education Planning Commission. In addition, there was the following staff: an Executive Director; a Coordinator of Studies; a Statistician; an economist; two UNESCO experts, comprising an economist and an educationist; a Finance Officer; an Administrative Officer; a documentalist and a librarian. Besides, the Institute could invite experts and specialists to deliver lectures and to participate in its programmes in the different fields covered by the courses to be conducted by it.

The Early Years

In the early years, UNESCO took a great deal of interest in promoting educational planning as a specialised activity. It organised a number of international conferences in different parts of the world, particularly in Africa, Asia and the Latin America, bringing together educators, sociologists, economists, administrators and statisticians, and collaborated with a number of national governments in setting up regional institutions for training in educational planning. It also set up an International Institute for Educational Planning (IIEP) at Paris.

Educational planning was really as old as educational administration. The newly independent countries of Asia and Africa were passing through a revolution of rising expectations, not only for food, clothing, housing and medical care, but also for education. The United Nations, by designating the 1960s as the "Development Decade", had given fresh impetus to the idea of educational planning. Studies of the economies of some of the advanced countries revealed that education was, perhaps, the single most important determinant of economic growth.

From its very inception, one of the key mandates of the Regional Centre and, later, the Institute was to organise training courses in educational planning. It was also to organise short seminars and expert meetings for participants from within the region and short-term courses for Indian educators, to which trainees from other Asian countries would also be invited. Further, it would advise and assist the Asian member states in the preparation of national courses in educational planning and administration in their own countries.

Objectives of Training Courses

The primary object of the training courses was to bring together senior officials from different countries of Asia to study the skills and techniques of educational planning and administration. By living and working together, the participants could exchange and analyse ideas and experiences; develop close insight into the educational programmes of different Asian countries and the techniques adopted by them for educational reconstruction as an important tool of general socio-economic development; get a deeper understanding of the interrelationships between different sectors of education and between the development of education, on the one hand, and the general socio-economic development of the country, on the other; and enrich their minds and increase their competence as planners and administrators by developing greater insight and a broader approach to educational programmes. UNESCO awarded fellowships to enable officers of member states to participate. At the same time, fellows sponsored by the host country, the UNICEF and other agencies of international cooperation, and by the Asian member states themselves could also be admitted to the courses.

Up to 1966, the Institute had worked on the region as a whole with no special emphasis on India. On February 10, 1967, a meeting was held to examine the possibility of adding an Indian wing, with financial help from the UNESCO, as follow-up action on the Report of the Indian Education Commission. The Institute, at this time, began concentrating on Indian education, as a prelude to becoming the National Staff College for Educational Planners and Administrators (NSCEPA) as recommended by the Education Commission. Towards this aim, it started concentrating on organising seminars, conferences and other academic activities with focus solely on India. Some significant issues were taken up.

Widening the Educational Base

A state seminar on 'School Improvement Projects and Community Support' was organised in 1969–70, highlighting the importance of community participation to increase the penetration of education. Professor N.D. Sundaravadivelu, the then Vice-Chancellor, University of Madras, made some valuable points on making education more widespread. He referred to Mahatma Gandhi's concept of *Gramraj* which, essentially meant that the village had to take the responsibility for its own welfare and upkeep without looking at any external agency. There could be no two opinions on the soundness of the philosophy and the vitality of the idea. He pointed out that the mind-set of the villager had undergone a change; although illiterate himself he understood the value of education, unlike his forefathers. He keenly wanted to educate his children and this desire could be used for the rebuilding morale, and for inculcating the spirit of self-help, self-reliance and self-confidence among the masses. Education could now be regarded as a birth right and essential for every citizen. Without it, democracy could not function efficiently and safely for long. This realisation prompted the Constitution-makers to make it a Directive Principle in the Constitution. It was mandated upon the State to provide free and compulsory education up to the age of 14. Very wisely, a lower age limit was not given.

With the spread of education, more and more children from poorer families started going to school. The result was that instruction was not merely confined to those who could afford a square meal but was extended to those who were even poorer. To educate a starving child was next to impossible as hunger and the consequent inattentiveness considerably affected the capacity to absorb and benefit from classroom teaching. The same circumstances adversely affected the participation of the children in co-curricular activities. Under these circumstances, the children of the poor, however well-equipped by nature, could not do as well as those children whose wants were adequately and properly satisfied. Hence, said

Dr Sundaravadivelu, as long as conditions of existence were not the same, it would be a mockery of the promised equality of opportunity to only give access to schools and make education free without any further support.

If the children of the poor had to benefit fully from schooling and if the nation's money and efforts were not to get wasted, it was necessary to ensure that they received at least one square meal in a day. This was essential if the expenditure on education was to be meaningful. Dr Sundaravadivelu wondered whether it was possible to divert resources to a School Meals Programme and also to seek community help for this. He took the example of the villagers of Nagalapuram who had consulted among themselves and decided to donate grain to organise a scheme for giving mid-day meals to poor children in their school. From there, the idea of free meals, organised by local donations, spread far and wide and was enthusiastically implemented in many villages.

The time-honoured hospitality and charity of the Indian villagers found one more channel of expression. The rich and the poor, the literate and the illiterate vied with one another in contributing their mite. Housewives showed the way by setting apart a handful of rice each day for this. Farmers took the movement further by donating grains at the threshing field itself. Children also did their bit. In an elementary school at Avinashi, Coimbatore District, the movement was launched with each pupil bringing a match-box full of rice for a few days. In certain high schools, the entire student community contributed a handful of rice once a week. Cash donations flowed freely from salaried and monied persons alike.

Many of these elementary schools were so starved of many essential requirements that often they did not even have a decent place to function from. Some of the sheds in which they were housed were sadapologies, being more suitable for cattle than for future citizens. There were schools, which had buildings but these were in a sorry state of repairs, without the barest equipment or teaching aids. In spite of these impediments, the brave schoolmaster tried to teach young children, many of whom were first-generation learners. Children could not be meaningfully educated in these conditions. And when schooling was substandard it could only produce substandard entrants to high schools and colleges. All efforts to improve the standard of education have to, of necessity, start from the bottom, from the elementary schools. The deficiency has to be made good even at the foundation. Since these problems required immediate redressal, it was necessary to think along unorthodox lines.

A Pilot School Improvement Project was attempted in a compact block with about 40 elementary schools. The first stage was a comprehensive survey of the actual condition of each school in that area keeping in view the normal requirements of an elementary school with regard to accommodation, furniture, equipment, teaching aids, library facilities, sanitary provision, space for play activities and gardening, not only for the present but also for the future. This survey revealed the actual deficiencies in each school. The people in the school, village and the neighbourhood were apprised of these deficiencies at formal or informal meetings. The teachers, acting as catalytic agents, persuaded the villagers to come forward, either individually or jointly, to provide the suitable and adequate needs of the school, according to their respective capacities. This novel idea caught the imagination of the people and the response was spontaneous and generous. After the villagers had undertaken the task to provide various requirements, a conference of the people, donors and teachers was held at the headquarters of the block where the articles presented to the schools were exhibited. The conference and the exhibition demonstrated to society the possibility of quick and widespread reconstruction through self-help. It thus created an ownership of the people in the school and, hence, the desire to maintain and upgrade it.

The Importance of District Level Planning

Another national seminar was held in New Delhi from February 11 to 13, 1970, on "The Role, Function, Recruitment and Training of District Education Officer." The District Education Officer occupies a key position in the educational administration of the state but his role and functions differs from state to state. Since the District Education Officer played a key role in the expansion and development of education through planned activity, it was realised that the system of his recruitment and training had to be reviewed and suitably modernised to equip him for the emerging tasks of development. The seminar was, therefore, designed to deal with the statement of the present position by the state and union territories: the role and function of District Education Officers; the recruitment of District Education Officers; and the training of District Education Officers.

In the inaugural address, Professor M.V. Mathur, Director, AIEPA, emphasised the need of educational administration as education had become the single largest organised activity of society since independence. India had one of the largest educational systems in the world. It was, therefore, of paramount importance that due attention be given to the proper recruitment and training to those who managed this massive enterprise.

The issues were taken up by Mr S. Chakravarti, the Education Secretary, who pointed out that the district was becoming more and more the unit of developmental planning. Hence, it was necessary to give appropriate training to the District Education Officer to not only become professionally competent in his own field, but also to play a significant role in the general community development in collaboration with other departments. Therefore, District Education Officers could also be recruited from universities and research departments. Provisions had also to be made for in-service training and orientation courses to instil, in the officers, attitudes and knowledge which would contribute to their becoming developmental generalists.

This was reinforced by Professor Rao in the valedictory. He also suggested that, as an experimental measure, some of the primary schools could be staffed by graduate teachers and freed from inspection. Similarly, some good secondary schools could also be exempted from routine inspection. Another pivotal issue was of teachers and how vital it was to build their levels of competence. Professor Rao stressed the importance of academic and professional competence of teachers. He suggested that, as a pilot project, about 50 talented young graduate teachers from each district could be selected and given facilities for post-graduate education at the State expense so that, after completing their higher education, they might return to teaching and do their work with greater confidence.

Thus, in the early years of its inception, the focus of the Institute was on meeting the challenges of education with optimum utilisation of scarce resources and, as such, immense importance was attached to planning and training of personnel to make effective implementation possible. Planning was not to be taken as just something related to the economic field, but also something that could be used in almost every sphere. For instance, there was not only economic planning but also social planning and, within that too, there were areas such as public health and education that required further planning. In any developmental sector, therefore, planning could refer to a whole range of activities beginning from the simplest enunciation of a goal or a purpose to the formulation of complex interlocking programmes including their evaluation and review. What all planning activities, however, shared in common was that essentially they were all directed towards eliminating or reducing shortages, or increasing supplies of one kind or another. The Institute was a living demonstration of the need of educational planning, particularly in the developing countries.

Towards the end of his tenure at the beginning of 1968, Dr Saiyidain evaluated the work of the Asian Institute. He wrote a philosophical farewell piece in which he narrated not only what was being done at the Institute, but also how it reflected the ideas and attitudes of society at large. In some ways, he felt that the work of the Institute in India was more difficult and complicated than that of the other three institutes of Educational Planning and Administration at Beirut, Dakar and Santiago de Chile, because the other regions were more compact and comparatively better integrated linguistically, culturally and politically. However, what made the work of the Institute more difficult also gave its members and participants a stimulating opportunity to practice the greatest art in life —the art of learning to live, think and study together the common or even differing problems of interest in an atmosphere of reason and mutual understanding.

An essential characteristic of intelligent planning was sensitiveness to the nature of the world, a proper assessment of the social order in which one was living and a vision of what was likely to be the shape of the future. Only then could planning become purposeful and ensure that the different schemes and plans formulated in various sectors did not work at cross-purposes, but strengthened and supplemented each other. Such harmonisation of the highly complicated structure of modern planning was possible only when persons and organisations concerned with it were knowledgeable about each other's activities and needs. Dr Saiyidain recalled one of the seminars, which had been organised by the Institute in December, 1967 in which a small effort had been made to initiate a dialogue between educational planners, economists and those concerned with the formulation of general planning policies and with the allocation of resources.

He referred to what he had said at the final functions of the alumni's Refresher Course a few days earlier. What was important in life was not so much what happened to the individual but what happened to the cause or the purpose which he was called upon to serve. It was important to ascertain whether the cause was really significant and whether the individual had the capacity to identity with it. An individual derived his significance from the nature of the cause, which he was privileged to serve because something of the greatness of that cause passed into his own personality. While talking of Mahatma Gandhi, Jawaharlal Nehru had once said, "We were all small men and women. To Gandhi belongs the credit of picking us up and using us in the great cause of freedom and the service of the masses. And it was under his leadership for such purposes that we gained some stature and some measure of the greatness of our cause." There were more than three billion human beings living on this earth who had potential significance. It could, however, become real when their gifts and talents, their integrity and devotion, their sincerity and humanism found expression in work which was valuable both for the individual and for the society of which he was a member. It was only when people were engaged in such causes, no matter in what hierarchical positions they were, and rated them higher than their personal interests, that there was a strong likelihood of much of the bitterness, narrowness and selfishness in their lives melting away.

The National Staff College for Educational Planners and Administrators (NSCEPA)

Apart from its studies and activities with the member states of Asia, the Asian Institute had started to emphasise educational issues in India since 1967. This was a prelude to the setting up of the National Staff College for Educational Planners and Administrators (NSCEPA) by the Government of India. It was registered on December 31, 1970 but came into effect from March 1, 1971. After it was established, the work being done at the Institute under the Indian Programme was transferred to the Staff College. However, the Institute continued to be actively involved in the implementation of the programme. The Staff College was fully financed by the Government of India.

The aims and objects of NSCEPA were to:

- Organise pre-service and in-service training, conferences, workshops, meetings, seminars and briefing sessions for senior educational officers of the Central and State Governments and Union Territories; training programmes for teacher-educators and administrators connected with educational planning and management; and orientation programmes and refresher courses for the university and college administrators with the approval of the University Grants Commission;
- Undertake, aid, promote and coordinate research in various aspects of educational planning and administration, including comparative studies in planning techniques and administrative procedures in the different states of India and in other countries of the world;
- Provide academic and professional guidance to agencies, institutions and personnel engaged in educational planning and administration;
- Offer, on request, consultancy service to state governments and administration;
- Act as a clearing house of ideas and information on research, training and extension in educational planning and administration services and other programmes;
- Prepare, print and publish papers, periodicals and books in furtherance of these objectives, and bring out a Journal on Educational Planning and Administration;

- Offer fellowships and scholarships in furtherance of the Staff College;
- Provide, on request, facilities for training and research in educational planning and administration to other countries, especially of the Asian Region.

To fulfil its mandate, the Staff College could collaborate with other agencies, institutions and organisations, including universities, institutes of management and administration and allied institutions in India and abroad.

The overall authority of the Staff College vested in its Council consisting of 23 members presided over by the Union Education Minister. The Director of the Staff College was the ex-officio Member-Secretary. It is evident from the aims and objects of the Staff College that the training of personnel was one of its most vital functions. But, the research component was also strengthened so that it could examine, report and recommend on issues pertaining to education in India at various levels from the district to the state and union territories and the centre. Hence, a great expansion of its activities took place as it undertook programmes both on the behalf of different government agencies at all levels, and on its own initiative.

The Second Decade of Development

The 1970s were the Second Developmental Decade. This was logical as expansion of knowledge was not only required, but was also ceaselessly happening. It was because of this realisation that the importance of life-long education was stressed upon and remains significant even today. The main objective was to acquaint educational administrators and planners with the theories and concepts of modern management; make them aware of the application of some of the modern management techniques to administration, in general, and to educational administration in particular; create receptivity for trying out some of these techniques; and promote studies and research in the application of modern management techniques to educational administration, particularly in the developing countries of the Asian Region.

The awareness of education as a tool of social transformation meant that there was a need to inculcate a commitment to, or identification with, fellow human beings. However, expansion alone could not solve the problem. It was not even a matter of improving standards as in some countries these were very good. The key problem was the widening gap between what the education system was supposed to do and what it was delivering. Society was rapidly changing and, with it, the expectations from education were also changing. This led to a universal demand for adopting unorthodox methods to improve education and meet the emerging needs.

Expenditure on education in India increased by about 10 to 15 per cent annually in the 1960s and 1970s, whereas the national income grew at about half that rate. It was therefore increasingly difficult to find additional money for educational development. While money decreased, demands on education continuously increased. This was true for all the countries of the world for different reasons. It gave rise to a feeling throughout the world that some new approaches to educational planning were required so that resources could be matched with the essential needs. It made education planning, administration and finances, very important and developing countries needed it more than the developed countries as they faced scarcity of resources.

Education could not merely be a matter of expansion as education without quality was useless. Standards of education at various levels had to be improved and educational policy-makers, planners and implementers had to be kept continuously abreast of the rapid developments taking place. This comprehensive educational revolution was not an easy task. It required new and effective knowledge about educational development through research and experimentation; an efficient system of educational planning and administration to engineer it into existence; the investment of immense additional resources; a national commitment together with vigorous and sustained effort; and, of crucial importance, a large band of dedicated teachers. Such an effort was particularly vital to Asia because more than half of the population of the world resided here.

Far-reaching changes in the content and structure had to be made to make it wider, more flexible and diverse. It meant:

- thorough revision and upgrading of curricula;
- adoption of new methods of teaching and evaluation;
- the full use of modern techniques and mass media, and preparation of thousands of competent teachers committed to national goals in the pursuit of knowledge and excellence and the welfare of students.

It was necessary to develop and extend the teaching of science and technology to a larger percentage of students to ensure that the middle and higher grade technical staff and research workers, which the Asian countries needed, were trained. The populations as a whole had to be helped to understand and master the environment for which scientific and technological thought provided the key.

A pre-condition for any kind of fruitful innovation was improved management at every level. Unless the educational systems were well-equipped with appropriately trained modern managers, who, in turn, had good information flows, modern tools of analysis, research and evaluation, and were supported by well-trained teams of specialists, the transition of education from its semi-handicraft state to a modern condition was not likely to happen.

This task assumed the highest priority in the national development plans for the seventies. Every nation in Asia had to accept the challenge and meet it in a way best suited to its own needs and resources. However, all such national efforts could be augmented through regional cooperation as that would enable mutually beneficial exchange of experiences. That was probably why comprehensive educational planning had become widely accepted as vital to the orderly and efficient development of education. UNESCO had declared educational planning to be one of its top priorities and had developed its programmes, mainly through ministers' conferences and technical meetings, by supplying educational planning experts to more than 80 countries, and by establishing regional and international training and research centres. Regional organisations and national institutions had also contributed substantially to the development of new concepts and methodologies in educational planning.

National Institute of Educational Planning and Administration (NIEPA)

In 1978, major re-structuring of the NSCEPA took place. Its name was changed to National Institute of Educational Planning and Administration (NIEPA). The Council, at its meeting held on August 10, 1977, constituted a committee under the Chairmanship of Mr Haribhau Joshi, the then Education Minister of Madhya Pradesh, with Dr Prem Kirpal and Mr P. Sabanayagam, the then Union Education Secretary, as members, and Director, NSCEPA as Member-Secretary to consider amendments to the Rules of the Staff College and make suitable recommendations. The Committee considered the matter in a meeting held on November 14, 1977 and recommended certain amendments to the Memorandum of Association and Rules of the Staff College. Those were approved by the Council at its special meeting held on October 19, 1978.

NIEPA was registered on May 31, 1979. Mr Suhrid Mukhopadhyay, the then Chief Visualizer of the Directorate of Advertising and Visual Publicity (DAVP), Government of India, designed the logo at the request of Professor Moonis Raza, Director, in 1981–82. The first logo was printed on the Annual Report of 1982–83.

While training and collaboration with other countries continued, research gained prominence. The faculty was reorganised as a team of academicians and educational administrators, engaged individually in specialised studies of areas and educational challenges and, at the same time, deployed in groups on particular tasks from time to time. As envisaged in the Perspective Plan, the academic work of the Institute was reorganised into eight Academic Units in October 1981 to help it develop expertise in specialised areas. This resulted in greater academic involvement and inputs in various training programmes and research. The units were:

1. Educational Planning
2. Educational Administration
3. Educational Finance
4. Educational Policy
5. School and Non-formal Education
6. Higher Education
7. Sub-National Systems
8. International

In 1985–86, the Distance Education and Educational Technology Unit was established taking the units at NIEPA to nine. It was created primarily to develop intervention strategies in planning and management of Distance Education and Educational Technology.

On becoming the National Institute of Educational Planning and Administration, an unprecedented growth took place in its activities in both training and research. Much of it was the result of the Perspective Plan that had been prepared under the leadership of Professor Moonis Raza. An effort was made to link training with the research projects. Studies were undertaken on Inspection and Supervision Practices and Proforma in some educationally advanced and backward states, cost of supply of education, ashram schools and the facilities for scheduled castes and scheduled tribes in Industrial Training Institutes (ITI), optimum teacher-pupil ratio, regional disparities in educational development, problems of educational planning, monitoring and development, problems of educational planning, monitoring and statistics in states and union territories, and norms for maintenance and development of educational services. All of them contributed significantly to the various training programmes organised by NIEPA at that time and were also seen to be helpful for its future programmes.

In 1982–83, the Institute diversified its training activities and started a number of new training programmes in educational planning, management, policy, education for the deprived and the handicapped and special programmes in areas of population, education, National Merit Examination and Vocationalisation of Education. A diploma course in educational planning and administration was also conceived as a regular systematic arrangement for the training of new District Education Officers in the country.

A review of the work and progress of the Institute was taken up in 1989 by a Committee constituted by the Government of India, Ministry of Human Resource Development, and the Department of Education under the Chairmanship of Shri P.K. Umashankar, Director, Indian Institute of Public Administration. The Committee collected information about the actual work done by NIEPA from 1989 with reference to the objectives laid down in the Memorandum of Association. Generally speaking, it was felt that NIEPA had done extremely well in fulfilling its objectives as identified in the Memorandum of Association.

The Achievements

NIEPA had conducted extensive in-service training programmes for various functionaries in the field of education. These had covered personnel in strategic positions such as district education officers, adult education officers, senior university personnel and others. Not only had the training programmes reached out to the various categories of educational planners and administrators, but they had also ensured that all the regions, states and union territories were covered. The feedback received from the states and union territories that had participated in the training programmes and, from some of the individual participants, was very positive as they all said they had benefited from the interactions. The pre-service training programme for education officers was also very successful. Normally, officers at these levels were rather reluctant to undergo long-term training in distant places, but that NIEPA should have been able to train 200 of them and also have special programmes for Andhra Pradesh, Assam and Uttar Pradesh, showed that the role of NIEPA had been accepted by the states. The Committee acknowledged that NIEPA had also more than fulfilled its objectives in organising pre-service and in-service training and other programmes for senior educational officers of the central and state governments, universities and college administrators. In regard to the training programmes for teacher educators, it was after 1986, when the National Policy of Education was implemented, that NIEPA had come into the picture by extending its training programmes to the functionaries of the District Institutes of Education and Training (DIETs). The personnel and training department was also happy with the one-week training programmes for IAS officers in NIEPA.

NIEPA had taken the initiative and done valuable work in preparing training materials and modules at various levels for different organisations. In any case, it was acknowledged that the Institute was steadily moving towards becoming the apex institution in the field of training. However, while it had not managed to arrange programmes for legislators, it had arranged discussion groups for top-level persons in the field of educational planning and administration. It had also rendered good professional support to the Central Advisory Board of Education, which was the highest policy-making body in the field of education.

Apart from training, the Institute had paid considerable attention to research and had conducted a number of studies. The fact that institutions such as, UNESCO, the IIEP, ICSSR and UGC had supported these efforts showed that they had confidence in NIEPA, and that they recognised it as an apex organisation, rendering significant service. The research projects, by and large, ranged around current and important issues in the area of educational planning and administration. Action research was also initiated and two projects were taken up that were of great importance. One was on the universalisation of elementary education and eradication of adult illiteracy and the other was on institutional planning.

NIEPA had provided academic and professional support services to important bodies such as the National Commission of Teachers, Finance Commission, Planning Commission, State Governments, State Institutions of Public Administration, NCERT and others. NIEPA was now being increasingly recognised as a significant professional institution in educational planning and administration and was readily consulted by state governments and other professional and academic organisations, including international organisations. NIEPA had made an impressive contribution to formulate the National Policy on Education. It was the recognition of the expertise and capabilities of its faculty that the Institute was made to shoulder a very heavy responsibility in this regard by the government.

NIEPA had gradually evolved as a clearing house of ideas and information on research, training and extension. These were disseminated through the Institute's Journal on Educational Planning and Administration, both in English and Hindi, apart from the published research work of the faculty. The Institute had also brought out a series of documents on various issues relating to different aspects of education. Some of the recent publications of the Institute, the Committee noted, touched on important issues in the field of educational planning and administration and attracted the notice of scholars and academic experts. The Institute also collaborated with other agencies such as UGC, universities and Institutes of Management in developing programmes and materials. The collaboration with UGC was detailed and extensive and covered a wide area of activities.

Although it had not yet developed the scheme of honorary fellowships for conducting research, NIEPA did confer associateships of the Institute in the field of its work. It also had a programme to give national awards for innovative concepts and practices, which was under review. In addition, the Institute had undertaken international training programmes and had organised them regularly for personnel from the Asia and Pacific Region, the Middle East and the African States. These programmes had been appreciated by the international bodies and were rated highly.

The Committee was of the view that NIEPA had moved in the right direction in fulfilling its training and research responsibilities. The objectives of the Institute had been fulfilled in ample measure, largely through the excellent leadership of its successive directors and the devoted efforts of the faculty and the staff. While individual areas of activities could be further developed, the Institute had, on the whole, made substantial contributions in its fields of competence and had secured recognition, not only among central and state governments and agencies, but also sister academic institutions within the country and abroad.

The Task Ahead

The Committee felt that the Institute was well poised to undertake a more significant role in educational planning and administration and could move to spending more time on research than it had thus far done. Of course, the Committee acknowledged that NIEPA had been under great pressure to expand its training activities and this had made inroads into the time available for research and consultancy. Nevertheless, the Institute had to move on to greater responsibilities and more challenging tasks. It was time for it to redefine its role and to sharpen its tools.

While reviewing the work of the Institute, the Committee had wide-ranging discussions and consultations with persons and groups that had been associated with NIEPA. These included former directors of the Institute, distinguished academicians, state secretaries and directors, and the faculty. Letters were sent out to the secretaries and the directors of the state governments and union territories and a questionnaire was sent to participants in courses conducted by NIEPA. Eminent educationists, who had been connected with NIEPA in one way or another, were interviewed separately by various members of the committee. The strengths and weaknesses of the Institute were identified, but it became evident that there were many more of the former than the latter. Valuable and constructive suggestions regarding NIEPA's future role had been made.

Views and Suggestions

One key suggestion was that there was need to develop a long-term perspective plan for NIEPA. A plan had been made in 1981 but it needed revision. It was felt that there was a lack of clarity about the future direction that the Institute had to take and the roles of its staff. In addition to a long-term plan, it was felt that NIEPA should plan its activities annually which would give them a focus.

It was stressed that NIEPA needed a perspective plan. As far as its training activities went, considering the different levels and the numbers of people that the Institute was required to train, it was difficult for it to undertake the training and orientation of even a sizeable portion of educational personnel in the planning and management of education without adopting alternate strategies. Among the major points that emerged from the review and deserve special mention were that the Institute had steadily moved towards becoming an apex institution in the field of training. While this had been useful and there was considerable continuing pressure to organise more training activities, the Committee felt that the Institute needed to assume more research responsibilities. At the time of the review, about 75 per cent of faculty time was being consumed by training activities. On the negative side, the Review Committee highlighted NIEPA's failure to arrange any training programmes for legislators despite this having found a clear mention in the objectives. Also pointed out was the Institute's inability to develop a scheme of honorary fellowships. It was accepted, nevertheless, that whatever may have been the difficulties and struggles, NIEPA had succeeded in becoming a clearing house of ideas and information on research, training and extensions.

The 2003 Review Committee found that while most of the recommendations of the 1989 Review Committee were being implemented, several significant ones had been left out. For example, the Empowered Committee had recommended that the NIEPA Council should set up a task force, "For the implementation on a time-bound basis of the recommendations of the Committee which are found to be acceptable by the MHRD." This had not been done although almost 14 years had elapsed. The plan to develop NIEPA as a centre of excellence had also not been worked out in specific details, with careful delineation of the tasks required to be accomplished, the modalities of doing so and the time frame for their implementation. Further, no long-term perspective plan had been given any meaningful shape that would develop NIEPA as a centre of excellence. No reorganisation of the structure had been done by reducing the number of units and although training effort was expected to be confined to experimental programmes and to training of trainers, the Institute had continued to train personnel at district levels, in District Institutes of Education and Training (DIETs) and in educational institutions.

The Committee, generally, accepted the assessment of NIEPA, articulated by the earlier (1989) Review Committee, and felt that its recommendations remained as relevant in 2003 as they had been in 1989. It was, therefore, regrettable felt the Review Committee of 2003, that many of the accepted recommendations had not been implemented or acted upon in the interim period of 14 years between the reviews of two committees.

The Review of 2003–2004 proved to be a watershed in the life of the NIEPA. The pivotal issue was to make the Institute a world-class organisation. It was suggested by the MHRD that perhaps the time had come to give the Institute the status of a 'Deemed to be University'. The Director of the Institute consulted the faculty. A meeting took place in February 2006 with the Director in the chair. The chief concern was what would be the implications of this move. The Director confirmed that the existing role and function of the Institute would remain the same and the 'Deemed to be University' status would be an add-on. The source of funding would also remain the same. The Institute could offer more research programmes and the proposed change could provide NIEPA the opportunity to prepare qualified and experienced human resource in educational planning and administration.

NIEPA to NUEPA

August 2006 was a landmark date for NIEPA as it became a Deemed University, the only University in the country completely dedicated to education, fully sponsored by the Government of India, but autonomous in character. The journey from the Regional Centre for the training of educational planning, administrators and supervisors to the establishment of NUEPA was a long and arduous one. Now that the centre had blossomed into a university, the only university in the country completely dedicated to education; fully sponsored by the Government of India, it was natural that, like any other university, it got the autonomy to design its own programmes and award degrees in accordance with the guidelines of the UGC. The change in status led to an exemplar shift in its philosophy, functioning and development. The focus shifted from being primarily a delivery mechanism to a resource institution. The emphasis moved from staff training to research and professionalisation of capacity-building efforts. In effect, the National University of Educational Planning and Administration (NUEPA) has become a research University with its aim of supporting human capacity building through research. It now had the opportunity to prepare qualified and experienced human resource in educational planning and administration.

Often the planning and implementation of reform programmes at the sectoral and institutional levels has been affected because of the lack of appropriate capacity of educational administrators. Many of the educational administrators in the country have been either untrained or ill-equipped to handle planning and management responsibilities. Hence, NUEPA, in its long journey, has been holding a large number of training programmes annually and gradually moving from individuals to training the trainers. Gradually, research too has got strengthened because NUEPA has to provide consultancy to the government and other organisations both in India and abroad. This entails not only taking stock of the situation, data collection and sponsored studies, but also research-oriented towards policy formulation, meeting of new challenges and planning for the future. Continuous strengthening research at NUEPA would help to design even more effective capacity-building programmes for educational functionaries and for policy formulation and implementation. This would have a strong impact on the functioning of the education system at all levels. The 'Deemed to be University' status facilitates the efforts of the Institute to expand and strengthen the pool of professionally trained human resource.

It could now develop specialised human resource in the area of educational planning and administration which, for decades, has been scarce in the country as very few universities offer specialised programmes in this area. The M.Phil., Ph.D. and post-doctoral programmes offered by the Institute as a University would provide, to a large extent, the required human resource to meet the increasing demand on account of educational reforms. The new initiatives including the Centre for Policy Research in Higher Education enable NUEPA to be a resource for planning for education at all levels from school to university. The Digital Archives have the potential to providing yeoman service to Indian education for researchers in India and abroad. Hence, NUEPA will undoubtedly contribute towards multiplying the number of qualified educational planners and administrators in the country. It is now coming closer to vindicating the vision and objectives for which it had been set up in 1962. However, must consciously resist becoming only a think tank for the Ministry of Human Resource Development but provide academic space to all researchers anywhere in India and the world. It has the capacity to stimulate discussion and debate on educational issues, provide solutions and offer a long-term view encompassing the historical perspective to build on for a vision for the future.

Part - II

5

Indian Higher Education: Challenges of Globalisation and Emergence of the Private Sector

Contemporary Public Higher Education in India

The situation in higher education is not very encouraging in India. While there has been a massive expansion of higher education after independence, making it the third largest after the USA and China, it is very inadequate in terms of access, equity and quality. Currently, it provides access to around 17–18 per cent of the relevant population (numbers vary) and efforts are being made to reach about 25–30 per cent by 2017. To do it in the public sector alone might be extremely difficult and so the private sector might need to be co-opted. This is because the financial requirement as estimated in the Twelfth Five-Year Plan is about 413 thousand crore rupees. About 21 million seats need to be created and over 140 million children still need development. There is just no way in which public finance can meet this requirement but the task has to be undertaken if economic development has to go forward. It is also important to note that currently India spends about 1.1 per cent of its GDP on higher education, while South Korea, over two per cent and USA over four per cent. Of course, there are several countries that spend on higher education; but the simple point is that India has to spend far more on higher education than public finance has the capacity to allocate.

Increasingly, the relationship between higher education and economic development has been established the world over leading to the "massification" (literally, taking to the masses) of higher education and moving towards its universalisation. This has linked it firmly with employability raising questions about relevance and quality of higher education. The need to simultaneously expand to increase access, create equity and tackle the issues of relevance and quality by upgrading existing institutions has put a strain on the resources available for the public funding of higher education. This has led to the emergence of the private sector in higher education that has prioritised subjects, such as engineering, medicine, management, media, law, applied sciences, and technology together with subjects related to the service industry and skill development. Social sciences and humanities are facing neglect, which get emphasised as more and more higher education moves to the private sector.

There is also an acute need for research for knowledge formation and its dissemination in which boundaries between disciplines get blurred. All this means that the way we think of the organisation, financing, governance structures, and delivery systems of higher education have to be revisited with regard to State-funded institutions and the emergence of the private sector, which has grown while policy for it has lagged behind.

In India, the strains in the system are more than evident with only a few research universities at the top while the bottom does not adequately fulfil the requirements of demand and so has little time to devote to relevance and quality. Skill formation is inadequate and too dysfunctional to meet the requirements of a growing and diversifying economy. While IITs and IIMs may be internationally competitive, they are only niche institutions, which cater to a very small percentage of the student population. One of the fundamental causes of the malaise is, perhaps, what Professor Altbach points out when he says that the mass of institutions of higher education have no clarity of vision about their purpose and aim. The universities are neither provided resources nor do have the mandate to build a distinctive and innovative profile, which is essential for successful academic systems. So, they continue as an undifferentiated mass repetitively producing more of the same. If there was clarity on what different institutions are attempting to deliver, then their funding sources and patterns could also be diversified.[1]

The accountability in the system is so diffuse and distributed that no one can be held responsible for delivery and outcome. This leads to mediocrity. It is only natural because most academic arrangements in India have been derived from British colonialism and were not meant to be effective or to encourage quality. The most affected is undergraduate education as the affiliating system puts the undergraduate colleges under the universities with their highly bureaucratised and controlled environment. It impedes innovation as they have to follow the common centralised policies without any autonomy. The universities, in turn, receive their funding from the government. So while they have formal autonomy, they too are basically under the control of Central or State governments. Also, they have been politicised which makes them ideologically blinkered and contentious. All this has made issues of quality assurance very ambiguous.

The Emergence of the Private Sector

What was the societal and systemic response to this situation? At least two things happened:

- It led to the emergence of a very substantial private sector that has stepped in to absorb the rising demand for higher education, especially in areas of professional and management education.
- The government itself realised that it was not able to meet all the financial requirements of the demand and tacitly recognised the need to involve the private sector.

Therefore, it allowed private education to enter the public sector universities and colleges through mechanisms, such as self-financing courses that run concurrently with public-funded programmes. The self-financing institutions are affiliated to public universities and they now far outnumber the public-funded colleges. Most of them are from the southern States of India. Many private deemed universities have emerged, which indicates that the government seeks private help and lacking a transparent policy or legislation, has taken this route to enable private institutions to flourish.[2] Another group of private institutions in the non-university sector is run by private and corporate initiatives like NIIT and APTEC. By law they cannot award degrees but they attract students because of the quality and relevance of their programmes and the training that they offer.

By the 1980s, because of economic and political factors student preference shifted to professional programmes over academic disciplines, particularly in areas related to engineering, medicine, management, computer applications and others. Finding a vacuum and sensing an opportunity, private providers took to the professional sector in large numbers and did well. They were supported by an unarticulated paradigm shift in the government itself. This can be seen from the various policy statements that emerged at this time.

The National Policy on Education, 1986, stated:

> Resources to the extent possible will be raised by mobilising donations, asking the beneficiary communities to maintain school buildings and supplies of some consumables, raising fees at the higher levels of education and effecting. Some savings by the efficient use of facilities... all these measures will be taken not only to reduce the burden on State resources, but also for creating a greater sense of responsibility within the education system.

The position was reiterated in 1992[3]

The first indications that policy on the private sector would reach the realms of implementation came in the recommendations of the Eighth Plan (1993–1997), which discouraged the opening of new universities and colleges. It endorsed that private sector and voluntary agencies be involved in the opening and running of higher education institutions with proper checks to ensure standards and facilities. Higher education institutions were to be made as self-financing as possible. The protests of the academic community were muted with the assurance that the quality of education would not be compromised. Earlier, the Report of the CABE on Gnanam Committee (1992) had also stated:

> It will not be possible for the State government to fund adequate resources to create endowment funds for each university. Universities, however, should make efforts to raise their own resources but must be ensured that there are no conditions attached like preference on admission, etc. Raising of resources should not affect academic standards and universities should lay down guidelines for the same.[4]

This position was not unique to India. It was in keeping with what was happening globally and had been stated by the International Commission for Education for the twenty-first century in 1996 in its report "Learning the Treasure Within."

> It is not only justifiable but also desirable to raise money from private sector in order to ease the pressure on national budgets. Private funding can come from a variety of sources, contribution...by families and students towards fees.[5]

In 1997, the Ministry of Finance in its white paper on public subsidies called higher education as "non-merit" good. This was significant because it could have long-term consequences for public financing of higher education as it made individuals the main gainers from it and hence not deserving of public subsidies. This is an old and on-going debate. If higher education is a public good, it must be completely supported by the government because society benefits by the education of the citizen.[6] It improves human capital, encourages civic involvement and boosts economic development. The private good or "non-merit" counter argument is that higher education largely benefits the individual and therefore students should pay a significant part for their post-secondary education. Perhaps there is truth in both points of view and the answer need not be an either/or proposition. In that case, a policy in which both can co-exist can be formulated. This has not been done so far in the public domain as a national policy.

The government was more than aware of the resource constraints and tried to address the problem by introducing the Private Universities Establishment and Regulation Bill in August 1995 in the Rajya Sabha. The Bill was referred to the Standing Committee for obtaining its views on involving the private sector. However, it just faded away. Since the matter continued to be discussed at various forums, the HRD Ministry set up a core group in 1999 for their views and recommendations on various issues pertaining to higher education. Nothing came of it probably because it was politically contentious and the private sector was also very resentful to some of the provisions of the proposed bill like those pertaining to an endowment fund, regulation by the government bodies, and free education to one-third of the students. The Birla-Ambani Report of 2001 also suggested the involvement of the private sector, minimal subsidies for higher education and the resources so saved to be used for school education.

The Eleventh Plan had a massive increase in the outlay for education and several new initiatives were envisaged, which were expected to lead to substantial expansion of higher education by establishing Central universities, world-class universities and colleges in every district. But even if this could all be implemented, massive inputs were needed from the private sector to meet the demand for higher education. An even larger outlay was expected in the Twelfth Plan but this did not happen. However, given the increase in secondary education, India's youthful demographic profile, and the existence of an already large private sector, a clear policy on private higher education and acceptance of public private partnership has to emerge.

There is resistance to privatisation from a vociferous and influential section of society, which is a hindrance in formulating a concrete national policy towards private higher education and its role. The contention of this section is, that education has never been a commerce in India, and hence private higher education with its aspect of commercialisation is opposed to the ethos, tradition and sensibilities to the nation. But these contentions are not reflected in ground reality. For example, medical care even more than education should be the responsibility of the government, but the moment one is sick there is rush for the best private nursing home. There is obviously some hypocrisy here, which is evident in the education sector as well. Flourishing coaching academies, tutorial colleges and parallel colleges collect substantial fees for unregulated academic programmes and these are willingly paid. Fees are also willingly paid for the sought-after schools and computer institutes but when it comes to formal higher education, even a minimal increase in fee is fiercely resisted.

Massification of Higher Education

Massification of higher education across the world has been attempted through both the public sector and the private sector. In Japan, over 77 per cent of education is private; while in South Korea, it is higher. Philippines has over 70 per cent private higher education. The private sector educates more than half the population in countries such as Mexico, Brazil, and Chile. Private universities are expanding in Africa, China and India too have significant private sector. Western Europe does not have a large private sector except for in Portugal. In the USA, the perceived bastion of private education, its role has reduced with the massification of higher education. The fall of communism has brought significant higher education to the countries of the former USSR and to the large majority of Central and East Europe. A few of these countries have only a tiny private sector, but in several others, it peaks at around 25–30 per cent. It is mainly in the developing countries that the demand for private education is very strong probably due to the desire of using education and human resource development to accelerate economic growth.[7]

The Impact of Globalisation and Democracy

The demand for higher education is being driven by at least two factors: globalisation and democracy. Globalisation can be seen as, "The widening, deepening and speeding up of worldwide 'interconnectedness'. It is the overarching international system shaping the domestic politics and foreign relations of virtually every country. It involves the inexorable integration of markets, nation-states and technologies to a degree never witnessed before—in a way that is enabling individuals, corporations and nation-States to reach around the world farther, faster, deeper and cheaper than ever before, and in a way that is also producing a powerful backlash from those brutalised or left behind. We have gone from how big is your missile to how fast is your modem? We have gone from a variety of economic ideologies to a choice between, free market vanilla and North Korea."[8] While the polarities may not be as extreme as are made out here, but in today's context as Henry Feignenbaum observes, it is taken as axiomatic that education and spread of knowledge are essential to increase international competitiveness because national and global economies are interconnected and based on information and its exchange.

It is no wonder that internationally there has been much debate and discussion on higher education. October 1998, for instance, was a very significant year for the world of higher education as representatives of 128 nations responsible for education, including higher education, met for the first time in Paris under the auspices of UNESCO to discuss issues of common concern and to agree on the general direction that higher education must take in the twenty-first century. The Conference was unanimously of the view that a renewal of higher education was essential for the whole society to face the challenges of the twenty-first century. These included intellectual independence of individual creation and advancement of knowledge; and education and training to shape responsible enlightened citizens and qualified specialists, without whom no nation could progress economically, socially, culturally, or politically. The Declaration of the World Conference emphasised that since society was increasingly knowledge-based, higher education and research had become essential components of the cultural, socio-economic and environmentally sustainable development of individuals, communities and nations. The development of higher education, therefore, ranked as among the highest national priorities of nations throughout the world because without it, the required human resource could not be created.

The Conference was preceded by a widespread mobilisation of partners, national policy-makers, institutional leaders, professors, researchers, students, professional sectors and others. Regional conferences were held in Havana in November 1996, Dakar in April 1997, Tokyo in July 1997, Palermo in September 1997, and Beirut in March 1998. Findings, declarations and plans of action of these conferences provided inputs for the Paris Conference of October 1998. These were complemented by studies and analyses undertaken by some 50 governmental and non-governmental organisations charged with preparing a series of thematic debates on important issues of higher education. Twelve debates were structured around three main domains:

1. Higher education and development as requirements for the world of work. Under this were to be considered higher education and sustainable human development contributing to national and regional development; and higher education staff development as a continuous process.
2. New trends and innovations in higher education that encompass students' vision of higher education for a new society. These would include the use of new information technologies, challenge and opportunities in research, and the contribution of higher education to the education system as a whole.
3. Higher education and its relationship with culture and society. It would have under its umbrella, women and higher education; promoting a culture of peace, mobilising the power of culture; autonomy and social responsibility and higher education.

At the Conference itself the delegates dealt with issues pertaining to the changing missions of higher education in the twenty-first century. These included interaction of higher education with society; the impact of the change process on higher education together with diversification; increased flexibility of systems and promotion of lifelong learning; and access to higher education. All these factors provided elements that went into the Declaration and Framework for Action that the Conference adopted at the end as "World Declaration on Higher Education for the Twenty-First Century: Vision and Action" and "Framework for Priority Action for Change and Development of Higher Education." The Conference resolved that, "Beyond its traditional functions of teaching, training, research and study, all of which remain fundamental", higher education must "promote development of the whole person and train responsible, informed citizens, committed to working for a better society in the future." It has led to intense activity around the world as country after country has tried to assess the role of higher education in development and what needs to be further done.

In 2000, the Task Force on Higher Education and Society was convened by the World Bank and UNESCO to bring together some of the world's foremost education and development experts. Based on research, intensive discussion and hearings conducted over a two-year period, the Task Force concluded that without more and better education, developing countries would find it increasingly difficult to benefit from the global knowledge-based economy.[9]

Globalisation is intimately connected to democracy and the empowerment of individuals who seek opportunities in an increasingly shrinking world. As Friedman points out, two major events have been responsible for this. One is the end of the Cold War, which has also been a struggle between two economic systems—capitalism and communism. Second is the fall of the Berlin Wall on November 9, 1989. Now there is primarily one system in the world and while there may be many variations of it keeping in view the local milieu, everyone has had to orient and adapt to it one way or another. With the spread of democracy, regulated or centrally planned economies have become an idea of the past. Henceforth, more and more economies would be governed in consonance with interests, demands and aspirations of the people, that is, from ground up rather than by planning from top down.

Friedman states the three great eras of globalisation:

1. From 1492 when Columbus set sail opening trade between the Old World and the New World, lasting until around 1800. It shrank the world from large to medium. Globalisation was about

countries and muscle. The driving force was, "Brawn how much muscle, how much horse power, wind power or later, steam power your country had and how creatively you could deploy it."

2. The second era of globalisation was roughly from 1800 to 2000; interrupted by the Great Depression and World Wars I and II. This shrank the world from medium to small. The key agent of change in this era, the dynamic force driving global integration, was multinational companies. The multinationals went global for markets and labour, spearheaded first by the expansion of Dutch and English joint-stock companies and then the Industrial Revolution. In the first half of this era, the impetus was given by falling transportation costs, thanks to the steam engine and the railroad; and in the second half, by falling telecommunication costs because of the development of technology. The global economy matured because there was enough movement of goods and information from continent to continent to create a global market, and global arbitrage in products and labour.
3. The third phase of globalisation began in around 2000. With it, the world shrank further from small to tiny and simultaneously flattened the playing field. The new found power for individuals to collaborate and compete globally gives this phase of globalisation its unique character is. The new information technology has made us all next-door neighbours. It is now for individuals to ask themselves where they fit into the global competition and opportunities of the day and they can, on their own, collaborate with each other globally. The individual empowerment is the most important new feature of globalisation but companies, small and big, have also got newly empowered in this era and seek opportunities of growth and expansion for themselves.[10]

Individuals push for higher education as they see in it an attractive personal investment, which can bring them rich rewards in terms of long-term income and employability in comparison to individuals with lower formal qualifications. Both of these have contributed to the promotion of market elements in higher education particularly through increased privatisation, which has helped to meet the demand for massification, diversification and the increased access it requires. It has created heterogeneous and complex systems that are required to meet the new and diverse demand which has made it nearly impossible to maintain a pattern of detailed regulation of higher education. Hence, new forms of governance, financing, curricula and flexible delivery and evaluation systems are needed.

Apart from an increasingly integrated world economy, new information and communications technology, and the emergence of an international knowledge network, the English language has gained in prominence as an international language of communication and work. Without a common language, it is not possible to prepare students for the globalised world, the byproduct of which is internationalisation of higher education. This includes enabling students to study abroad, setting up branch campuses overseas, and internationalising the curriculum or engaging in international partnerships. Both these factors have contributed to the promotion of market elements in higher education, particularly through increased privatisation.

Early Private Higher Education

Resistance to private education however, continues, although it is resilient enough to persist and grow. India has had a long experience in this area. In colonial times, institutions of higher education were started with little or no support from the government. Motivated by their ideals and philanthropy, socio-religious trusts, societies and even individuals took the initiative. The Sikhs in the Punjab formed the Khalsa Diwan in 1873, which established Khalsa schools and colleges. Sir Syed Ahmad Khan founded the Mohammedan Anglo-Oriental College in 1877, which grew into Aligarh Muslim University in 1920. The Jamia Millia Islamia was founded by Dr Zakir Husain in 1920. The Arya Samaj founded a number of schools and the Anglo-Vedic College in Lahore in 1886. The Deccan Education Society was founded in 1880 and it started the Fergusson College. In Bombay, the Victoria Jubilee Technical Institute was founded in 1887 through local initiative. Dr Annie Besant of the Theosophical Society founded the Central Hindu College in 1909, which was later handed over to Banaras Hindu University Society. She joined Pt. Madan Mohan Malviya to establish the Banaras Hindu University in 1917. In 1921, Gurudev Rabindranath Tagore started Visva Bharti at Shantiniketan. Mahatma Gandhi motivated the establishment of several institutions in the 1920s —Gujarat Vidyapeeth, Kashi Vidyapeeth, and Tilak Maharashtra Vidyapeeth.

Rulers of the princely States also took a keen interest in higher education and contributed to establishing and developing universities like Mysore University (1916), Osmania University (1918) and Annamalai University (1929). Business houses too made their contribution to higher education and continued till much later after independence although philanthropy in this field largely died out after 1947. With the efforts of Jamshedji Tata, the Tata Institute for Science was established; now it is called Indian Institute of Science at Bangalore. Shri G.D. Birla initiated educational programmes at Pilani in the early 1900s, which culminated in establishing the Birla Institute of Technology and Science in 1964. B.M. Birla started the Birla Institute of Technology, Ranchi in 1955. Banasthali Vidyapeeth (1983), Thapar Institute of Engineering and Technology, Patiala (1985), and Bharati Vidyapeeth (1964) are all examples of private initiatives.[11]

The situation was not unique to India. Many of the earliest universities of Europe, too, were the products of non-governmental initiative during the second half of the Middle Ages.[12] They were set up as autonomous institutions by a royal or papal decree. They had a public orientation and were accountable to the secular or religious authorities. The distinction between the public and private spheres was not marked in medieval times and hence the dichotomy between public and private institutions was also less clear. It was only from the seventeenth century onwards when the modern State expanded and included higher education as its function and that it needed to train personnel for the various emerging spheres of State activity. Today, the private sector in a broad sense seems to be emerging similarly to meet the new demands of economy and taking over from the State-sponsored public education.

Contemporary Private Higher Education

Historically, private institutions were established as not-for-profit institutions, like the universities. However, recent private institutions are inevitably profit seeking. Even when 'for profit' institutions are not allowed, private institutions are usually for profit whatever may be their claim; and the regulatory mechanism is not able to deal with them. Further, most private institutions are not universities but specialised institutions that provide higher training in some specific fields of study. Research facility, especially in basic sciences is usually weak or often non-existent here, because of the large outlay it demands. However, in recent times, attempts to gain legitimacy have prompted them to show some research activity but it is largely cosmetic because it is difficult to find philanthropic sources of funding and these institutions have no access to public research funds. Therefore, whatever finances are required for research have to be cross-subsidised from teaching funds; this involves raising tuition fees, which are already high compared to public universities and therefore not a viable option. As the system matures, some amelioration may take place.[13]

Right now, most private higher education institutions cater to undergraduate demands, which satisfy the current needs of the labour market and bring immediate returns. However, high-end programmes demand heavy financial outlay, which in turn means very high fees. Since there are no takers for this, either the quality gets diluted or private education gets confined to the popular courses of social sciences, economics, business, management, and others.

The issue of quality becomes an urgent one for private institutions since they find it hard, if not impossible, to compete in terms of fees with public institutions. They also face problems of getting good teachers. Most of them have to rely on part-time teachers or the retired faculty from public universities. The dearth of faculty disturbs the teacher-student ratio that further dilutes the quality of teaching. Further, when teachers from public institutions 'moonlight', it creates tension between the two sectors with its own dire consequences. Public angst also rises against them because the lack of quality and high fees means that the employment returns do not match the individual investment and expectations.

At the policy level, expectations from private institutions are usually not met. Given that they have more flexibility, one would expect that they demonstrate increased diversification, both in terms of geographical reach and subjects taught, being more responsive to labour market demands. But, this does not happen because the very nature of private institutions compels them to gravitate to capital cities or major urban centres. The subjects get confined to those that are popular because of market demand. In fact, it is the public institutions that are geographically diverse because of the involvement of local and regional authorities. They also have the wherewithal to innovate if they could only get out of their straitjacket.

But whatever may be the constraints on private higher education, evidence seems to suggest that they are set to become a permanent feature on the higher education landscape. This is because higher education is likely to persist as an important priority in policy terms. The government may not be able to cope with the rising financial demands and expectations, and this will give a push to private higher education. There will also be financial challenges on how to expand the supply of higher education but these will be in both the public and the private sectors. Unless there is a policy that will take into its ambit the concerns of both sectors, the likely response will be the strengthening of market mechanisms which can increase the unregulated growth of privateness in the system. The consequence will be the commercialisation of higher education and the victims will be the stakeholders—teachers, students, and parents. Teachers will be underpaid, hired on a contractual basis, with their services being dispensed with during vacations. They will have career uncertainties. Students will not get quality education and parents will pay exorbitant fees in their quest for professional degrees for their wards. Therefore, it is vital to have a public policy with regard to private education in place to avoid the ills of commercialisation.

But this is a complex and controversial issue especially in countries where private institutions have remained minimal with ideological issues and public sentiment to grapple with.

Since private education usually gets a boost because of massification, initially at least, it tends to focus on the absorption of unfulfilled demand but gradually these institutions tend to position themselves as high quality/ high cost alternatives to mass/low-cost public higher education. In the course of time, they would not want to be seen as the second choice for those who do not get a place in the public sector institutions. In the post-massification phase, the demand absorption pattern can give way to niche institutions, which present alternatives to mass higher education rather than reinforcing it.

The Futuristic Vision

Private institutions will gradually seek greater legitimacy. The first endeavour will be to strengthen their teaching mission both in terms of programmes and faculty. They will also start paying more attention to research. Up to now the teaching element has been dominant but they will focus on research for legitimacy.[14] They will attempt to improve their academic pedigree with better qualified staff, increase the number of research centres affiliated to them, and develop good post-graduate programmes. In addition, they are also likely to develop good strong student support mechanisms because both academic quality and students are equally important to them.

Models for Private Higher Education

Many models for private education are already available in the country. There are at least four distinct ones:[15]

1. The Manipal model —provide access to students who can pay and who may not have got admission for various reasons in a public sector university. The Manipal Academy of Higher Education is a pioneering centre for self-financing higher education, managed and funded by private enterprise.
2. The marketing model —already existing institutions receive aid from the government (Central or State) and are allowed to start some professional courses at the undergraduate and postgraduate level on the self-financing pattern.
3. The sponsoring model —popular with the corporate sector in which it sponsors its managerial and executive personnel to enable them to update their skills and knowledge. For this, they

are attached to some leading institutions for a short period of training.

4. The franchising model —self-financing institutions have to select courses designed by the university and follow the teaching as per norms prescribed by the affiliating university. However, these colleges do not receive grants from the government. Guru Gobind Singh Indraprastha University, Delhi has a large number of privately-managed self-financing courses in different professional fields such as engineering, technology, management studies, medicine, pharmacy, education, law and others, affiliated to it.

Governments will increasingly develop accreditation and evaluation mechanisms, often as an instrument to curtail private institutions. This will gain relevance as for-profit institutions emerge — as they are already doing in many countries of the world and even as the not-for-profit ones behave like for-profit ones. Private institutions too will seek accreditation to legitimise themselves and proclaim their quality.

Need for Government Policy

The acceptance of private higher education will essentially depend on the role of the government, which has to be clear, and has to build a national consensus on the issue. Right now, there is divergence and the public percèption is negative with fair justification. At the same time, paradoxically the private sector continues to grow while policy lags behind. Therefore, benign negligence of the private sector or allowing its covert entry will not do. If the government needs the private sector for resource mobilisation and its other strengths, it has to facilitate it and see it as complementary to its task of discharging its responsibility of expanding the higher education base. If this is the perception, then potential private providers can be facilitated and given some incentives. For this to happen, the most important is appropriate legislation because it will embody the will of the State and bring about clarity on the rules of the game. It will save the private sector education from perpetual litigation and harassment. Security by legal action would constitute the first step in promoting quality private participation in higher education. Regulation implemented with integrity can lead to open and transparent policies that can attract big corporations with enough funds to establish quality institutions and staying power to not expect immediate returns.

Lacking a national legislation, many States have already enacted for establishing private universities — sometimes with disastrous consequences, as in Chhattisgarh. But State legislation is not enough. The national will must be made clear through a national policy; which should have basically three components:

- Promotion, which needs policies that stimulate private efforts through the expansion of higher education.
- Facilitation, which requires enacting of appropriate legislation.
- Regulatory control, which is needed to ensure good quality in private institutions as well as to safeguard against any exploitation of the gullible public.

Right now, higher education seems to be stuck in a quagmire. It is clear that India is affected by global trends but is unable to deal with them. If it has to meet the challenges, it has to systematically create an internationally competitive academic system. For this, it will have to rise above ideological biases and politics to reform its outmoded structures of academic governance structures and delivery systems and build a national consensus by a continuous Centre-State dialogue on higher education, both in the public and the private sectors. A tall order perhaps but without it, the Indian higher education system cannot deliver — neither nationally nor globally.

References

1. Altbach. Philip G. Pawan Agarwal (ed.). 2012. "Tiny at the Top," "A World-Class Country without World-Class Higher Education," "India's 21st Century Dilemma," "The Giants Awake: Higher Education Systems in China and India," "A Half-Century of Indian Higher Education," in *Essays by Philip G. Altbach*; New Delhi: Sage Publishers.
2. Powar, K.B. 2012. *Expanding Domains in Indian Higher Education*, pp. 147-181 New Delhi: Association of Indian Universities.
3. See National Policy on Education, 1986 and Programme of Action 1992, www.teindia.nic.in/Files/Reports/CCR/POA%201992.pdf. See also, National Policy on Education, 1986, www.ncert.nic.in/oth_anoun/ape86.pdf
4. Report of the CABE Committee on Gnanam Committee Report, Teindia.nic.in/mhrd/50yrsedu/g/52/4g/52450101.htm
5. Debres, Jacques.1996. *Learning: The Treasure Within*, UNESCO.
6. Srivastava, D.K. and H.K. Amar Nath. 2001. *Central Budgetary Subsidies in India*, New Delhi: National Institute of Public Finance and Policy.
7. Levy, Daniel, C. *An Introductory Global Overview: The Private Fit to Salient Higher Education Tendencies*, WP No. 7 September 2006, PROPHE Working paper series, http://www/albany.edu/dept.eaps/prophe.
8. Friedman, Thomas. 2005. *The World is Flat: A Brief History of Twenty First Century*, New York: Farrar, Straus and Giroux.
9. Sharma, Kavita A. 2008. *Internationalisation of Higher Education: An Aspect of India's Foreign Relations*, New Delhi: Gyan Publishing House.

10. Friedman, Thomas L. 1999. *The Lexus and the Olive Tree: Understanding Globalisation*, pp. 13-16. New York: Farrar, Straus and Giroux.
11. Sharma, Kavita A. 2013. *Sixty Years of University Grants Commission: Establishment, Growth and Evolution*, pp. 6-12. New Delhi: University Grants Commission.
12. Teixeira, Pedro. 2009. "Mass Higher Education and Private Institutions," *Higher Education to 2030*, Vol. 2, pp. 231-258. Globalisation OECD, Centre for Educational Research and Innovation.
13. *Ibid.* See also, Jochen Fried, Anna Glass and Bernd Baumgartl, 2007. "Shades of Privateness: Non-Public Higher Education in Europe," in *The Rising Role and Relevance of Private Higher Education in Europe*, pp. 585-664. UNESCO-CEPES.
14. Levy, Daniel C. *An Introductory Global Overview: The Private Fit to Salient Higher Education Tendencies*, WP No. 7, September 2006, PROPHE Working Paper series. See also, Daniel C. Levy, *Unanticipated Development: Perspectives on Private Higher Education's Emerging Roles*, WP No. 1, April 2002, PROPHE Working paper Series, http://www.albany.edu/dept/eaps/prophe
15. Powar, K.B. April 2013. *Expanding Domains in Indian Higher Education*, pp. 147-181. Turkish Online Journal of Distance Education – TOJDE April, 2013 ISSN 1302-6488 Volume: 14 Number: 2 Book Review: 2.

6

Research in Higher Education

The purpose of a university is usually the creation and dissemination of knowledge. This implies both teaching and research, but the two often share an uneasy space. When Humboldt, a German statesman, philologist and architect of the university observed that the purpose for both the teacher and the student is, "A common quest for knowledge",[1] he, in effect, abolished the problematic nature of the teaching-research link. Cardinal Newman, on the other hand, saw the university, "As a place of teaching universal knowledge", and as a source for, "the diffusion and extension of knowledge rather than advancement" questioning that, "If its object were scientific and philosophic discovery...why a University should have students."[2] But as expectations from them have evolved, universities have increasingly become research-oriented.

Clear ways on how to bring teaching and research together within a scholarship paradigm are still unresolved and very often universities themselves are confused about their mission. This link has also not been established in universities around the world. Universities that are research-intensive are uneasy about the balance between teaching and research because research inevitably gets privileged over teaching. Consciously or sub-consciously, research is considered a more 'professional' endeavour because it requires lengthy preparation while teaching is seen as a skill, a 'craft' that requires 'technique' rather than deep thought about the subject. The situation gets even more complicated because of private funding and grants for research, which give rise to what Mahmood Mamdani calls the consultancy culture by which universities seek to augment their resources through consultancy work done by the faculty, and the faculty, in turn, pursues research grants for the work in which the conclusion may not present the whole picture. This is sometimes done at the expense of teaching, leading to an imbalance in the system, and could result in a divorce between teaching and research, which should go hand in hand.[3]

Emergence of Universities and the State

The nature of universities is connected to the emergence of the modern State and the role it carves out for itself. Many of the earliest universities in Europe were the products of non-governmental initiatives during the second half of the Middle Ages. They were set up as autonomous institutions by a royal or papal decree. They had public orientation and were accountable to the secular or religious authorities that established them. The distinction between them arose from the seventeenth century with the rise of modern Nation-States and this got strengthened by the early twentieth century when the modern State expanded and included higher education as its function.[4]

The process began in the 1660s when the modern State came to regard the universities as the suppliers of qualified labour and so sought increasing control over them. The motivations for State control then were not very different from what they are today—politics and economics. As the functions of the State grew, new institutions were started or the existing ones were regulated so that they could be used to train new members of administration. By the nineteenth century, the autonomy of the university was impacted as the State sought to regulate the organisation of the universities, syllabi, teaching staff and students. The growing role of government funding of universities was accompanied by greater oversight over them. The ministries of education and similar public administrative structures were established and these exercised detailed control over university life.

A direct correlation can be seen in the expansion of the government's economic and social role and the government funding and control over universities. The social welfare State required highly qualified people such as teachers, social workers, doctors, engineers, accountants and others. This impacted syllabus formation and priority in the funding of types of programmes thus privileging some over others. It meant that expenditure on higher education became a budgetary and political priority and funding was made available for required skills and achievements in scientific research required for military, economic and social life. It also led to the need for mass higher education, as more and more workforce was required.[5]

This was the European pattern of higher education which was copied all over the world including India. With the rise of North America, the North American pattern, which is different from the European model because of the development of a federal State and its more limited role in the higher education, is also beginning to emerge. This has led to a system of federal grants together with private funding from commercial enterprises for research. It has obvious consequences for areas to be prioritised for research, interests of funding agencies in outcomes, together with economic and political consequences. For obvious reasons, India chose to follow the European model and more particularly the British model. Higher education was seen as a State responsibility and as an instrument for training the elite especially for civil service and public administration.

With the establishment of the relationship between higher education and economic development the world over, "massification" of higher education is taking place and is moving towards its universalisation. This has linked it firmly with employability raising questions about relevance and quality of higher education. The need to simultaneously expand to increase access, create equity and tackle the issues of relevance and quality by upgrading existing institutions and establishing new ones, has put a strain on the resources available for the public funding of higher education and given rise to private education. It has also prioritised subjects like engineering, medicine, management, media, law, applied sciences and technology together with subjects related to the service industry and skill development. Social sciences and humanities are facing neglect but without societal understanding, the fruits of research will not find successful application.

Globalisation has intensified the relationship between education and economy. It has demanded linkages between education and skill development and employability for developing the market economy. Education is seen as a means of material benefit to the individual and of material prosperity to the Nation-State through the agency of global markets. The marketisation of the world has shifted focus from values such as diversity and inclusiveness and moved towards homogenisation and material progress at a cost. The focus is on outcomes as universities get more corporatised and managerial.

Issues Pertaining to Research

Several questions arise over the issue of research. What kind of research is needed? What is the aim of this research? How can research be incorporated into teaching? At what level should the research programme begin? One thought is that there does not seem to be an obvious flow from research to teaching at least at the undergraduate level. This could partly be because of the way teaching is organised and partly because research yields such specialised knowledge that it is remote from what students need to know at the undergraduate level. But on the other hand, evidence can be given to show that there are advantages to learning in a research-rich environment. For that, however, a conscious and deliberate link needs to be established between teaching and research in a department.

But what kind of research do universities need to facilitate and to what end? What are the forces that drive this kind of research? What are the aspirations of the students enrolling in the universities? Has the kind of research being pursued led to imbalances in the outcomes and the privileging of some disciplines over others? What are the consequences of this in teaching, learning and its impact on society at large?

Opportunities in Research

Given the economic integration and individual aspirations, what kind of research needs to be done? As Hebe Vessuri points out, the three main challenges that face the world in the twenty-first century are: freedom from want, freedom from fear, and freedom for the future generations to sustain their lives on this planet.[6] Science, technology and innovation are central to successfully handling these challenges, but in some ways, they are also associated with causing them. They have led to the improvement of health, life expectancy and living standards, greater opportunities for information sharing and environmental remediation in many places around the globe. But they are also linked, in complex ways, to the current unsustainable development trajectories.

Unacceptable levels of disparity have been created because research efforts are unevenly distributed between different countries and regions. As Jens Revold points out, it is only a few industrialised countries that conduct the greater part of the world's research. This is problematic for developing countries that do not have the means or the education base to get a large share in the global research effort. Quite inevitably most of the research effort is directed at solving problems and answering questions that are related to the needs of industrialised countries, where the research is conducted. Applied to developing countries, their solutions may not be appropriate. Also, the developing countries may not even have the level of competency of education, research and technology required to benefit from the knowledge developed elsewhere.

Therefore, if the fruits of research have to reach developing countries, the developed countries must increase research funding to solve problems in countries that do not have the capacity to invest much in research. There is growing awareness, internationally, of the need to enhance the role of higher education, science and technology by embedding it as part of aid and development policies. Of course, there is no equal correlation between benefits of research and the efforts required to be put into research. It is not necessary for countries to necessarily share in the costs of developing technology to take a share to its benefits. The development of new technology may be costly but the price of using it may be low. Even to use the available technology, there has to be a broad knowledge base and therefore higher education is important.[7]

The way research endeavour has grown, it has led to the privileging of science, but is this the surest route to development or is there a need to also incorporate other routes? Development is a practical end sought to be achieved through research and its applications but the universalistic scientific approach without the national, social and cultural dimensions being factored in, can lead to problematic and even tragic results. Therefore, scientific endeavours should be linked to social concerns. Scientists have to be aware of the societal impact of their work if their research and its applications have to bring collective well-being and equity in society and salvage the Earth's environment.

Science is only a part of a richer whole and spaces have to be created to bring scientists and different audiences together in democratic spaces so that expert knowledge can become comprehensible and more widespread. This would enable plural perspectives to emerge on the pros and cons of application and increase informed awareness among citizens. Without it, the growth of higher education will not necessarily reduce social and economic inequalities. As Vessuri has pointed out, in weaker countries with inadequate capacity, and unstable political and social institutions, higher education in science and technology may actually widen the gulf between the knowledgeable and the ignorant; between the better off who can afford education through its formal structures and those who cannot. These disparities can develop domestically within nations and internationally among different Nation-States. The process started with the move towards open market policies in the 1970s, when greater emphasis was given to growth than to income distribution and social objectives. This was the wisdom of North America and the OECD countries and finally, it was followed by the whole world.

This has led to asymmetries based on the economic capacities of different countries. So while education, knowledge and research base of science has increased mainly in the developed countries, the same has not happened in the developing world. Vessuri presents some interesting figures. "There are only 94.3 scientific researchers per million people in the least developed countries (LDCs) against 313 in the other developing countries (ODCs) and 3,728 in rich countries (high-income OECD). Enrollment in university-level institutions (that is, tertiary school enrollment as a share of the corresponding age group) is only 3.5 per cent in the LDCs, against 23 per cent in ODCs and 69 per cent in rich countries. LDC governments are devoting only 0.3 per cent of their gross domestic product (GDP) to research and development, against 0.8 per cent in other developing countries and 2.4 per cent in rich countries. Five LDCs —Haiti, Cape Verde, Samoa, Gambia and Somalia—have lost more than half of their university-educated professionals in recent years because they have moved to industrialised countries in search of better working and living conditions. Asian LDCs received more than twice from workers' remittances than from official development assistance (ODA) in 2005; $7 billion in the former case versus $3 billion in the latter. For all the LDCs remittances amounted to some two-thirds of the total Official Development Assessment (ODA) of $18 billion received in the same year."[8]

Higher education and science have to be more evenly distributed around the world and there is a need to develop certain features that have largely been absent in the post-colonial and semi-colonial world. Universities cannot just do neutral science research. They must build a foundation of civic and democratic values to build social cohesion and purpose. They must create knowledge that not only leads to economic growth, but also to an understanding of how to overcome racial and ethnic tensions, dogmatism and religious extremism that often become concomitant to it because of its unevenness. This requires immediate attention to cultural diversity in higher education and research within the framework of globalisation. This does not mean merely increasing the population of the under represented social groups in a campus population. It implies building knowledge systems that give an understanding of diverse values, policies, practices, traditions, resources and living knowledge systems outside the formal structures so that students and faculty, who have been excluded up to now, can become part of the knowledge resource and provide keys and solutions that have eluded thought and policy up to now.

This brings us to what, Mahmood Mamdani, speaking in the context of Africa says: the central issue is that we are still dealing in the framework of the Western paradigms derived from the values of Enlightenment, whether we extol its virtues or critique it. As he points out, while it may be vital to understand Enlightenment, if it is exclusively a European phenomenon, it excludes Africa. By the same token, it also excludes Asia. The central question, therefore, is whether universities in Africa and Asia can be founded on those values.

The Enlightenment framework, as Mamdani points out, presents a single model derived from the dominant Western experience and reduces research to a mere demonstration of whether societies around the world conform to that model or deviate from it. This has to be challenged because discordant experiences, whether Western or non-Western, cannot be dehistoricized or decontextualised to somehow make them fit into the dominant Western experience.[9]

Formulation of the Research Problem

A vital key to research is the formulation of the research problem as thoughts, formulations and solutions flow from it. Therefore, it cannot be decontextualised from where it is situated or its processes and outcomes will be of no relevance to the society it seeks to serve. Research has to have a dual engagement; one, a critical engagement with the society at large; and the other, a critical grasp of disciplinary literature worldwide, so that the key debates within the literature can be identified and the specific queries can be located within those debates.

This was perhaps the mission of Anil K. Gupta from Indian Institute of Management (IIM), Ahmedabad. He challenged the dominant developmental paradigm in which the role of the State or civil society was only to provide what poor people lack —material resources, opportunities for gains in skills or resources or employment. Strategies of development do not build upon a resource in which poor people are often rich; it is the knowledge that they possess. They are not 'resource-poor people' simply because they do not have material wealth. Their resource is their knowledge that has enabled them to innovate and survive, particularly in high risk environments. Their knowledge he says blends the secular with the sacred, reductionism with holism, short-term options with long-term ones, specialised with diversified strategies in pursuits that might be individual or collective material, or in non-material pursuits. This was reflected in the environmental ethics of these communities. Writing and working consistently on this area for over two decades, Gupta points out that higher the physical, technological, market or socio-economic stresses that they go through, the more the greater the disadvantaged communities and individuals generate innovative and creative alternatives for resource use. The innovations could originate in both traditions and in modern awareness. They could be evolved by communities or by individuals. Usually it was the joint endeavour of communities that led to the widespread indifference towards the entrepreneurial potential of the knowledge rich but economically poor people.

To remedy this, Gupta created an extensive knowledge network that connected innovation, enterprise and investment in an institutional context, known as the Honey Bee Network. It worked on certain basic premises:

1. The knowledge could not be exploitatively taken away. To prevent this from happening, he created the Society for Research and

Initiatives for SustainableTechnologies and Institutions (SRISTI) that supported the Honey Bee Network. The vision statement was a link of six 'Es'—ethics, equity, excellence, environment, education and efficiency in enterprise.

2. The intellectual property rights of the poor were protected by ensuring that the formal sector could use their knowledge without acknowledgments, citations and prior informed consent.
3. The people-to-people learning was strengthened by ensuring that communication was in the vernacular. Similarly, the documentation and dissemination of these innovations was in local languages.
4. Finances were sought on the premise that the knowledge network for sustainable technological options operationalised through Honey Bee Network could approach and seek or attract investments from any part of the world. This could also lead to a flow of innovation and research not only from the North to the South, but also from the South to the North.[10]

Balance between Teaching and Research

'Relevant' research would be different in different domains and yet form an integrated ecosystem. It would have to take in both the local and global to form a continuous whole, and teaching would have to be organised accordingly. Teaching and research have to be seen as a continuum. There is no real dichotomy between the two if the connection is seen not between research and teaching as between research and learning. Research can probably be seen as a process. It is a form of learning. At one end of the spectrum is information transfer that takes the form of lecturing or slide presentations and at the other end is enquiry into a problem by individuals or teams. Therefore, integrating research and learning is really about inculcating skills of enquiry and research into students. This is much more important educationally than providing students with content knowledge, which is now freely available in different media both print and electronic.

To enable this to happen, teachers have to know more than just their subject. They must also know how in its transmission it can become understood or misunderstood. In any case, what is the meaning of understanding? As Brew says, they need to know how individuals experience the subject. Seen thus, researchers and teachers have much in common because researchers are essentially involved in "meaning-making activity" or "making sense of chaos and translating this into culturally accepted explanations." But increasingly, the learning process in higher education is also being seen as meaning-making or "constructivism." It is a process of helping students to construct knowledge rather than simply transmitting it to them. The emerging pedagogical goals and emphases, therefore, is "not objective knowledge" which is outside the learner and which can be obtained through multiple sources "but the subjective processes of the learner" and the acknowledgement that "learning always takes place in a particular context." Hence, Brew concludes, "that research and teaching can be viewed as being in a symbiotic relationship."[11]

This involves not only knowledge, but also skills of self-management, communication, team working and interpersonal skills. It involves looking for similarities and differences between disciplines. Techniques and approaches, such as group projects, interactive lectures, problem-based learning and information literacy initiatives, can beneficially cross-disciplinary boundaries with relative ease. And this can start from the undergraduate level. It is in essence an ecosystem of knowledge, a shared quest between the teachers and students that integrates the local knowledge resource base with the cutting-edge research and technology. This requires a paradigm shift and economics is not the only thing standing in the way of the much-needed change in the way we deliver knowledge and conduct research. As Ravetz said, it is more the inertia of those intellectual structures that define and regulate our thoughts whether we call them paradigms, frameworks, or mental models, and these have to be recognised by those who attempt to change them. If science has to address problems with regard to sustainability, it has to be produced in a way that allows it to be linked more easily and rapidly to action communities. In the process, it may be reformulated and even transformed through multiple dialogues and interactions among the individuals, groups and institutions that generate and ultimately apply new scientific and technological knowledge. The implementation of new knowledge and the technical capacities by different social actors whether it is governments, natural resource managers, industry, and society in general should not be a final phase in a research programme. It has to be an integral part of it, right from formulating the research problem.

We must insist on the critical importance of linking the various scales of interaction. Locally focused studies and actions often have limited value if they do not account for the action of higher-level forces on the immediate local dynamics. This limited understanding of multi-scale interactions is one of the main obstacles to progress. "Advances in the modelling of complex systems and new integrated assessment methodologies afford new opportunities to overcome traditional disciplinary compartmentalisation and to aid in decision-making under conditions of persistent uncertainty."[12]

If all disciplines are as seen as a continuum, then there has to be a commitment to local and regional knowledge production, rooted in relevant linguistic and disciplinary terms, with a critical and disciplined reflection on the globalisation of modern forms of knowledge and modern instruments of power. Rather than oppose the local to the global, the global has to be understood from the vantage point of the local. Research will then have to try to understand alternative forms of aesthetic, intellectual, ethical and political traditions, both contemporary and historical, the objective being not just to learn about these forms, but also to learn from them. This is crucial because one of the major bottlenecks has been the insularity of formal research systems towards informal innovations. As Anil Gupta would put it, research stations or laboratories dedicated and designed to work under the leadership of knowledge rich, economically poor people are yet to be set up. Research and Development (R&D) for the poor cannot be just an attempt to identify "appropriate technologies" or some other variants of sub-optimal solutions. The best of the formal and informal sector have to join hands to compete in the marketplace at all levels without privileging one over the other.

References

1. Cited in George Lueddeke, 2008. "Reconciling Research, Teaching and Scholarship in Higher Education: An Examination of Disciplinary Variation, the Curriculum and Learning," *International Journal for the Scholarship of Teaching and Learning*, Vol. 2, January, 2008.
2. *Ibid.*
3. Mamdani, Mahmood. 2011. "The Importance of Research in a University." Keynote at Makarare University Research and Innovations Dissemination Conference, Hotel Africana, 11th April, 2011.
4. Teixeira, Pedro. 2009. "Mass Higher Education and Private Institutions," *Higher Education to 2030*, Vol. 2: Globalisation, OECD.
5. *Ibid.*
6. Vessuri, Hebe. "The Role of Research in Higher Education: Implications and Challenges for an Active Future Contribution to Human and Social Development," *Higher Education in the World*,
   http://upcommons.upc.edu/bitsteam/handle/2099/8119/vessuri.pdf?sequence=1.
7. Jens Revold, "Research and Higher Education in Developing Countries", Speech by State Secretary, Jens Revold, Norway, 12.2.2008. http://www.regjeringen.no/en/dep/kd/News-and-latest-publications/Speeches-and-articles.
8. *Ibid.*
9. Mamdani, Mahmood. "The Importance of Research in a University." www.pambazuka.org/resources/importance-research-university
10. Gupta, Anil K. "Honey Bee Network." www.sristi.org/cons/?q=en/book/print/519. This article summarises the essential vision that has motivated Gupta and

the structures he has established to encourage and mainstream the grassroots knowledge and innovations.

11. Cited by George Lueddeke, "Reconciling Research, Teaching and Scholarship in Higher Education: An Examination of Disciplinary Variation, the Curriculum and Learning." *Op.cit.*
12. Cited by Hebe Vessuri, "The Role of Research in Higher Education: Implications and Challenges for an Active Future Contribution to Human and Social Development." *Op.cit.*

7

Internationalisation of Higher Education: An Aspect of India's Foreign Relations*

There is, generally, little thought in India that higher education can be an important instrument in furthering its external relations. While the Ministry of External Affairs (MEA) recognises the importance of soft-power diplomacy, it is only beginning to recognise the benefits of internationalisation of higher education. The universities need far greater awareness. Internationalisation of higher education has largely been triggered by the impact of globalisation, the exodus of Indian students to foreign universities, the setting up of centres by foreign universities in India to recruit students, the availability of degrees through the Internet, and other such factors.

There is increasing consensus that if India has to emerge as a global leader, it must gain pre-eminence in the field of education. It cannot compete with the developed world in military might; in spite of its fast-growing economy, it cannot acquire in the near future the equivalent economic muscle. Although it has a sizeable educated and skilled middle class, all social indicators show that there is still a long way to go before India can be counted amongst the developed countries. India can however, gain pre-eminence and be seen as a significant global actor in the field of development of human resource. Thanks to the groundwork done immediately after independence in establishing institutions for scientific, technical, agricultural and medical education apart from the liberal university education and the subsequent rapid increase in the education system, India has emerged as a developer of skilled human resource. What used to be

* This is extracted from the author's book: Sharma, Kavita, A. 2008. *Internationalisation of Higher Education: An Aspect of India's Foreign Relations*, Delhi: Gyan Publishing House. Research for it was done through the Centre for Policy Research with financial support from the Ministry of External Affairs.

lamented as brain drain is now seen as human capital. Developing countries, too, look to India for help in enhancing their human resource. This was understood in post-independence India and it led to the establishment of institutions such as the Indian Council for Cultural Relations (ICCR).[1]

The first Education Commission of India, popularly known as the Kothari Commission (1964–66), had emphasised that knowledge is international and there should be no barriers to obtaining it from anywhere in the world. However, India cannot remain at the receiving end of the pipeline forever. It has to make its own contribution as an intellectual and cultural equality in efforts to extend the frontiers of knowledge. This, as the Kothari Commission pointed out, required a large-scale programme for discovering and developing talent and the creating centres of excellence in higher education that can compare favourably with the best in the world. It is through education that India can grow and find its place in the comity of nations.

India's Educational and Cultural Diplomacy

Educational and cultural diplomacy received some attention in India through ICCR and its programmes and through other educational exchanges but it was not been foregrounded to any large degree. Obviously, there was some understanding of it immediately after India's independence. This is obvious from India's efforts to provide educational support to the newly independent countries of Africa in spite of its own straitened circumstances, by sending teachers and giving scholarships to students to study in India. Many African students who pursued higher education in India went on to occupy very important positions in their home country. Earlier, during the colonial administration, Indians had become teachers in many developing countries such as, Burma or Myanmar and Fiji, and in East Africa in Uganda, Kenya and Tanzania. Hence, India already had a well-recognised base but it was not built upon to the extent that it could have been. India's over 20 million-strong diaspora is also attracted to the country of their forefathers. Many students who come to India from Fiji, Malaysia, Mauritius, Sri Lanka and some countries of Africa and the Caribbean for education belong to the Indian diaspora. They have a strong emotional attachment to India and can be important goodwill ambassadors. However, the university system has to be sensitised to this and the educational institutions have to play a vital role.

Even cultural diplomacy cannot be effective without educational institutions and organisations being a part of the delivery system. India has, for example, spent huge sums of money on organising "Festivals of India" in different parts of the world but these have made a limited impact or have even reinforced the "Exotic India" image because there has been little or no backing with education programmes to create an in-depth understanding of the country and its people.

Indian Council for Cultural Relations (ICCR)

While cultural diplomacy has received sporadic attention, educational diplomacy has hardly received any. Although there is some writing on the subject, it has not been foregrounded in foreign policy discussions or in the education sector. The MEA has initiated whatever initiatives have been taken in this area, but does not seem to meaningfully impinge on the consciousness of either the Ministry of Human Resource Development (MHRD) or the University Grants Commission (UGC) or the universities or other decision-making bodies in the field of higher education.

After independence, India was inevitably drawn into the mainstream of international activities. While internally the government and its leaders grappled with problems of economic, social and cultural development, India began to play a leading role abroad in the sphere of international peace and amity. To attain these objectives, many major academic and educational programmes were initiated in ICCR. Some of these were scholarship schemes for overseas students, with emphasis on developing countries; establishing and maintaining chairs and professorships for Indian studies abroad; presenting books, audio-visual material, art objects and musical instruments; annual organisation of the Maulana Azad Memorial Lecture and the Maulana Azad Essay Competition; and organising other programmes on behalf of the MEA. In addition, the ICCR brings out several publications, organises and participates in international seminars and symposia, among other such activities. Numerous academic-related programmes indicate awareness about education as the medium through which culture and values can be disseminated. The belief is that overseas students help in building bridges of understanding and developing a better appreciation of India. They have enormous potential to spread goodwill for India in their home countries.

This vision led the MEA to put several programmes in place. For example, the Government of India provides fifty scholarships each year to deserving Bhutanese students in different professional streams such as Medicine, Engineering, Law, Nursing, Agriculture, Dentistry and others. In addition, ambassador's scholarships are awarded to meritorious and deserving Bhutanese students after they have been admitted to various schools and colleges in India. There is the Technical Cooperation Scheme of the Colombo Plan, through which the Government of India provides comprehensive and integrated training to foreign participants to upgrade their administrative and technical skills. There are other programmes such as the SAARC scholarship scheme and a six-week professional course for foreign diplomats, the latter being run three or four times a year by the Foreign Service Institute of the MEA.

Indian Technical and Economic Cooperation (ITEC) Programme

The most important is the Indian Technical and Economic Cooperation (ITEC) programme run by the MEA.[2] It was launched by a decision of the Cabinet on 15 September, 1964 as a bilateral programme of assistance. Its chief architect was Jawaharlal Nehru, who was also the Minister for External Affairs at the time. Through ITEC and its corollary Special Commonwealth Assistance for Africa Programme (SCAAP), India has shared, since independence, its developmental experience with 156 countries in Asia, East and Central Europe (including Russia), Central Asia, Africa, Latin America and the Pacific.

The ITEC, embodying the spirit of South-South Cooperation for mutual benefit, is response-oriented. While in the early 1960s, India could not give grants-in-aid to match those of developed countries, its strength lay in its skills of human resource and technology that were more appropriate for developing countries than those of developed countries. The six components of the programme: training in India of nominees of ITEC partner countries, both civilian and military; projects and project-related activities such as feasibility studies and consultancy services; deputation of Indian experts abroad; study tours; Aid for Disaster Relief (ADR); and gifting or donation of equipment at the request of ITEC partner countries. Although ITEC is essentially bilateral, occasionally the resources have been used for financing trilateral and regional programmes, for example, under the UN Economic Commission for Africa (UNECA), United Nations Industrial Development Organisation (UNIDO) and the Group of 77. The African-Asian Rural Development Organisation (AARDO) and G-15 are also helped by ITEC with training and project support. Also, special and customised programmes have been designed for regional and multilateral groupings, such as the Association of Southeast Asian Nations (ASEAN), Bangladesh, India, Myanmar, Sri Lanka, Thailand Economic Cooperation (BIMSTEC), African Union (AU), Caribbean Community and Common Market (CARICOM), the Commonwealth and the World Trade Organisation (WTO).

India spends about Rs 500 million annually on ITEC activities, and has provided over US$ 2.5 billion worth of technical assistance to developing countries, including its neighbours, since 1964. Over 45,000 people have participated in ITEC programmes, attending courses in various disciplines. Many of them work in important positions in their home countries. In addition to the training courses, ITEC takes its participants to "Outstation Study Tours" to introduce them to India, its democratic system, culture and historical heritage. It brings home India as a vibrant democracy with a strong pluralistic flavour, which provides a model of development to many developing countries. The ITEC programme also demonstrates India's role and contribution in South-South Cooperation.

Internationalisation of Indian Higher Education

The Indian higher education system is now recognised as one of the better systems for producing talented human workforce. Various agencies connected with education have begun to seriously look at the merits and demerits of the internationalisation of higher education in India. The National University of Educational Planning and Administration (NUEPA) established by the Union Ministry of Human Resource Development, is a premier organisation dealing with capacity building and research in planning and management of education not only in India, but also in South Asia. It deliberated upon issues pertaining to globalisation and the response to internationalisation of education in a national conference held in New Delhi in August 2004.[3] It felt that challenges of quality; modes of supply; access and equity in higher education; responses to General Agreement on Trade in Services (GATS) and WTO; matters pertaining to identity, culture and curriculum; and other concerns of the nations receiving foreign higher education needed to be addressed.[4] On the one hand, there was recognition of the benefits that internationalisation of education could bring but there were also serious apprehensions leading to ambivalence of attitude.

The Association of Indian Universities (AIU), too, held roundtables on internationalisation of higher education, at the University of Mysore in February 2001 and at Guru Nanak Dev University in Amritsar in February 2002.[5] The recommendations of neither roundtable viewed the internationalisation of education as a soft power, but noted that in the new knowledge era, internationalisation of higher education had to be done if India was to be counted as a knowledge society. There was a realisation that internationalisation would lead to an improvement in the quality of education, promote Indian culture abroad, generate goodwill and understanding, and yield financial benefits. It was recognised that partnership and networking were essential for enriching the teaching-learning process and for improved quality of research. Hence, it was necessary to act in earnest without further delay. The government, academic institutions and AIU were all urged to take the necessary steps to promote

Indian higher education internationally. The Amritsar recommendations built on the "Mysore Statement" and reinforced it.

In the Tenth Plan (2002–07), UGC made internationalisation of higher education one of its thrust areas and projected a vision for promoting Indian higher education abroad as a response to the phenomenon of globalisation. The Chairman of UGC set up an Expert Committee to encourage the free flow of students from other nations to India and vice versa. Subsequently, a Standing Committee of UGC for the Promotion of Indian Higher Education Abroad (PIHEAD) gave its report in January 2004. The UGC identified several countries for targeting to attract international students to India. Based on country profiles (demographic and economic) and taking into consideration, the present state of their higher education and training system, skill gaps, programmes for offer need to be identified. After this, issues like academic calendar, equivalence and matters relating to curriculum, language skills/maths skills/subject combination, etc. are sorted out. There is a need to create a fit on what is being offered and what is sought.[6]

The PIHEAD Committee emphasised that globalisation was a dominant feature of the twenty-first century because of which integration of societies was taking place. This gave rise to major challenges in interaction between individuals, groups, and even with nature. The committee noted that the Indian education system had not yet acquired the capacity to cope, as it catered largely for domestic needs. Although India had certain advantages because of its low-cost delivery system, English as the medium of instruction, and its huge technological and management resources, it had yet not harnessed its immense potential of reaching out to foreign students. Unlike in the developed countries, the number of international students in India was decreasing. The Committee recognised that internationalisation would necessarily be a relatively slow process as both institutions and individuals have to be made aware that cooperation with universities in different countries was beneficial to both. The stakeholders needed to understand that internationalisation did not imply a dilution of the national culture and ethos, but actually resulted in the strengthening of these by learning from others. The Committee detailed the steps that had to be taken to make Indian higher education attractive abroad while at the same time strengthening it from within to build capacity to internationalise. Unlike some of the advanced English-speaking countries, particularly the USA, the UK, Canada and Australia that had made concerted efforts to attract international students, India had done little in this direction. It was therefore, necessary to formulate a national policy and adopt consistent strategies that would encourage Indian institutions to admit international students.

There were several constraints to international students becoming a part of Indian university campuses. Under the government policy, dictated in part by the apex court, educational institutions were permitted to admit a limited percentage of students to educational programmes in technical and professional fields. There was a need to seriously rethink this matter.

It was also felt necessary to create a nodal agency to coordinate the efforts and activities of Indian universities as they attempted to internationalise their education. This would mean establishing a Consortium for International Education to identify select universities and institutions of higher learning, keep in view standards, infrastructure and performance; help in projecting Indian universities/institutions in other countries and function on their behalf; act as a clearing house for information on courses offered, availability of seats, the fees charged, the financial assistance available, and look at the possibility of on-campus housing accommodation for individuals and families. Publication and distribution of guides and handbooks for promoting international education programmes in the country was also a necessary function. Coordinating education and training international students of the universities/institutions of higher learning in the country and building a network, to liaise, collaborate, and interact with relevant institutions, individuals and other agencies within and outside the country, and promoting international education cooperation programmes was another envisaged function.

The Consortium could also help Indian universities/institutions of higher learning in obtaining approvals of the various central government ministries for different international education cooperation programmes by promoting, coordinating and monitoring jointly the affairs of international students with the Indian universities/institutions. It could also represent Indian universities/institutions at international fairs on higher education and organise similar fairs in India. In addition, the Consortium could develop norms and guidelines for ensuring quality in international education and do all other things incidental or conducive to the attainment of the main objects of any of them.

To further the recommendation of the PIHEAD Committee, the Committee for the Promotion of Indian Education Abroad (COPIE) was set up, which in turn decided to form two sub-committees. One was to be headed by the UGC Chairman; Chairman, AICTE; Director, National Assessment and Accreditation Council (NAAC); Secretary-General AIU; Chairman, CBSE and representatives of Confederation of Indian Industry (CII); Ministry of External Affairs (MEA); Indian Council of Agricultural Research (ICAR); and Ministry of Health, with the mandate to identify universities/courses with potential to attract foreign students; to improve their standards; and to promote Indian institutions in targeted countries through Indian missions, Educational Consultants India Limited (Ed.CIL). The second sub-committee was to be a standing committee of COPIE and to act as a clearing house for all proposals of Indian institutions either for setting up their campuses abroad or for entering into twinning arrangements with foreign educational institutions. The sub-committee was to receive all proposals from the MHRD and place them, along with their recommendations, before the COPIE for a final decision. It appears from the deliberations of the Committee that there was consensus on attracting foreign students to undertake degree and study programmes in Indian universities. The Committee, in addition, suggested that focused "Study India Programme" (SIP) in Indian universities for students from developed countries should be initiated. It also endorsed proposals such as: (a) initiation of "twinning" academic arrangements with foreign universities, (b) setting up of foreign campuses of Indian universities, and (c) creation of special education zones for running of teaching and learning programmes exclusively for foreign students through Consortia of Indian Universities.[7]

The Committee was of the view that Indian education needed to target the African and South East Asian countries as they represented a client group distinct from Europe and the USA. Also, special efforts were needed to export education to the countries of the Middle East. However, the Committee overlooked Central Asia, particularly the former Soviet Republics, which have the advantage of proximity and with whom India has historical, cultural and civilisation links. The Committee emphasised one great advantage that education in India was affordable.

Following the recommendations of the PIHEAD Committee, together with those of other committees, UGC together with some universities has been participating in the NAFSA conferences since 2004. While participation in the NAFSA conferences is an important step in the direction of internationalisation of higher education, the question was whether the structure of higher education in India was ready for it. Unless the ground was prepared and systemic changes were made, raising expectations at such a conference without the ability to deliver could be counter-productive and detrimental. Even this effort was put on hold as not much movement in this direction was evident.

International Student Mobility: The Indian Situation

In spite of many positive policy decisions and recommendations in the last few years from the AIU, NUEPA and UGC, the ground reality is that the population of foreign students is very small in India. This is despite the fact that India has the third-largest system of higher education in terms of enrollment after China and the USA.

Pawan Agarwal estimated 12,263 international students in higher education institutions in India in 2003–04, but he noted that a better figure would be about 15,000 students, given the lacunae in the maintenance of records in most universities. This analysis was based on his combining the data for 82 universities collected by the AIU for 2003–04 with the projected data from 83 universities collected by UGC in 2005 for 2001–02. Out of 308 universities that existed in 2003–04, 109 reported no international students and 34 did not respond.

With an annual estimated growth of eight per cent, the number would be about 17,500 in 2005–06. More than 90 per cent of the students came from developing countries of Asia and Africa, with two-thirds were from Asia and one-fourth from the African countries. Only eight per cent came from other countries. Thirty per cent of students were from South and Central Asia and 20 per cent from North Africa and the Middle East. There were some students from the Caribbean and Latin America. Nepal sent the highest number of students to India followed by Bangladesh, Malaysia, Kenya, Sri Lanka, Iran, Mauritius, Ethiopia, the USA and Oman. This showed that the percentage of students from high-income countries was extremely low in India.[8] According to Agarwal's findings, in 2003–04, three-fourths of international students were enrolled in Arts (28 per cent), Science (26 per cent) and Commerce (22 per cent). There were 72.53 per cent of students in the undergraduate programmes and 17.8 per cent were doing post-graduation. Twenty-eight per cent of students were girls. The number of students from developed countries was very small and they largely came for "short term study abroad programmes" in order to get a cross-cultural experience. Many advanced countries have instituted policies to encourage students to study abroad for a short time. This is especially true of the USA where study abroad is very popular.

According to Achuthsankar S. Nair, the Director of the International Affairs of Kerala University, there has been a 35 per cent jump in the foreign students coming to India in the last three years. Currently, there are about 75,000 foreign students. Africa, Afghanistan and Iran have triggered this rise. Affordability and comparative quality makes India a favoured destination for students from these regions.[9]

The author did a survey in 2007–2008 to find out the favoured destinations for foreign students. Over 60 per cent of international students in India enrolled in just 10 out of the 274 universities that reported having international students. These are a mixture of both public and private institutions. The largest numbers attended the Manipal Academy of Higher Education (MAHE), Bangalore University, University of Pune and the University of Delhi. The other popular destinations, according to Agarwal, are Bharati Vidyapeeth and Symbiosis in Pune.While these findings were largely substantiated, there were also other destinations that were found to be popular like the University of Mysore and the CMR Institutions in Bangalore. Largely, as Agarwal points out, students prefer metropolitan towns in western and southern India. While MAHE, Bharati Vidyapeeth and Symbiosis, all private deemed universities actively recruited foreign students, public-funded universities and colleges were generally more conservative. Perhaps, the three exceptions were the Universities of Pune, Bangalore and Delhi, together with their affiliated colleges. It was found during the survey that most educational institutions did not have either the mind-set or the organisational infrastructure to cope with foreign students in terms of physical space and human resource. The best equipped seemed MAHE, CMR and Osmania University. Some more universities were making an effort to internationalise their campuses such as the Sardar Patel University at Vallabh Vidyanagar; but in others, the number of foreign students had declined.

The Roadblocks

What are the impediments in the way of international students coming to India? Some are obvious: paucity of institutions of higher education, lack of resources leading to inadequate physical and academic infrastructure, and there being little or no consciousness in the majority of the institutions that the diversity of student population is a desired goal to be actively pursued. Access to higher education is only about 17–20 per cent. This implies that at least 80 per cent of India's population has no access to higher education. As the Indian economy strengthens, the domestic demand for higher education increases; this leads to higher enrollment numbers. Not only is there a lack of institutions, but also inadequate funding. India spends less than 0.5 per cent of GDP on higher education, while the recommendation is of an expenditure of 1.5 per cent out of a total of at least six per cent of GDP for education overall. This goal has yet to be reached. As per the National Knowledge Commission, even this may not suffice for the massive expansion of higher education that is required, in which case, other possibilities need to be explored to complement the increase in public expenditure. Further, even the small amount that is spent on higher education is very unevenly distributed. Nearly one-third of the institutions do not get any government funds. Of the remaining, only about a half get central funding. The small numbers of institutions that cater for less than two per cent of the students get 85 per cent of the central funds. The rest receive pitifully small amounts and have to depend on the state governments for funding. Many of them are in perpetual financial problems. This is not healthy for higher education itself and also makes it much less attractive to foreign students.

India's External Relations and the Education Sector

It would be useful to examine how education cooperation can help India's foreign policy objectives. High priority has always been accorded to relations with neighbours. There is already a fair amount of cooperation with most of the members of the South Asian Association for Regional Cooperation (SAARC) except Pakistan. Recognising the importance of education in promoting regional cooperation, during the summit at Dhaka, held on 12 November 2005, India proposed establishing a SAARC University. It would be useful to accelerate the decision-making process for early fruition of the idea. This apart, India needs to take the lead in promoting student and faculty exchange programmes with universities in SAARC countries.

Nepal and Bhutan already enjoy a special status in Indian universities. Students from these countries, for example, are eligible to get admission in Delhi University even on scoring five per cent less than the basic eligibility for Indian students. India being the education destination for the people of Nepal has played a positive role in India-Nepal relations. But it has not been possible to accommodate the demand of a large number of Nepalese students, particularly for professional courses. MAHE has opened a Medical College in Nepal; unfortunately, its full potential has not been realised because of political turbulence there. In a deemed university like MAHE, the Nepalese students could have been accommodated in India itself but excessive regulatory framework in India made Nepal a more attractive destination. The institution in Nepal also attracts students from India and some other foreign countries.

India is the first choice destination for higher education for the Bhutanese, who look to it to play a significant role in the development of human resources in their own country. Bhutanese society is gradually opening up and education there is bound to grow. It is essential that India plays a key role in helping educationally in human resource development and thus shaping attitudes towards India in a newly democratic Bhutan.

With regard to Sri Lanka, while education has played a positive role in India-Sri Lanka relations, its full potential has not been realised because of paucity of seats and institutions in India. Apart from general education,

Buddhist studies need greater attention. A number of Sri Lankans come to study Buddhism in India. It is necessary to remember that the Buddhist clergy plays an important role in Sri Lanka's national affairs. Special attention should be paid to Buddhist studies because of the large number of Buddhist countries in the world, which expect India to provide the lead in areas of Philosophy and Comparative Religion. There is only one centre of Buddhist studies in Varanasi, but many more can be developed and departments of Philosophy need to be strengthened.

India has little or no educational links with its neighbours on the east and west. Bangladesh sends a large number of students to India. However, India is unable to meet their huge demand for professional and vocational courses. There is hardly any faculty exchange between universities in Bangladesh and Indian universities and few, if any, joint research projects. Such initiatives will not only enhance cooperation in the field of education, but also help develop better understanding. Because of linguistic commonality, it should be possible to develop close links between academic institutions of the two countries, especially with universities in West Bengal. With Pakistan this area has been a closed one. As part of the confidence-building measures, it would be worthwhile to begin with small steps like faculty exchange in this field.

The greatest expectation of war-ravaged Afghanistan from India is help in developing human resource for reconstruction, including education facilities. The government has realised the importance of education in promoting Indo-Afghan relations and has started a special scheme for training Afghan students in India. This is a challenge because war has interrupted the educational processes there and created imbalances in societal structures; but if India can meet the challenge, then it will be an important aspect of India's cultural diplomacy towards these strategically important neighbours. The Prime Minister of India has offered massive aid in human resource development to Afghanistan. A number of Afghans have studied in India earlier, including President Hamid Karzai. The impact of his educational experience in India was visible in the affection with which he remembered his teachers at the Himachal Pradesh University from where he did his post-graduation in Political Science.[10]

India's cultural relations with South East Asia are among the most fascinating fields of history. This interaction goes back over two thousand years and has left a lasting impression on almost every aspect of life in a number of countries of the region. There is probably no other example in history of such peaceful cultural cross-fertilisation for over two millennia. The "Look East" policy, formulated during Prime Minister Narasimha Rao's regime, was a major foreign policy initiative in the post-Cold War era. Relations with the member countries of Association of Southeast Asian Nations (ASEAN) are the cornerstone of the "Look East" policy. Recognising the close cultural ties between the regions, India had also taken the initiative of launching, "Mekong-Ganga Partnership" with the ASEAN countries.

Education has played an important role in independent India's relationship with a number of South East Asian countries, particularly Malaysia, Thailand and Singapore. With the other countries of the region, stronger educational links can be built. A large number of Indian teachers teach in Brunei, but there is little or no educational contact with the Philippines and Indonesia. A few Indonesian students have come to India on ITEC and ICCR scholarships, but keeping in view the large population of the country and its growing needs for skilled human resource, this relationship can be developed.

A large number of Malaysian students came to study in India till the end of the 1980s. Many of them went on to occupy high positions in Malaysian society. These students played an important role in the all-round development of Indo-Malaysian relations. The Malaysian University Graduate Association (MAYUG) of university graduates from India has been active in promoting Indo-Malaysian ties. They have made a mark in academics, law and engineering. A large majority of doctors in Malaysia have been trained in India. However, the number of Malaysian students has been declining since the early 1990s. A meeting with some alumni indicated several reasons for this:

- Malaysia has developed its own institutions.
- Alternate destinations such as Australia, New Zealand and Singapore have also emerged.
- With growing affluence, bright Malaysian students have started enrolling in larger numbers in universities in the USA and UK.
- There have been problems of equivalence and recognition of Indian degrees, which have not been addressed by India. On the contrary, because of pressures on them, Indian institutions have become more inward looking. The Indian regulatory framework has also contributed to this decline.
- MAHE has opened a campus in Malacca to overcome the difficulties created by the rigid regulatory framework of higher education in India.

However, discussions with a number of Malaysian academics and other members of the civil society make it evident that interest in Indian higher education remains. Only a more proactive policy is required.

There has been close cooperation between independent India and Thailand in higher education. The situation in recent years resembles that of Malaysia. Discussions with alumni as well as their academics show that it is possible to revive the relationship. People of Indian origin in Thailand have a particularly strong interest in quality education in India. It is noteworthy that Shivnath Rai Bajaj has given an endowment of one million baht to start an India Study Centre at the Thammasat University.

A number of students from Singapore came to study in India till they developed their own high-quality educational infrastructure. Currently, the majority of Singapore students who go abroad prefer universities in the developed world, particularly the USA. The Singapore government, too, is vigorously developing the country as a destination of higher education. However, it is still keen to collaborate with India, as can be seen from the initiatives taken for a campus of IIM Bangalore in Singapore. Singapore is also keen to have links with the IITs and on student-exchange programmes. For this, it has been interacting with good Indian universities such as Delhi University.[11]

Vietnam, Cambodia and Laos as a group have had close cultural links with India. Vietnam, a strategic partner in ASEAN, looks upon India to play a major role in the development of its human resource. Vietnam is amongst the highest recipients of ITEC fellowships and is particularly keen for cooperation in the field of IT Education. The National Institute of Information Technology (NIIT) has established its presence in Vietnam. Some self-financing Vietnamese students have also started coming to India for management and other professional education. Given the high growth rate of Vietnam's economy, the trend could grow. The position of Laos and Cambodia is somewhat similar to that of Vietnam. Given the cultural affinity with these countries, there is room for strong linkages with them in the field of education.

Central Asia is another region with which India has had strong civilisation and cultural links. India also enjoyed considerable goodwill with many countries that formed part of the earlier Soviet Union. These countries are in transition. Their most important requirement is development of human resource. Because of traditional links and the respect that India enjoys as a knowledge economy, they are keen on India's assistance in the field of education. Geographic proximity and affordability are important factors in favour of India. Some students from the former Soviet Union have started coming to India mostly on ICCR and ITEC fellowships. However, these countries would have a growing middle-class community in the coming years, which would be keen on quality education. This would create further opportunity for collaboration in the education sector and could lead to the strengthening of ties. Even the former Soviet Union used education as an important tool of diplomacy, particularly in its relations with developing India. Many Indian scientists and doctors were trained in the former Soviet Union.

Like South East Asia and Central Asia, India also has traditional ties with West Asia. A number of students from Iran and the Arab and Gulf countries have studied in India. Many Arab students would look towards India if quality education was available because culturally they would feel more comfortable here than in the West, especially after the events of September 11, 2001 in the USA. They look at other options and India is necessarily one of them. Collaboration in education would ensure that the traditional people-to-people contacts between India and West Asia are strengthened. Although the rich students prefer to study in Europe and America, Dubai has realised the potential of providing quality higher education and so has taken the initiative to establish a Knowledge City to meet the educational needs of the region. There was a similar recommendation in the Report of the High Level Committee to establish Special Education Zones in India but the idea has not been taken forward. Ironically, many Indian institutions are setting up campuses in the Dubai Knowledge City. BITS Pilani, Mahatma Gandhi Institute and MAHE are already there. Some students from India, too, have started enrolling in these campuses. India's loss of opportunity could be Dubai's gain.

Africa has always been special to India because of their common struggle against colonialism. The architect of India's foreign policy, Jawaharlal Nehru, accorded very high priority to relations with Africa. Under this policy, India extended scholarships to a large number of African students. Salim Ahmed Salim, who did his undergraduate studies from Delhi University, was Foreign Minister of Tanzania and later Prime Minister and Secretary of the Organisation of African Unity (OAU) during 1989–2001. The educational support given by India generated enormous goodwill for the country among African leaders. Unfortunately, because of inadequate follow-up and lack of proper institutionalised mechanism, India and Africa could not realise the full potential of this aspect of their relationship. Human resource remains a major constraint in African development efforts. Except in South Africa, the educational infrastructure of most African countries remains very inadequate. India's help in developing education for quality human resource can be a major factor in Indo-African ties.

Relations with the European Union are high on India's foreign policy agenda. Both sides recognise the potential role of education in the development of bilateral and Indo-EU relations. India and the UK have historical ties and at one time, the UK used to be the education destination for elite Indians. That has been replaced by the USA but during his visit to India, Gordon Brown, Chancellor of the Exchequer, announced the setting up of an educational fund to ensure cooperation in this field. France and Germany, too, are beginning to look into student exchange programmes with India.

Similarly with the USA, India has had long-standing ties that kept a dialogue of academics and thinkers in place even during the height of the Cold War. Cultural and educational diplomacy, as an exercise of soft power, declined in the US after the disintegration of the Soviet Union, but the events of 11 September 2001 and the Iraq War have once again brought it to the fore. Besides, the growing Indian economy and closer political Indo-American ties have created an interest in India among American universities. The most effective and popular mode of academic collaboration is that of exchange programmes at various levels.

The Way Forward

The education sector is an effective and unobtrusive mode of creating proper understanding of India among young people. Developing countries look to India to take a lead in helping them to develop their own human resource. With India's economic growth in a democratic framework, the developed world is interested in understanding the country through student exchange programmes and faculty and research linkages. The diaspora want to understand and retain their cultural heritage. They look to India to create opportunities for doing so in addition to normal academic exchange and linkages in which, too, it can help. Education should, then, be an integral part of economic assistance given by India to the developing countries. It has the expertise, the cultural understanding and environment, together with the educational infrastructure that has the potential to deliver. However, the university system does not have much sensitivity to this aspect, so there is little motivation to act. Besides, the system itself has problems of both numbers and resources, creating its own challenges. When it is called upon to provide for one more sector, it responds with fatigue and inertia. So what can be done?

Since the MEA is the most aware of the potency of soft-power options of foreign policy, it needs to sensitise and create understanding among other agencies, such as the MHRD, UGC and universities themselves. Once the MEA begins to emphasise education and its consequent soft-power benefits, it must draw up a calendar of events to sensitise others. It needs to collaboratively hold seminars and other academic events with institutions, such as NUEPA and the various departments in universities, both central and state, especially where foreign students advisors are already there. Unless there is sensitivity in education administration and faculty members, the ground cannot be prepared for implementation.

It will be argued that most universities face a resource crunch, both physical and academic, because of which they are not able to cope with domestic demand; how can they be asked to accept foreign students? This, however, is not unique to the education sector. In spite of domestic requirements, India gives aid and assistance in different forms to various countries and institutions. It also makes investments that are not necessarily important to immediate societal amelioration. If it is accepted as policy that the education sector is significant in contributing to India's external relations, adequate provision will have to be made for it. The internationalisation of education has already been accepted as a desired goal by the universities in the "Mysore Statement" and the subsequent "Guru Nanak University Conference". The UGC has recommended a 15 per cent intake of foreign students over and above the sanctioned seats in every educational institution. It was a thrust area for UGC in the Tenth Plan and several initiatives were taken. However, financial allocations have to be made to realise this recommendation of the UGC. Efforts need to be made to improve standards of educational institutions. In any case, all foreign students are not to be given scholarships or financed by India. Many of them are self-financing and actually contribute additional resources where they are enrolled. This is evident from the experience of, say, the University of Pune and from the deemed universities that are more proactive in this regard.

India has a diaspora of over 20 million people spread in 110 countries. In the Pravasi Bharatiya Divas held from the 7 to 9 January 2007, the Government of India recognised the role of education in strengthening ties with the Indian diaspora. It announced the acceptance of a long-standing demand of overseas Indian communities to establish an NRI university.[12] The idea of a South Asian University that was put forward by Prime Minister Manmohan Singh at the SAARC Summit in Dhaka highlighted the urgency of the need to develop cooperation through the education sector.

Conclusion

It is increasingly being accepted that one important role of education is bridge building. It would be natural for India to take the lead in education.

If India wants to become a global player, it must not only be a consumer of knowledge but also produce it. This was the vision of the Kothari Commission, as well. Indian education must contribute to the country's societal well-being and also provide leadership in knowledge generation. To do this, it must harness the academic talent that exists in the country and enlist the services of its educational institutions to create a world of ideas with intellectual leaders who create bonds between India and the world.

References

1. ICCR was envisaged by its founder president, Maulana Abul Kalam Azad as an organisation that would foster and strengthen cultural relations of India with the world. See (online Web)*http://www.iccrindia.org*
2. See (Online Web)*http://itec.nic.in*
3. In recognition of the pioneering work done by NUEPA in the field of educational planning and administration, the Government of India has empowered it in August 2006 to award its own degrees by way of conferring on it the status of Deemed to be University. See (Online Web)*http://www.nuepa.org*
4. See Report of the Conference on Internationalisation of Higher Education: Issues and Concerns, held on 26th and 27th August 2004, New Delhi: NIEPA, 2004. See also Pawan Agarwal, "Higher Education Services in India and Trade Liberalisation", in Rupa Chanda (ed.), 2006. *India's Trade in Services: Prospects and Strategies*, New Delhi: Wiley.
5. See *www.aiuweb.org*. K.B. Powar (ed.) 2001. Internationalisation of Higher Education: Papers presented at the Roundtable on 'Internationalisation of Higher Education', organised by the Association of Indian Universities at the University of Mysore on February 26-28, 2001, New Delhi: Association of Indian Universities.

   K.B. Powar (ed.) 2003. Internationalisation of Higher Education: Papers presented at the Roundtable on 'Internationalisation of Higher Education', organised by the Association of Indian Universities in association with Guru Nanak Dev University on February 25-27, 2002, New Delhi: Association of Indian Universities.
6. See (Online: Web)*URL: http://www.ugc.ac.in/new_initiatives/Preface.html*
7. Committee for the Promotion of Indian Education Abroad (COPIE) Report.
8. Agarwal Pawan, "Higher education Services in India and Trade Liberalisation," Chanda Rupa ed. India's Trade in Services: Prospects and Strategies, New Delhi: Wiley, 2006.
9. Achuthasankar S., "Enhancing Foreign Student Inflow a Game – Changes in Higher Education," New Indian Express, 31st March 2014.
10. See (Online: Web)*URL: http:// www.hindu.com/2006/11/16/stories/2006111616414OO.htm*
11. Nguyen Dy Nien, *URL: http:// www.hindu.com/ersity.*
12. Nguyen Dy Nien, *URL: http:// www.hindu.com/ersity1/16/stories/2006111616414OO.htm*, India's Foreign Relations.docx 2, p. 7.

8

Affirmative Action in India: The Caste and Class Conflict

Introduction

The confusion between 'caste' and 'class' is embedded in 'The Constitution' itself. It has led to multiple interpretations and court cases. For example, Art. 15(4) uses both terms when it talks of "Scheduled Castes" and "socially and educationally backward classes." The question is: are the latter the same as backward castes or are 'backward classes' and 'backward castes' two distinct categories? The loose drafting has become as T.T. Krishnamachari, in a lighter vein prophesied it would, "a paradise for lawyers." These issues have been exhaustively dealt with in two landmark cases, the *Indra Sawhney* case and the *Ashok Thakur* case. A nine-judge bench of the Supreme Court sat for each of these two cases.

The Constitution gave special rights to two categories of people among others, namely the Scheduled Castes (SCs) and Scheduled Tribes (STs) on the one hand and the Other Backward Classes (OBCs) on the other. The term 'Backward Classes' (BC) was used in two senses: one, as a generic term to mean all backward classes including the SCs and STs; two, it means all those not included in the category of SCs and STs. The Constitution itself does not make these terms clear. The Scheduled Caste is really a euphemism for the erstwhile 'untouchables'. These are "castes, races or tribes or parts of or groups within castes, races or tribes" that are notified under Art. 341 of the Constitution. Similarly, Scheduled Tribes are "tribes or tribal communities or parts of or groups within castes, races or tribes that are notified under Art. 342." Scheduled Castes were those who had a low ritual status in the traditional Hindu hierarchy and hence suffered severe disabilities. Scheduled Tribes suffered disabilities both because of their isolation and also low hierarchical position in society. The two groups were designated by a Presidential order in the first instance, which could only be subsequently modified by an Act of Parliament.

The SCs and STs were obviously placed on a different footing from the OBCs. This can be seen from the widespread provisions pertaining to them in the Constitution. For example, Articles 15, 16, 17, 46, 330, 333, 335, 338, 338A, 339, 341 and 342 are just some of the articles that seek to protect the rights of SCs and STs so that the disabilities caused by centuries of discrimination and inhuman treatment can be gradually overcome by the term. As has been pointed out in the Indra Sawhney case *[1992 Supp (3) SCC, pp. 20-772]*, SCs and STs are a category by themselves and the Constitution permits protective discrimination to compensate them. The issue of special provisions for the SCs and STs was not a contentious one. It was generally recognised that they had to be compensated for their current deep-seated disabilities consequent to centuries of inhuman treatment. What was contentious was the issue of 'backward' classes and that has not yet been resolved.

The original draft Article 10(3) which corresponds to the present Art. 16(4) stated "Nothing in this article shall prevent the State from making any provision for the reservation of appointments or posts in favour of any class of citizens who, in the opinion of the State, are not adequately represented in the services under the State." Initially it did not contain the word 'backward'. Rather it said 'any class of citizens'. The word 'backward' was inserted by the Drafting Committee at a later stage.

In his speech to the Constituent Assembly, Dr Ambedkar outlined the position as follows.[1]

He explained that three points of view had to be reconciled: (1) The principle of equality of opportunity for all citizens. (2) If this principle was to be operative, there should be no reservation of any sort for any class or community at all and all public services should be placed on the same footing of equality. (3) Opinion was the demand of those communities, which had till then not had representation in the State. These were the backward communities. In an attempt to reconcile the three explained by Dr Ambedkar, some qualifying phrase like 'backward' was needed as otherwise the exception made in favour of the rule of equality would eat up the rule itself. For example, said Ambedkar, if reservations were made for a community or a collection of communities, the total of which came to something like 70 per cent of all the posts under the State and only 30 per cent were retained as unreserved, the first principle, namely, of equality before law and equality of opportunity would not be satisfied. Therefore, only a minority of seats could be reserved if it had to be effectively consistent with the first principle. A qualifying term like 'backward' would ensure that. Hence, the Drafting Committee introduced the word 'backward', which did not originally find a place in the fundamental right in the way in which it was passed in the Assembly. But Dr Ambedkar did not spell out what was meant by 'backward'. That, he said, should be left to each local government to determine. So, according to him, a backward community was one that was backward in the opinion of the government.

K.M. Munshi explaining the position of the drafting committee said that they strove to secure two things: first, they wanted to achieve the highest efficiency in the services of the State which would enable effectiveness and promptness; second, to ensure that the really backward classes should be given opportunities to be a part of the State services. K.M. Munshi went on to explain that this was important because "State services give a status and an opportunity to serve the country and this opportunity should be extended to every community even among the backward people." That being so, he said, they tried to find some generic term and found 'backward class' to be the best. He went on to say: "When it is read with Art. 201, it is perfectly clear that the word 'backward' signified that class of people – does not matter whether you call them untouchables or touchables, belonging to this community or that – a class of people who are so backward that special protection is required in the services...."[2]

The Background

The issue of what constitutes backward classes had been going on much before the terms came to be used in the Constitution. Both Christophe Jaffrelot and Marc Galanter have given a detailed history of how reservations in jobs came about and who were the beneficiaries. At the time of independence, says Galanter, the term "backward classes" was not yet fixed in its meaning. The Fort St. George Gazette No. 40 of NW. 5, 1895, mentions grant-in-aid to schools for a list of 'backward classes' that includes most of the 'untouchable' castes. The term was used in 1880 for illiterate or indigent classes who were entitled to allowances to study in elementary schools. The terms were often used to mean depressed classes, untouchables, aboriginal and hill tribes, criminal tribes and others. That is, it was used to cover a wide range of castes and communities.[3]

Jaffrelot explains that the expression 'backward classes' first appeared in 1870 in Madras Presidency where there had been a non-Brahmin movement made up of lower castes except for the untouchables.[4] The British Government in Madras had grouped together the *shudras* and the untouchables under the label of backward classes swelling their numbers from 39 to 131, between 1871 and 1920. The aim was to provide for positive discrimination. But in actual fact they were different categories as the stigma of untouchability made the depressed classes a separate group. In 1925, "castes other than depressed classes" became a separate group.

Positive discrimination was being followed in favour of lower castes both in British India and some princely states prior to independence, particularly where the sovereign came from a *shudra* caste. For instance, in Kolhapur, Maharashtra, when Shahu Maharaja of Maratha dynasty, which belonged to the caste of farmers ascended the throne in 1895, he introduced an egalitarian quota policy as he was concerned about the domination of Brahmins over the administration. By 1902, he had already reserved 50 per cent of vacant positions for backward castes. The most developed policy was in Mysore where again the sovereign was a shudra and wanted to bring down Brahmin dominance in his kingdom. He asked Leslie Miller, the British president of the State's High Court to assess the problem and suggest ways to remedy it. Miller recommended reserving half the posts in the highest civil service to the 'backward classes,' by which he meant "all communities other than Brahmins, who are not now adequately represented in the public service." This can be termed the First Commission for Backward Classes.

The British too, were trying to improve the representation of these groups in elected assemblies with ever-increasing powers. Some would see it as the usual divide and rule policy, but it led to the 1919 reforms because of which seven seats of the Bombay Legislative Council were reserved for the Marathas and 28 out of 65 seats for non-Brahmins in the Madras Council were occupied by the untouchables and the *shudras*. This enabled the Justice Party that claimed to speak for non-Brahmins to win the 1920 elections and form the government in 1921 when it reserved 48 per cent quota for non-Brahmins. In 1930, the State Committee in Bombay devoted careful consideration to the question of nomenclature. They noted that in 1924, the term Depressed Classes had been given a wider meaning to include: "Aboriginal Tribes and the Criminal Tribes and some other wandering and backward castes...(which had) resulted in much confusion of thought in this Presidency, as in ordinary usage the phrase Depressed Classes is taken as meaning the untouchables...whereas they do not form half of this new and enlarged grouping of Depressed Classes." The Committee recommended that 'depressed classes' should be used for untouchables, which will coincide with the existing common practice. They proposed that the wider group should be called 'backward classes' which should be divided into Depressed Classes or untouchables; Aboriginals and the Hill tribes; and Other Backward Classes including wandering tribes. They felt that the groups then called Backward Classes should be renamed "intermediate classes."

The Divisiveness of the Caste-Class Argument

The issue of caste and class has been a divisive one as is evident from the First Backward Classes Commission of independent India known as the Kaka Kalelkar Commission set up in 1953.[5] Its report, given in 1955, was not accepted in the Parliament. This was because the four criteria it set up to determine backwardness all found a common denominator in caste. The four criteria were: a degraded status, lack of education, under-representation in civil service and in the fields of trade, commerce and industry. It prepared a list of 2399 backward castes or communities for the entire country and 837 of these were classified as the 'most backward'. Some of the most noteworthy recommendations of the Commission were:

(1) Undertaking caste-wise enumeration of population in the census of 1961.

(2) Relating social backwardness of a class to its low position in the traditional caste hierarchy of Hindu society.

(3) Treating all women as 'backward'.

(4) Reserving 70 per cent seats in all technical and professional institutions for qualified students of backward classes.

In addition, minimum levels of representation were provided for different levels of service to OBCs.

The Commission could not present a unanimous report as the five members dissented on various issues. Three were opposed to linking backwardness with caste. One was passionately for equating caste with backwardness. The Chairman Kaka Kalelkar himself was ambivalent by the time the work of the Commission came to an end. He realised and himself unveiled the dangers of recommendations based only on caste. He also understood that by so doing, the Commission had created an ambiguity about affirmative action programmes for religious communities like the Muslims and Christians, which theoretically did not accept caste but in which caste divisions persisted. However, by then he had no option but to go along and accept caste as the predominant criterion in ascertaining backwardness.

The government did not accept the Commission's report although it laid it before each House of the Parliament together with the Memorandum of Action taken. Regarding the issue of caste as criteria, the Memorandum stated that while it could not, "be denied that the caste system is the greatest hindrance in the way of our progress towards an egalitarian society," but "the recognition of the specified castes as backward may serve to maintain and even perpetuate the existing distinction on the basis of caste." On the issue of the recognition of a large number of castes and communities as backward, it was pointed out, "if the entire community, barring a few exceptions has thus to be regarded as backward, the really needy would be swamped by the multitude and hardly receive any special attention or adequate assistance, nor would such dispensation fulfil the conditions laid down in Art. 340 of the Constitution."[6]

After this, the government made efforts "to discover some criteria other than caste which could be of practical application in determining the backward classes." The Deputy Registrar General was asked to conduct a pilot survey to see if backwardness could be linked to occupational communities instead of caste. Such a survey was taken but it failed to throw up the desired criteria. The matter was also discussed at a Conference of State Representatives on April 7, 1959 and subsequently reviewed by the Ministry of Home Affairs; but no consensus emerged.

The Central Government ultimately took a decision that no all-India lists of backward classes could be drawn up, nor any reservation made in the Central Government service for any group of backward classes other than the SCs and STs. A letter was then sent by the Ministry of Home Affairs to all the State governments stating, "While the State Governments have the discretion to choose their own criteria for defining backwardness in the view of the government of India it would be better to apply economic tests than to go by caste."

The then Home Minister G.B. Pant in fact argued that development efforts would lead to "the establishment of our society on the socialist pattern," an evolution with which "social and other distinctions will disappear." In 1961, Pant added another argument, informing heads of the states not to initiate policies in favour of OBCs at the federal level as positive discrimination measures would have the drawback of penalising the most capable and deserving people, and would therefore hinder efficiency in the administration and business.

The rejection of the First Backward Class Commission report led to intense debate on the place of caste in Indian society and the role of positive discrimination policies in this context. The socialists were in the forefront of this debate. Drawing on both Marx and Ambedkar, Lohia maintained that caste rather than class was the basic unity of Indian society. He did not agree that the Nehruvian vision of socialism would be enough to combat inequalities because even after collectivising land and nationalising industry, the upper castes would continue to dominate on the basis of skills that had been handed down from father to son for thousands of years. The lowest castes, according to Lohia, not only needed socio-economic redistribution but also had to shed their feelings of inferiority.

Two visions have been clashing here. One is to reduce the emphasis on caste and the other to insist on caste as a prime determining factor. Nehru coined the phrase "Other Backward Classes" implying classes other than the untouchables and the tribes. But he used the word classes rather than castes and this paradigm ambiguity and ambivalence has been at the core of the controversy arising out of reservation as a mode of affirmative action. It lies at the heart of the somewhat uneasy interpretations of Art. 15(4) and Art. 16 (4) that fetter unbridled equality rights. The matter has kept coming up in the courts regularly.

The Balaji Case

A number of challenges to reservation in jobs and admissions to educational institutions followed before the Court after the rejection of the First Backward Class Commission. The first to be hit was Mysore in *M.R. Balaji vs. State of Mysore (AIR 1963 SC 649)*. The state had set up an expert committee to identify criteria for classifying backward classes but the committee felt that the only practicable method of doing this would be on the basis of caste. It divided the backward classes into backward and more backward. Based on its recommendations, Mysore reserved 50 per cent quota for OBCs, over and above 15 per cent reserved for STs and 3 per cent for STs. For OBCs, 50 per cent quota was split into 28 per cent for BCs and 22 per cent for More Backward Classes (MBCs). The total reservation came to 68 per cent leaving only 32 per cent in the merit pool. All this was done under Art. 15 (4) of the Constitution.

The Government order was declared invalid on four grounds:

1. Caste, poverty, occupation and place of habitation were some of the relevant factors for determining social backwardness and not caste alone. The court did not also agree with the way educational backwardness was determined.
2. Caste though relevant in the Indian society, could not be made the sole or dominant test to determine social backwardness as that would perpetuate the vice of caste system in society.
3. Sub-classification of backwardness into backward and more backward was not constitutionally permissible.

4. The total reservation of 68 per cent for SCs, STs and BCs was held to be excessive. A limit of 50 per cent reservation was laid down.

The judgement was pivotal because following it, positive discriminatory measures in several states based on caste alone were overturned.

The Second Backward Classes Commission: B.P. Mandal

The Second Backward Classes Commission was set up in December 1978. It was popularly known as the Mandal Commission after B.P. Mandal who chaired it. It gave its report in December 1980.[7] It was aware that the First Commission had not formulated any objective criteria for classifying OBCs. Hence, the members of the Commission undertook measures like questionnaires to state and central governments and the public; toured the country extensively, took evidence of legislators, eminent public figures, sociologists and others; did a country-wide socio-educational survey; got reports by specialised agencies prepared on some important issues, analysed census data, and took other such measures. However, these actions were challenged as performed so superficially that they could not be seen as certain in determining the backward classes. This contention was upheld in a couple of minority opinions in the Indra Sawhney case. J. Kuldip Singh, in particular, pointed out the flaws in methodology and hence the findings in fairly great detail in the Indra Sawhney case.

This Commission too made caste synonymous with social backwardness. Castes, it said, were the building bricks of the Hindu social order for centuries and this has resulted in a close linkage between the caste ranking of a person and his social educational and economic status. The evolution of society in such a highly stratified manner gave the higher castes deep-rooted vested interests in the perpetuation of the system. It concluded that the low ritual caste status of a person had a direct bearing on his social achievements.

However, in the absence of caste-based census since 1931, it was forced to project its conclusions pertaining to the castes to be included as backward classes on the basis of that census. It identified 3743 castes, about 1500 more than in the First Commission, as OBCs, representing 52 per cent of the country's population. Noting that quota totals had to be kept below 50 per cent because of the Supreme Court order in the Balaji case and that there already existed 22.5 per cent reservation for the SCs and STs, an additional 27 per cent reservation was recommended bringing the total to 49.5 per cent.

The Commission dealt with the question of equality rights guaranteed under Art. 14 of the Constitution by countering that equality was a double-edged weapon. It placed the strong and the handicapped on the same footing but social justice required that unequals could not be treated on the same footing. To treat unequals as equals was to perpetuate inequality. 'Equality of opportunity' and 'equality of treatment' placed the weak and the strong on par and to that extent, it amounted to denial of social justice. In fact, 'equality of results' had to be the acid test of society's egalitarian pretensions.

As far as merit was concerned, the Commission said that it was largely a product of favourable environmental privileges. A higher rating in an examination did not necessarily reflect higher intrinsic worth of the examinee. Hence, merit and equality had to be viewed in their proper perspective and the element of privilege duly recognised and discounted. It accepted that the apprehensions regarding the drop in the quality of government services owing to large-scale induction of SC, ST and OBC candidates may be justified up to a point, but felt that it could not be said that all candidates selected on merit were honest, efficient, hard-working and dedicated. At present, top echelons of all the government services were manned predominantly by open competition candidates and if the performance of the bureaucracy was anything to go by, they had not exactly covered themselves in glory.

Hence, the Commission recommended the creating of special educational facilities for upgrading the cultural environment of the students in a phased manner in selected areas, containing high concentration of OBCs. Particular emphasis had to be placed on vocational training. Special coaching facilities also needed to be provided to enable the quota students to catch up with students from the open category. In addition, it recommended a reservation of 27 per cent for OBCs. This reservation should apply to all government services as well as technical and professional institutions, both in the Centre and the States.

The Commission took up the argument that when 52 per cent of the population belonged to the category of OBCs, the recruitment of a few thousands every year against reserved vacancies was not going to produce any perceptible impact on their general condition. On the other hand, the induction of a large proportion of employees against reserved vacancies would considerably impair the quality and efficiency of the government services. It also considered the contention that the benefits of such reservations would be skimmed off by those sections of OBCs who were already well off and the really backward sections would be left high and dry. Another proposition advanced against reservation that the Commission dealt with was that the policy of large-scale reservations would cause great resentment among those meritorious candidates whose entry into services would be barred as a result thereof.

The Commission said that these arguments were advanced by the ruling elite, which was keen on preserving its privileges and hence were partisan. An essential part of the battle against social backwardness, it said, was to be fought in the minds of the backward people. In India, government service had always been looked upon as a symbol of prestige and power. Increasing the representation of OBCs in government services, would give them an immediate feeling of participation in the governance of the country. When a backward class candidate becomes a Collector or a Superintendent of Police, the material benefits accruing from his position were limited to the members of his family alone but the psychological impact of this phenomenon was tremendous. The entire community felt socially elevated and came into the mainstream of society.

The chief merit of reservation was not that it would introduce egalitarianism amongst OBCs when the rest of the Indian society was seized by all sorts of inequalities, but that it would erode the hold of the higher castes on services and enable OBCs in general to have a sense of participation in running the affairs of the country. The Commission conceded that reservation for OBCs would cause a lot of heartburn to others, but this could not operate as a moral veto against social reform. When the higher castes constituting less than 20 per cent of the country's population subjected the rest to all manner of social injustice, said the Commission, it must have also caused a lot of resentment in the lower castes. Now that the lower castes were asking for modest share of the national cake of power and prestige, a chorus of alarm was being raised by the ruling elite. Hence, it is obvious that the essential agenda was primarily of power sharing and the educational and economic amelioration was only secondary.

The Indra Sawhney Case

The Report of the Commission lay in cold storage. When Indira Gandhi came to power in 1980 after the Janata government rule, she did nothing about it. However, when the Janata Dal returned to power in 1989, its leader V.P. Singh, who had earlier been with the Congress, announced its implementation. It caused widespread agitation and intense resistance. Multiple writ petitions were filed and finally, the matter came up before a nine-judge bench in the pivotal Indra Sawhney case that was decided in 1992. The idea was to settle the issue once for all as earlier too the court had not spoken in one voice. But this was not to be because once again it was a split 6:3 judgement, leaving the room wide open for more interpretations and litigation.

An Office Memorandum was issued on August 13, 1990 by which 27 per cent vacancies in civil posts and services were reserved for the Socially and Educationally Backward Classes (SEBCs) in direct recruitment. Those among the SEBCs who were recruited on the basis of merit in an open competition, on the same standards prescribed for the general candidates, were not to be adjusted against the reservation quota of 27 per cent. Since lists of such castes and communities had been prepared by both the Centre and the States and they varied, only those that figured in both the lists were to be considered. This Office Memorandum was modified by that of September 25, 1991 by which in the 27 per cent reserved posts, preference was to be given to candidates belonging to the poorer sections of the SEB candidates. In case a sufficient number of such candidates were not available, then the unfilled vacancies would be filled by other SEB candidates. Further, 10 per cent of the vacancies would be reserved for other economically backward sections of the people who were not covered by any of the existing schemes of reservation.

These Memoranda were based on the recommendations of the Mandal Commission. Fourteen questions were raised before the court of which some questions had several parts. The most relevant for our purpose were those pertaining to the meaning of the term 'backward classes'; whether these classes could be identified on the basis of caste alone; whether backwardness had to be both social and education; whether 'means-test' could be used to identify backwardness; whether backwardness could be identified only on the basis of economic criteria; whether the backward classes could be further subdivided into backward and more backward; to what extent could reservations be made and what was the concept of positive action and positive discrimination.

By a majority judgement, the Court directed the Government of India and the governments of the States and the Union Territories to constitute, within four months, a permanent body for examining and recommending upon requests inclusion and complaints of over-inclusion and under-inclusion in the lists of other BCs of citizens. The advice tendered by this body would ordinarily be binding. The government was to also specify within four months, the relevant and requisite socio-economic criteria to exclude socially advanced persons/sections, called the 'creamy layer' from OBCs. The Office Memoranda were to be implemented subject to the exclusion of the 'creamy layer'. That reservation could only be for the initial appointment and the category based on only economic criteria was held invalid.

Subsequent to the judgement, posts for OBCs were reserved in public appointments funded by the Central Government. However, the issue has kept coming up and no finality has been achieved. These issues, together with others dealing with private sector involvement in higher education, once again reached the Supreme Court in 2002. They were then dealt with by an eleven-judge constitutional bench of the Supreme Court in October 2002 in *T.M.A. Pai Foundation and Others vs. State of Karnataka*, popularly known as the Pai Foundation case. The current matter is then but a link in the long chain of adjudication on the issues pertaining to access and equity in higher education.

Ashok Kumar Thakur vs. Union of India and Others (2008)

Following Arjun Singh's announcement and the passing of the Act 5 of 2007, reserving seats in centrally-funded higher education institutions including professional institutions, some sections of the Act have been challenged in the Supreme Court. The issues are similar to the ones that had been adjudicated upon almost fifteen years earlier in the Indra Sawhney case, concerning: definitions and criteria of backwardness; the merit factor; and economic factors in determining backwardness, which had to be both social and educational.

The broad contentions of the petitioners are as follows:

- The Union of India has failed in performing its constitutional legal duties towards its citizens.
- The effects of the Act would have wide-ranging ramifications that would ultimately divide the country on caste basis.
- It would lead to chaos, confusion and anarchy that would have a destructive impact on the peaceful atmosphere in the educational and other institutions and would seriously affect communal harmony.
- The constitutional guarantee of equality and equal opportunity would be seriously prejudiced by the proposed reservation and it would violate the equality provisions under Art. 14 of the Constitution.
- The quotas are nothing but vote banks.
- Merit would be sacrificed.
- The Act has been passed on the basis of unfounded and unsupportable data about the number of OBCs in the country.

In this regard, it was pointed out that in the Indra Sawhney case the Supreme Court itself had recognised the concept of the 'creamy layer' amongst the advanced OBCs that were to be kept out of preferential treatment. The projected 52 per cent had also not been fully approved at that time and the State had been directed to constitute a permanent body by March 15, 1993 to examine and recommend the inclusion and exclusion in the lists of backward classes of citizens. Consequently, the National Commission for Backward Classes Act 1993 was enacted and the National Commission for Backward Classes was set up. However, there were flaws in its functioning.

- The definition of 'backward class' was contested. Under Section 2(i) of the Act, 'backward classes' were defined to mean classes of citizens other than the SCs and STs as may be specified by the Central Government in the lists. Under Section 2(i) of the Act, 'lists' mean those prepared by the Government of India from time to time to make provision for reservation of appointments or posts in favour of BCs who in the opinion of the government are not adequately represented in government services. In any case what exactly does "Other Backward Classes (OBCs)" mean has not been decided on any acceptable basis on the parameters provided in the Backward Classes Act.
- Section 11 of the Backward Classes Act provides for a revision of lists but this has not been done. On the contrary, additions are being made in it. The rationale of 27 per cent reservation is based on the assumption that 52 per cent of the population consists of BCs. However, it has been highlighted that there has never been a caste-based enumeration or tabulation since 1921; so, the 52 per cent projection is not reliable. Reference was made to the figures provided by the National Samples Survey of India and the National Health and Family Survey by the Government of India's own departments that show the hollowness of the claim of OBCs being 52 per cent of the population. The number of socially and educationally backward classes had to be arrived at after a careful in-depth analysis.
- It was also pointed out that under Ss. 2 (g), 3 (iii), 5 (1) (2) and (6) of the Act, 27 per cent of the seats were being reserved for OBCs out of the permitted strength. But since the foundational basis was weak, the introduction of the reservation was not acceptable neither

in a staggered manner nor by the notion that the number of unreserved seats would be kept at the same levels.

- The constitutional validity of the 93rd amendment that came into force with the insertion of Art. 15 (5), with effect from 20.1.2006, was challenged and it was prayed that certain sections of the Act promulgated as a consequence be declared invalid.
- It has been further contended that the effect of judgements in *M. Nagaraja and Others vs. U.O.I.* (2006 (8) SCC12) and *Nair Service Society vs. State of Kerala* decided on 23.02.07 has not been considered. It has been emphasised that what was relevant eight decades back could not be of current relevance.
- In the Indra Sawhney case, the Supreme Court overturned the concept of backwardness as outlined in the Balaji case (*M.R. Balaji vs. State of Mysore*, 1963) and followed in the Janaki Prasad Parimoo case (*Janaki Prasad Parimoo vs State of J.K.*, 1973), distinction was made between Arts. 15 (4) and 16 (4) of the constitution, which had been more or less equated in these two cases.
- In any event, it was contended, that the 'creamy layer', which had to be kept out was of great relevance and significance. The criteria and lists made under Art. 16 (4) could at best be used to provide a rough and ready rule for Arts. 15 (4) and (5) but that did not take away the care of S.11 in the Backward Classes Act. The National Commission for the Backward Classes had put out no report subsequent to 3.2.2005 and hence the whole exercise by the Central Government had been done in a great hurry. Since there was no database after the 1931 census, the government should have first tried to create one before acting on the presumption that 52 per cent of the population belonged to OBCs. The Act itself requires the determination of socially and educationally backward classes to be made by the government made under S. 2 (g).
- Further, no methodology had been laid down for such a determination, as caste alone can not be the basis for identification. It can only be a starting point. The following documents were also referred to, which show that the figures arrived at by the union were erroneous:

  (a) The National Sample Survey Organisation survey of 1999–2000 that shows that the present educational level is directly proportionate to a person's economic condition.

(b) S.11 of the National Commission for Backward Classes Act, 1993 which says that the Central Government would undertake revision of the lists in order to exclude those classes who have ceased to be backward.

(c) Standing Committee on Social Justice and Empowerment chaired by Sumitra Mahajan (2005–2006).

(d) 186th Report of the Parliamentary Standing Committee of Human Resource Development submitted to the Parliament on 1.2.2006.

(e) Annual Report of the National Commission for Backward Classes, 3.2.2005.

(f) Report of the Oversight Committee constituted under the orders of Prime Minister on 27.5.2006.

The Office Memoranda of 1990 and 1991 with respect to reservation for BCs in government jobs could not stand forever as that would make S.11 of the Backward Classes Act, which calls for revision of lists after a period of 10 years, redundant. Since the lists have not been revised, their figures were doubtful. The K.C. Vasanth Kumar case (*K.C. Vasanth Kumar vs. State of Karnataka*, 1985 Supp. SCC 714) was also referred to wherein it was stated that the policy of reservation for employment and education should be necessarily reviewed. Also, that the time had come to review the criterion for identifying SEBCs ignoring the caste label. Identification was an imperative requirement and the 1931 data could not be used. It was also pointed out that the Mandal Commission itself had found two equi-distributed groups: (a) intermediate OBC and (b) depressed OBC. It was emphasised that when the Mandal Commission arrived at the figure of 52 per cent population of OBC, it had added the population of non-Hindu communities. Besides, the management of social backwardness had to be dynamic. This meant that measures adopted as a remedy had to be time-bound and renewable.

Contentions of the Government

The Additional Solicitor General, arguing on behalf of the Government of India stated:

- All the issues that were being raised had already been settled in the Indra Sawhney and the Rajendran cases [*P. Rajendran vs. State of Madras*, (1968) 2SCR 786].
- Reservation did not violate the basic structure of the Constitution as it was an integral part of the principal of equality where inequality existed.

- There was nothing unconstitutional in specifying SEBCs in terms of caste on the basis of criteria evolved for such a purpose.
- Reservation was not anti-merit.
- In the absence of data, there was no alternative but to project the proportion of SEBCs from the 1931 census.
- The Mandal Commission had not relied upon the 1931 census to arrive at the figure of 52 per cent as the population of the BCs but on multiple approaches in the contemporary context and not in the context of 1931.
- The Ministry of Social Justice and Empowerment was in charge of the subject and issued state-wise lists. Once issued, these continued to be in force and were binding for any or all purposes, subject to modifications, deletions, additions from time to time in accordance with the Backward Classes Act and in the light of Indra Sawhney Case.

Interim Orders of the Court

On hearing the contentions of both sides, the Court held that a survey of the entire population on the basis of an acceptable mechanism was necessary. This had also been accepted by the Additional Solicitor General. What may have been relevant in the 1931 census could have some contemporary relevance, but it could not be the deciding factor. The Court had already observed in the Nagaraja case that backwardness had to be based on objective factors and inadequacy or representation in public-funded appointments had to factually exist. Also, care had to be taken that forward castes did not get included in the backward caste lists.

Even in the Indra Sawhney case it had been repeatedly emphasised that the list of BCs cannot be mechanical, prepared without relevant data or for extraneous reasons. Justice Pandian had observed that before it could be concluded that a caste was backward or inadequately represented in services, it was necessary to show the existence of circumstances relevant to the formation of such an opinion. If such an opinion suffered from non-application of mind or formulation of collateral grounds or was beyond the scope of the statute or based on irrelevant and extraneous material, then it was challengeable. Justice Sawant had also pointed out that there was need for proper application of the mind to facts and circumstances, the field being examined, the post and the extent of existing representation and the requirement to balance representation. Similarly, speaking on his own behalf and three others, Justice Jeevan Reddy had said that opinion in regard to backwardness and inadequate representation had to be based on relevant material. Likewise, there had to be periodic examination of these lists that could lead to the exclusion of a class if it ceased to be socially backward or was inadequately represented in the services. *Once backward, always backward was not acceptable*. In any case, the Court said in its interim order that the 'creamy layer', as explained in the Indra Sawhney case, was not irrelevant. Nowhere else in the world did castes, classes, or communities queue up to gain backward status. This truth was recognised in the Indra Sawhney case as a stark reality.

Equality, said the Court, was a fundamental substantive norm that was the characteristic feature of many democratic constitutions. In societies with diversity or where there had been past discrimination against groups of people, the norm of equality necessitated affirmative action. That may have been the underlying object of Art. 15. The Court noted that whatever may have been the philosophical foundation of its origin, caste had become a rigid hierarchical system that caused immense social and economic exploitation of a section of the population. The late nineteenth and early twentieth centuries had seen the rise of social reform movements for the amelioration of the plight of these sections of society. The equality provisions of the Indian Constitution were intended to be proactive means of social engineering and thus the system of reservation had developed.

The Court said that it had focused on Arts. 15(4) and 16 (4) several times earlier. Equality of opportunity was not simply a matter of legal equality or the mere absence of disabilities. It had to be the presence of abilities. Hence, wherever there was inequality in fact, legal equality only tended to accentuate it (*Dr. Pradeep Jain vs. Union of India*, AIR 1984 SC 1420). In the Indra Sawhney case, it had been accepted that the State was constitutionally empowered to enact affirmative action measures for backward classes according to certain underlying principles in the identification of which, caste could be used as a proxy. However, differentiations and classifications could not be unduly unfair to the persons left out of the favoured group. Also, the policy of reservation could not and should not be intended to be permanent or perpetuate backwardness.

The Court also asked the question whether a different form of preferential treatment other than quotas could be employed. Although it had been submitted that the number of seats available for the general category would not be affected, there was really a broader issue involved. If the seats could have been increased in the absence of reservation, these could have gone to the general category. Also, if the whole exercise was only to be undertaken over a period of three years, during which there would be a staggered increase in seats, then a firm data should have been first evolved.

Another important factor said the court, pertained to the 'creamy layer'. In the Nagaraja case, it was said that the main issue was the 'extent of reservations'. In each case, the State would have to show compelling reasons, namely, backwardness, inadequacy of representation, and overall administrative efficiency before making provision for reservation. The State was not bound to make reservations as the provisions were only enabling ones. It could if it wished to, but then it had to collect quantifiable data showing the backwardness of the class and the inadequacy of the representation of that class in public employment in addition to compliance with Art. 335. Further, even if the State had compelling reasons, reservations could not be so excessive that they exceeded the ceiling limit of 50 per cent or were extended indefinitely.

Following the Nagaraja case, the issue of 'creamy layer' was reiterated in the Nair Society case. It was stated that, "the creamy layer principle was one of the important limits on State power under the equality clause enshrined under Arts. 14 and 16 and any violation or dilution of the same would render the State action invalid." It went on to say, "We reiterate that the ceiling limit of 50 per cent, the concept of creamy layer and the compelling reasons, namely, backwardness, inadequacy of representation and overall administrative efficiency are all constitutional requirements without which the structure of equality of opportunity in Art. 16 would collapse." The Court said, "In Indra Sawhney, this court has, therefore, accepted caste as the determinant of backwardness and yet it has struck a balance with the principle of secularism which is the basic feature of the constitution by bringing in the concept of creamy layer." It affirmed that the determination of creamy layer was a part of the constitutional scheme. It was a necessary bargain between the competing ends of caste-based reservations and the principle of secularism. Therefore, it would have to be examined in detail whether the stand of the Union of India that the creamy layer rule was applicable only to Art. 16(4) and not to Art. 15(5) was based on any sound foundation.

What the Court really did was to scrutinise the government's plans to extend reservation by 27 per cent though quotas to OBCs. Initially, the reservation was to have taken effect from the academic year 2006–2007 and also no plans had been drawn up to increase the number of seats. Thus, the number of seats available in the general or unreserved category would have been reduced. By asking the government to answer a series of questions to justify the extension of reservation, the Court has tried to balance the equality rights of all individuals with group rights of the underprivileged.

The Final Judgement

The much-awaited final judgement in the Ashok Thakur case was pronounced on 10/4/08 by a five-judge Constitutional Bench led by the Chief Justice of India. Four different judgements were handed down, but there was broad agreement on several issues. On other points, there were differences. Also, there was a lot of obits leaving room for further legal challenge.

An important question was whether the 93rd amendment of the Constitution was against its 'basic structure'. The Chief Justice upheld the validity of the amendment as inserted in Art. 15(5) of the Constitution in so far as it did not violate its 'basic structure' with regard to the state-maintained institution. He left the question of its validity with regard to private institutions open to be decided when a case came up. The Chief Justice explained that this was an enabling provision that could cover both state-funded and private educational institutions, whether aided or unaided, but it excluded minority institutions established under Art. 30(1) as they belonged to a separate category. All the petitions have challenged Act 5 of the 2007 that flows from the Constitutional amendment that provides reservations of seats for STs, SCs, and SEBCs in Central Educational Institutions. The latter have been defined under 8.2(d) of the Act as institutions established or incorporated by or under the Central Act or set up by an Act of Parliament or Deemed Universities maintained by or receiving aid from the Central Government or institution maintained by or receiving aid from the Central Government or educational institutions set up by the Central Government under the Societies Registration Act, 1860.

It was pointed out that Act 5 of 2007 was not intended to provide reservations in 'private unaided' educational institutions and none of the private unaided institutions had challenged the 93rd amendment itself. In the absence of such a challenge, it was not proper to pronounce upon the constitutional validity of that part of constitutional amendment. However, Justice Bhandari chose to categorically state that imposing reservation on unaided institutions would violate the basic structure of the Constitution by stripping citizens of their fundamental right under Art. 19(1) to carry on an occupation. T.M.A. Pai and Inamdar approved that the establishment and running of an educational institution fell under the right to an occupation. The right to select students on the basis of merit was an essential feature of the right to establish and run an unaided institution. Hence, reservation was an unreasonable restriction that infringed this right by destroying the autonomy and essence of an unaided institution. The effect of the 93rd amendment was to abrogate Art. 19 leaving the basic structure altered. To restore the basic structure, it would be necessary to severe the reference to "unaided" institution in the 93rd amendment. Hence, the Chief Justice only dealt with the validity of the 93rd amendment as so far as it related to state-maintained and -aided educational institutions. But Justice Dalveer Bhandari upheld the validity of the 93rd amendment only with regard to publicly-funded institutions.

Citing the Indra Sawhney case, Justice Bhandari observed that reservation was to be given to BCs until they ceased to be backward and not indefinitely. Justice Sawant had stated in the Indra Sawhney case that society did not remain static. Industrialisation and urbanisation had led to the advancement of the underprivileged on political, social and economic fronts especially after the commencement of the Constitution. Also, the social reform movements and the spread of education had made at least some individuals and families in the BCs gain sufficient means to develop their capacities to compete with others in every field. Therefore, they could no longer be called backward, whatever be their original birthmark. It could hardly be argued that once a backward, always a backward. Such a position would defeat the very purpose of the special provisions in the Constitution for the advancement of BCs, which is to enable them to compete with forward classes as equal citizens.

The Parliament and the legislature in the country could not transgress a basic feature of the Constitution, namely the principle of equality enshrined in Art. 14 of which Art. 16(1) was a facet. If the creamy layer was included, it would be the same as the forward castes getting the benefit of reservation. It would be a breach not only of Art. 14 but of the basic structure of the Constitution. Therefore, the non-exclusion of the creamy layer or the inclusion of the forward castes would be totally illegal.

Further, it was held that Art. 15(4) and 15(5) were not mutually contradictory. Art. 15(4) was introduced when the "communal G.O." in the then State of Madras was struck down by the Supreme Court in Champakam Dorairajan's (AIR 1951 Med. 130) case. In the Unni Krishnan (1993), ISCC 645 case, the court had held that Act 19(1) (g) was not attracted for establishing and running educational institutions. However, in the later T.M.A. Pai case, the court reversed its earlier position and held that the right to establish and run educational institution was an occupation within the ambit of Art. 19(1)(g). The scope of the decision in the Pai case was later explained in the P.A. Inamdar (AIR 2005, SC 3226) case where it was held that the state had no control over unaided institution and that they were free to admit students of their own choice. This necessitated the 93rd Constitutional Amendment Act, 2008. Hence, the areas of operation of Art. 15(4) and 15(5) were different and not mutually contradictory. Justice Raveendran agreed and added another reason to reject the challenge to Art. 15(5) saying that otherwise it would make Art. 15(4) also inoperative or ineffective. It was also said that the exclusion of minority institutions was not violative of Art. 14 of the Constitution as these formed a separate class whose rights were protected by other constitutional provisions.

The key question was whether Act 5 of 2007 was constitutionally valid in view of the definition of 'Backward Class' and whether the identification of such 'Backward Class' based on 'caste' was constitutionally valid. To answer this question, the Chief Justice did an elaborate discussion of the definitions and concept of 'caste' and 'class' given by some leading sociologists. The overall conclusion was that 'caste' was the wholly predetermined status that men were born into without any hope of changing it. This was the situation in Hindu Society. Every Hindu necessarily belonged to the caste of his parents and remained in it. No accumulation of wealth and no exercise of his talents could alter his caste status. Marriage outside his caste was prohibited or severely discouraged.

A 'class' on the other hand, enjoyed certain privileges over others in society. When such a 'class' was more or less rigorously closed or enjoyed hereditary privileges, it was called 'caste'. In the early sociological theories, caste had been used to mean class, indicating hereditary or rigid status and occupation. On the other hand, it is possible that within a certain caste group, there is marked inequality of status, opportunity, or social standing which then defines 'class' within that particular 'caste'. For example, not all Brahmins are engaged in highly respectable employment. Neither are they all wealthy. A Brahmin may be a servant to a member of the lower caste or a servant to a rich Brahmin. Hence, within a single caste group, there may be some classes or groups who have more dignity, social influence, and social esteem than others. A caste is not characterised merely by typical or occupational characteristics of individuals who are part of it. It is characterised by its codes and close-knit social controls. In classes, however, such close-knit social controls may not exist and there may also be great disparity in occupational characteristics.

A social class, therefore, is a homogeneous unit from the point of view of status and mutual recognition, whereas caste is homogeneous from the point of view of common ancestry, religious rites and strict organisational control. Thus, caste is closed as opposed to class both in the organisational and biological sense. It emphasises rituals and regulations pertaining to cleanliness and purity. In this, it differs radically from the secular nature and informality of social rules. In a social class, exclusivity would be based primarily on status. Hence, social classes divide homogeneous populations into layers of prestige and esteem and the members of each layer are able to circulate freely within it. In a caste, however, the social distance between members is because they belong to entirely different organisations. Therefore, it may be said that caste is a horizontal division, while class is a vertical one.

It was pointed out that the National Commission for the Backward Classes and the State Commissions for Backward Classes had prepared a list based on elaborate guidelines and these had been framed after studying the criteria/indicators framed by the Mandal Commission and by the commissions set up by different State Governments. The various commissions had held public hearings before they finalised the lists. The National Commission held 236 public hearings. Also, during its functioning, it had recommended 297 requests for inclusion and rejected 289. Also, it had taken into consideration detailed data with regard to social, educational, and economic criteria. It had looked into whether there has been improvement or deterioration in the condition of the caste or community being considered for inclusion during the past twenty years. Hence, the lists of socially and educationally backward classes of citizens were not being prepared solely on the basis of caste and therefore, it was not violative of Act. 15(1) of the Constitution.

Next came the question of the exclusion of the creamy layer. The SEBC have been identified by applying different and multiple criteria, though the list is based on caste for convenience. But within the castes listed there may be affluent sections that cannot be included in the list of SEBs. There may be a segment in that caste that is economically advanced and does not require the protection of reservation. The petitioners contended that the principle of the 'creamy layer' should be strictly applied to SEBCs and the principles of exclusion should be same as developed in the Indra Sawhney's case. The Chief Justice disagreed with the contention raised by the respondents that if the 'creamy layer' was excluded, there may be practically no representation for a particular backward class in educational institutions because those left, that is the non-creamy, may not have risen to the level or standard necessary to get admission even within the reserved quota. The Chief Justice asserted that if the creamy layer was not excluded, the identification of SEBC would not be complete and any SEBC without the exclusion of 'creamy layer' may not be in accordance with Art. 15(1) of the Constitution. He upheld the criteria of the government as given in the Office Memorandum dated 8.9.1993 following the Indra Sawhney case to provide for reservation of 27 per cent for OBCs. In addition,

Justice Bhandari wanted the government to periodically revise the Office Memorandum so that changing circumstances could be taken into consideration while keeping the constitutional goal in view. He also urged the government to exclude the children of former and present Members of Parliament and Members of the Legislative Assemblies. The Office Memoranda, he said, should be amended accordingly.

Justice Raveendran also concurred on this issue while adding his own reasoning. His argument represents a greater paradigm shift from purely caste-based quotas to the inclusion of other criteria than those of others. He pointed out that the Supreme Court in a series of discussions in cases such as, *M. R. Balaji vs. State of Mysore* [1963 Supp.(1) SCR 439]; *R. Chitralekha vs. State of Mysore* [1964 (6) SCR 368]; *State of Andhra Pradesh vs. P. Sagar* [1968 (3) SCR 595]; *Janaki Prasad Perimao vs. State of Jammu and Kashmir* [1973(1) SCC 420]; *State of Kerala vs. N. M. Thomas* [1976(2) SCC 310] and *K.C. Vasanth Kumar vs. State of Karnataka* [1985 Supp. SCC 714] has explained social and educational backwardness. All have laid down one common principle that caste cannot be made the sole or dominant test to determine backwardness. Doing so would make it an invalid determination. These decisions have recognised that caste cannot be equated with class and that all backwardness, whether social or educational is ultimately and primarily due to poverty or economic conditions.

The principle of 'creamy layer' however, said the Chief Justice, could not be applied to SCs and STs as they were to be treated as a separate category. Nobody had even disputed the identification of such classes. Justice Bhandari agreed with this. In addition, Justice Pasayat said that a notification should be issued by the Union of India for the determination of BCs. This can only be done after the exclusion of the creamy layer for which necessary data must be obtained by the Central Government from the State Government and Union Territories. Such a notification would be open to challenge on the ground of wrongful exclusion or inclusion. Hence, norms had to be fixed according to the peculiar features in different States and Union Territories.

The other important question was what should be the educational qualification beneath by which a class could be considered educationally backward. The petitioners had contended that reservation or any other affirmative action could be made for the advancement of only SEBCs of citizens or SCs and STs and the educational standard to be addressed should be matriculation or 10+2. There were many in the castes included in the BC list who had this much education and so had to be treated as educationally forward. Hence since Act 5 of 2007 was intended to give reservation to students in higher institutions of learning, it was not permissible under Art. 15(5). What is being pointed out by the petitioners is really a contradiction between individual and group rights. Certain individuals in a BC may have completed their schooling. Were they also to be given the benefit of reservation? They were themselves not educationally backward but their class as a whole might be.

The Chief Justice did not agree with this argument, but the judgement does not really provide a conclusive answer to this problem. It only states what should be the minimum educational attainment of a class below which it would be considered educationally backward. He said that at the time of independence, the basic idea was to improve primary and secondary level education but now after a period of more than fifty years, it could not be said that the BCs shall be determined on the basis of their attaining education only to the level of 10+ 2 stage. Justice Pasayat said that while determining backwardness, graduation (not technical graduation or a professional qualification) should be the standard yardstick for measuring backwardness. He also felt that in order to strike a constitutional balance, it was necessary and desirable to earmark certain percentage of seats out of the permissible limits of 27 per cent for socially and economically backward classes.

Justice Bhandari spent a long time in pointing out that school education had been neglected and that primary and secondary education had to be looked after if reservation in higher education was to be made effective. He also felt that once a candidate graduated from a university, he was educationally forward and so ineligible for special benefits under Art. 15(5) for post-graduate and any further studies thereafter. Here he talked only about the individual and not about the group as a whole leaving the matter inconclusive.

Following Indra Sawhney case, Justice Bhandari acknowledged that caste had to be accepted as a valid criterion but he felt that if reservation in education was to stay, it had to adhere to the basic tenet of secularism; that is, it should not take caste into account. As long as caste was a criterion, we would never achieve a casteless society. Exclusively, only the economic criterion should be used. He urged the government that for a period of ten years, caste and other factors such as occupation, income, property holding and similar measures of economic power may be taken into consideration but only to be able to achieve the constitutional goal of a casteless and classless society in India.

Caste, pointed out by J. Raveendran, had divided this country for ages and hampered its growth. The effect of reservation, to begin with, seems to perpetuate caste and it has had some undesirable consequences. In the pre-reservation era, people wanted to get rid of the backward tag, either social or economical. But post-reservation, there was a tendency even among those who were 'forward' to seek the 'backward' tag in the hope of enjoying the benefits of reservation. When more and more people seek the backward tag, the country stagnates. Further, if reservation was not to become a crutch, a periodic review was necessary. This was emphasised by the Chief Justice as well who said that there shall be a review every five years.

In addition to the issue of creamy layer, the factor of merit was introduced for the first time into the social engineering. Justice Pasayat said that the Central Government must examine the desirability of fixing cut-off marks in respect of OBCs, in relation to those required from the general candidates. By way of illustration, he indicated that five marks grace could be extended to such candidates below the minimum eligibility marks fixed for general categories of students. This would ensure that quality and merit did not suffer. If any seats remained vacant after adopting such norms he said, they should be filled up by candidates from the general category. For Justice Bhandari, the concession could go up to 10 marks.

An analysis of the different opinions expressed seems to indicate a paradigm shift from 'caste alone' to include parameters like income, education, family background, and others that have always arisen as subtends throughout but have got submerged in caste-based reservations. However, the ratio leaves certain areas extensively discussed in individual orders, ambiguous or unstated leaving it open to further challenge.

As expected, the judgement went back to the Supreme Court within a month on whether there could be quotas for OBCs at the postgraduate level.[8] Multiple petitions were filed. After the Supreme Court upheld the validity of Art. 5 of 2007 subject to the exclusion of creamy layer in the determination of OBCs, the Ministry of Human Resources, Government of India, issued an Office Memorandum on 20.4.2008 for the implementation of reservation for OBCs in accordance with the judgement. One Soyan Guha challenged this Office Memorandum with respect to the admission of OBCs in IIM, Calcutta. The Pan-IIM Alumni Association challenged it in the New Delhi High Court and Youth for Equality and two others in the Mumbai High Court in respect to OBC admissions in IIT. The common contention was that a candidate who had done graduation could not be counted as educationally backward and so was not entitled to reservation in post-graduation. The Calcutta High Court granted a stay of the implementation of the Government's order against which the Government filed an appeal in the Supreme Court and also asked for all the petitions to be transferred to the Supreme Court as the issues were the same. The Supreme Court vacated the stay given by Calcutta High Court and allowed provisional admission to post-graduate courses subject to the outcome of the case. The primary issue that has emerged is one of individual rights and their relationship to group rights. It is not new and goes straight to the heart of the Constitution within which lies the contradiction that in this case has come to a head.

References

1. Cited in *Indra Sawhney vs. Union of India* [1992, Supp. (3) SCC, pp. 20-772].
2. *Ibid.*
3. Jaffrelot, Christophe. 2003. *India's Silent Revolution: The Rise of the Low Castes in North Indian Politics*, Delhi: Permanent Block. See also, Christophe Jaffrelot, *The Politics of OBC*, http://us/6621.mail.com/you/showletter

   Marc Galanter, *Competing Equalities: Law and the Backward Classes in India,* Delhi: Oxford University Press.
4. Jaffrelot, Christophe. *India's Silent Revolution* and *The Politics of OBC.*
5. Kalelkar, Kakasaheb. 1955. *Backward Classes Commission Report.*
6. Jaffrelot, Christophe. *The Politics of OBC*. Op.cit. Also, cited in *Indra Sawhney v. Union of India*. Op. cit.
7. Mandal Commission, Report www.ncbc.nic.in/user_Panel/userviewaspx?TypeID=1161.
8. Three petitions separately filed in the High Courts of Delhi, Bombay and Calcutta have all been transferred to the Supreme Court to be heard together as they all are concerned with the issue of quotas in post-graduate courses. The three petitions are *PAN-IIM Alumni Association and Others v. Union of India* (May 2008); *Youth for Equality and other v. Union of India* (April 2005); and *Sayan Centre vs. Union of India* (May 2008).

9

Religious Minorities, Sachar Committee and Affirmative Action

Introduction

The issue of individual rights versus group rights in the Constitution is not merely confined to Scheduled Castes (SCs) and Scheduled Tribes (STs), but also to religious groups. By the time the Constituent Assembly met, there had been a long history of distrust among Hindus and Muslims that had culminated in the partition of the country. One of the basic questions facing the members of the Constituent Assembly was whether a list of rights should be included in the Constitution and the overwhelming feeling was that it was absolutely necessary to do so for at least two reasons:

1. After the excesses of the colonial rule, Indians in general wanted their rights spelt out.
2. Various minority communities believed that their safety depended on including measures to protect their group rights and character in the Constitution.

Congress itself had demanded written rights throughout the independence movement and it could not therefore, reject their incorporation when it was itself coming to power. Britain had also often claimed that it had a special obligation to protect the minorities as Indians could not get justice from other Indians. This claim had to be refuted. Sardar Patel told the first meeting of the Advisory Committee:

> It is for us to prove that it is a bogus claim, a false claim and that nobody can be more interested than us in India, in the protection of our minorities. Our mission is to satisfy every one of them....At least let us prove we can rule ourselves and we have no ambition to rule others.[1]

As part of protecting minority rights, the freedom of religion was included in the Fundamental Rights together with special provisions relating to the protection of script and culture and the rights of minorities to maintain their own educational institutions. However these rights were considered fundamental and enforceable by the courts, Assembly members realised that they could not be absolute. The question was to what extent and in what way could they be limited: (i) Attach provisos to particular rights and provide for their suspension under certain circumstances; (ii) Qualify individual rights by allowing the State to intervene for certain social purposes. For example, freedom of religion could not come in the way of social reform. The right to equality could not prevent the state from making special provisions for the less privileged sections of society.

Education and Minorities

The framers of the Constitution were fully aware of the importance of education and there was a detailed debate on whether it should be made a fundamental right. In spite of strong opinion in favour of making it a justiciable right, it could not be made a part of enforceable rights primarily because the State lacked the resources to cope with the immensity of the problem. However, it did find a place among Fundamental Rights for the minorities as they were given a fundamental right to establish and administer educational institutions of their choice, primarily through Articles 29 and 30. In *Arya Samaj Education Trust, Delhi vs. the Director of Education, Delhi Administration, Delhi*, the Court dealt with the question of whether the Arya Samaj was a 'minority' under Article 30. In doing so, it traced the history of Article 30(1) as it came to be incorporated in Part III of the Constitution. Under Article 30(1), only minorities whether based on religion or language, have the right to establish and administer educational institutions of their choice. Therefore, in the case of a religious minority it implies: (i) the existence of a minority, (ii) it being based on religion, and (iii) the basis being 'religion' in the sense in which the word is used in Article 30(1).

Originally, the draft of the Fundamental Rights was submitted with the Report of the Sub-committee on Fundamental Rights on April 16, 1947 to the Constituent Assembly. It did not contain any provision corresponding to Article 30(1). However, K.M. Munshi submitted a letter in which the rights now contained in Article 30(1) together with some other rights were proposed to be conferred on "national minorities....based on religion." Munshi explained that the genesis of his proposal lay in the minority rights embodied in the Polish Treaty of June 28, 1919, which became a part of the Polish Constitution. After the First World War, the problem of national minorities in Europe was sought to be settled by the Treaty of Versailles, the Polish Treaty being a part of the settlement. Munshi's proposal was accepted by the Sub-Committee on Minorities and annexed to its interim report. Later, in para 18 of the draft of Fundamental Rights contained the provision corresponding to the present Articles 29 and 30 of the Constitution. In this draft, both these rights were conferred on "minorities".

The Drafting Committee, however, distinguished between the right of any section of citizens to conserve their language script or culture later embodied in Article 29, and the right of all minorities based on religion or language to establish and administer educational institutions of their choice, later embodied in Article 30. Why the word "minorities" was omitted from the draft fundamental right relating to the conservation of language, script or culture was explained by Dr Ambedkar:

> The term "minority" was used therein not in the technical sense of the word "minority" as we have been accustomed to use it for the purposes of certain political safeguards, such as representation in the Legislature, representation in the services, and so on. The word is used not merely to indicate the minority in the technical sense of the word, it is also used to cover minorities which are not minorities in the technical sense, but which are nonetheless minorities in the cultural and linguistic sense. For instance, for the purposes of this Article 23, if a certain number of people from Madras came and settled in Bombay for certain purposes, they would be, although not a minority in the technical sense, cultural minorities. Similarly if a certain number of Maharashtrians went from Maharashtra and settled in Bengal, although they may not be minorities in the technical sense, they would be cultural and linguistic minorities in Bengal. The article intends to give protection in the matter of culture, language and script not only to a minority technically, but also to a minority in the wider sense of the term as I have explained just now. That is the reason why we dropped the word "minority" because we felt that the word might be interpreted in the narrow sense of the term, when the intention of this House, when it passed Article 18, was to use the word "minority" in a much wider sense, so as to give cultural protection to those who were technically not minorities but minorities nonetheless.[2]

Dr Ambedkar made an important distinction between the technical and the non-technical sense of the word "minority." In the technical sense, it was used in connection with reservations for minorities in legislatures and services. Muslims, for instance, were such a minority. But even a part of the majority community, the Hindus could become a linguistic minority when people from one linguistic area migrated to another. That is the non-technical sense of minority. Because of the potential confusion that the two interpretations of the word could cause, the word 'minority' was dropped from Article 29(1) and replaced by "any section of the citizens."

The problem of minorities before the Constitution related only to those who claimed to be separate from the majority on the basis of religion: Muslims, Christians, and Sikhs. No section of Hindus was treated as a minority. The attempt of the British to separate the SCs from the Hindus was defeated by the combined efforts of Mahatma Gandhi and Babasaheb Ambedkar. The word 'community' denoted either the majority community, that is, Hindus by religion, or the minority communities based on a religion separate from Hinduism such as Islam, Christianity, and Sikhism. That was why the words,'communal award', 'communalism', 'communal reservation', and 'communal', in the Indian context, always referred to the community based on religion. The non-political sense of community as based on language acquired significance only later.

The meaning of the words "based on religion" in Article 30(1) is only or principally the adherence to one of the many religions and not a sect or a part of any religion. The other features of the minority are subordinate to this main feature. 'Religion' in the context of Article 30(1) refers to the well-defined religions of India — Hinduism, Islam, Sikhism, Christianity, Jainism, among others. Thus, minorities were given a fundamental right to establish and administer educational institutions of their choice while education for all up to the age of fourteen years was placed under the Directive Principles. It became a Fundamental Right in 2002.

In spite of having the right to establish and administer educational institutions of their choice, there was persistent demand among religious minorities for reservation for the 'lower' castes in their religions. As Harish K. Puri pointed out, one of the major demands by the twenty-two members of the Sikh members of the East Punjab Legislative Assembly in 1848 was to secure for the former 'untouchables' who had converted to Sikhism the same rights that would have been available to them if they had not converted.[3] They gave a memorandum to the Advisory Committee on fundamental rights minorities, pleading that the lower castes in the Sikh community be included in the list of Scheduled Castes. Vallabhbhai Patel, the Chair of the Committee, remarked in the Constituent Assembly:

> Really as a matter of fact, these converts are not Scheduled Castes or ought not to be Scheduled Castes; because in the Sikh religion, there is no such thing as untouchability or any classification or difference of classes.

And so when these proposals were brought to us, in fact, I urged upon them strongly not to lower their religion to such a pitch as to really fall to a level where for a mess of pottage you really give up the substance of religion. But they did not agree.[4]

The Committee accepted the plea of the Sikh leaders but Patel remarked: "I concede this is a concession. It is not a good thing in the interest of the Sikhs themselves. But till the Sikhs are convinced that this is wrong, I would allow them the latitude."

In 1953, the demand for the Punjabi Suba was raised. Master Tara Singh and Shiromani Akali Dal wanted that all 'untouchables' who had converted to Sikhism be included in the list of SCs so that they would be entitled to the benefits of reservation. When eventually the demand was conceded, it was hailed as a victory for the Sikhs forgetting that it had been a matter of pride for them that they did not believe in the Hindu caste system.

There have been demands for quotas for Dalit Muslims and Christians too. Justice Ranganath Misra's report on the status of Dalit Christians stated that a caste was a social concept and did not have any religious basis. Therefore, the SC status should be delinked from religion and the group be made religion-neutral like the STs. The Report recommended that all groups and classes among the Muslims and Christians whose counterparts among the Hindus, Sikhs or Buddhists were included in the Central or State Scheduled Caste list be taken into the Scheduled Caste net.[5] Further, any such group or class among Muslims and Christians that has been placed under the OBC be transferred to the SCs. Since the Constitution guarantees the freedom of conscience and religion as a fundamental right, a person in the SC list cannot be removed from it simply because he changes his religion.

A Public Interest Suit filed in the Apex Court sought equal rights for all Dalits, irrespective of religion. The Government of India drafted an amendment bill to the Constitution to include Dalit Christians and Muslims in the list of Scheduled Castes but this was not passed in Parliament. Support was sought to be garnered from the National Commission for the SCs and STs, but the appeal was rejected in February 2007. The acting Chairperson Fakirbhai Vaghela said that once an individual adopted Islam or Christianity, he did not face the social stigma of untouchability and hence did not fall within the purview of reservation. The Social Justice Ministry proposed that in the case of inter-caste marriages, "If either of the parents belongs to such a caste (SC) and the other parent belongs to neither SC nor ST but professes one of the religions which a person belonging to SC may profess," he or she may be treated as SC. This meant that a child from mixed parentage had to have one parent of the reserved category and the other parent of the non-reserved category had to either be a Hindu, Buddhist or Sikh because only the followers of these three faiths were eligible for SC status. This was to preclude Christians and Muslims from availing of Dalit status through mixed parentage.

A recent judgement by the Supreme Court (*K.P. Manu vs. Chairman, Scrutiny Committee for Verification of Community Certificate*, 2014) has once again brought the issue of Dalit Christians to the force. A scheduled caste certificate was denied to K.P. Manu on reconversion by the Scrutiny Committee constituted under the Kerala (Scheduled Castes and Scheduled Tribes) Regulation of Issue of Community Certificates Act, 1996 on grounds that K.P. Manu's grandfather had converted to Christianity and since then the family had remained Christians. Manu himself was married to a Christian. It was Manu's great grandfather who belonged to the Hindu Pulaya Community which is a Scheduled Caste community. The question arose whether Manu on reconversion could be taken back into the Pulaya Community fold and considered as a Hindu Pulaya. The High Court ruled that this was not possible. The Supreme Court while overruling the High Court dealt with two principles that were germane to the issues. One was that a court can look into the notification by the President and the Act of the Parliament under the Scheduled Castes and Scheduled Tribes Order (Amendment) Act, 1976 and the schedule appended to it to find out whether the castes, races or tribes are parts or groups within the caste, races or tribes, especially scheduled castes for the purpose of the constitution. This was a matter of fact. The second was whether a person born to Christian parents, who initially belonged to the scheduled caste, can go back to his caste after reconversion.

As far as the second principle is concerned, the Supreme Court examined the various cases that had been dealt with by the courts and ruled that it was the community that had the final say as far as the acceptance of the person after reconversion was concerned. In this case, the community had wholeheartedly accepted him and so Manu, on reconversion, could go back to his caste and all that went with it. This order once again reopens the debate on reservation for Dalit Christians.[6]

The Sachar Committee Report

Since Muslims are the largest religious minority of India and constitute the second-largest religious community after the Hindus, the government felt the need to get authentic information about their social and economic status to plan, formulate and implement specific interventions, policies and programmes to address issues relating to their socio-economic backwardness. A High Level Committee chaired by Justice Rajinder Sachar, was constituted in March 2005. It was to prepare a report on the social, economic and educational status of the Muslim community in India and analyse:

- The geographic areas where the Muslims of India lived, their patterns of economic activities, their assets and levels of income, employment and socio-economic development compared to the other communities of India.
- The proportion of Muslims in the OBCs list out of the total OBCs as provided in different states of the country.
- Access of the Muslim population to education and health services, infrastructure, bank credit and other government services compared to the other communities of India.[7]

The Committee was then to identify the various sectors that required government intervention to address issues relating to the social, economic and educational status of the Muslim community. Social stratification among Muslims was recognised and they were not treated as a monolithic block. The Committee looked at the various indicators on at least two levels: for Muslims as a whole and for the different classes within the Muslim community as social stratification within it was accepted.

The Muslim Population in India and Its Distribution

According to the 2001 Census, there were 138 million Muslims out of a total population of 1029 million; 13.4 per cent of the population spread across India. State-wise population of Muslims: Uttar Pradesh, West Bengal, Bihar and Maharashtra over ten million; Kerala, Andhra Pradesh, Assam, Jammu and Kashmir and Karnataka—five to ten million; Rajasthan, Gujarat, Madhya Pradesh, Jharkhand and Tamil Nadu—three to five million; Delhi, Haryana and Uttarakhand—one to two million; Punjab and Orissa—less than one million. Except for the last two, the larger States had larger populations of Muslims.

There was also big variation in the density of the Muslim population in different districts. Ten districts of West Bengal, five of Uttar Pradesh, three of Jammu and Kashmir and seven of other States each had a population of over one million Muslims. In 51 other districts, their population was between half and one million. Thus, about half the population lived in these 76 districts. There were 593 districts in India, of which nine were predominantly Muslim constituting 75 per cent of the population and 11 districts constituted 50–75 per cent. Roughly 13 per cent of Muslims resided in these 20 districts. Twenty-two per cent of the total Muslims lived in thirty-eight other districts spread across the states which had 25–50 per cent Muslim population. One hundred and eighty-two districts had 10–12 per cent Muslim population and all of them together accounted for nearly half the population. There were 77 other districts with just 1 per cent or less Muslim population. Further, 30.7 per cent of Muslims lived in urban areas compared to the national average of 27.8 per cent. The age profile of Muslims appeared to be younger with 27 per cent in the 0–10 age group compared to 23 per cent overall and 14.7 per cent in the 10–14 age group compared to 12.1 per cent overall.

The population distribution of the Muslim community was important because the Report observed that in the predominantly Muslim areas both the physical and educational infrastructure was poor and needed to be developed and strengthened. The Census of 2001 showed that hardly any banking facilities were available in the densely-populated Muslim areas. The Sachar Committee Report cited a Reserve Bank study to show that 44 minority districts did not have banking facilities, which affected their access to credit and in turn adversely impacted other spheres including education.

The standard of living of Muslims seemed to indicate deprivation in many areas. For example, the consumption levels of the majority of Muslims in urban areas resembled that of SCs/STs, at a monthly per capita expenditure of Rs 400 to Rs 500; about half the urban Muslim population had an expenditure of Rs 300 to Rs 600. Poverty in the urban Muslim population was the highest among the various socio-religious categories at a Head Count Ratio of 38.4 per cent, while it was better in the rural areas.

The Muslim OBCs

The Sachar Committee recognised the social stratification among Muslims detailed their conditions as a whole and according to the different categories among them. The social structure of the Muslim community clearly showed an inherited and occupation-based, hierarchical ordering and the following of endogamy, similar to the Hindu caste system. The Census of 1901 listed 133 such social groups. The present-day Muslim society is divided into two main classes:

1. Ashrafs, who trace their ancestry to foreigners such as the Arabs, Turks, Persians and Afghans.
2. The Ajlafs, who are converts.

The Ajlafs are further divided into three classes:

1. Upper class Hindus who converted to Islam.
2. Middle class converts.

3. The Arzal or lowest classes converted from the erstwhile 'untouchable' castes with 'unclean' occupations.

Since the Constitution's SCs were restricted to Hindu groups with 'unclean' occupations, the Ajlafs (equivalent to Hindu OBC) and Arzals (equivalent to Hindu SCs) were called Muslim OBCs and were placed within the general OBC list.

According to the 55th Round of the NSSO, the population of Muslim OBCs was 31.7 per cent, while the 61st Round gave 40.7 per cent OBCs of the total Muslim population. While in most States, the majority of Muslims are now listed as OBCs, in West Bengal, the number is miniscule. Except for Lakshadweep, where almost the entire ST population is Muslim, and Himachal Pradesh, where seven per cent of the STs are Muslim, they do not have much of a representation in the ST list. This is despite the fact that ST status is given irrespective of religion.

Higher Education and Employment in the Muslim Community

According to the Sachar Committee, only about seven per cent of the Indian population over 20 years of age were graduates or diploma holders. But among the Muslims, the percentage was just 3.6, while only 0.4 per cent had technical education. The figures were somewhat similar to those for SC/ST. Technical education is particularly important for Muslims as a substantial numbers are engaged in artisanal activities in which technical training would improve their economic status. The gap in the Graduate Attainment Rate (GAR) between Muslims and 'all others' has widened from the 1970s onwards, and while the Muslims initially had a higher GAR than the SCs/STs, the gap has been closing, as the GAR for the SCs/STs have been increasing. There is a very real possibility, therefore of the SCs/STs overtaking the Muslims. This is already apparent in some states.

The proportion of Muslims in undergraduate courses in the universities in India was just nine per cent, which was lower than their share of the population and also lower than the figures for ST and SC students. While Muslims were more likely to take up science and commerce streams, their presence in engineering and medical colleges was extremely low. In postgraduate courses, the Muslim presence comprised only 2 per cent compared to 24 per cent for OBCs and 13 per cent for SCs/STs, as they were more inclined to take up professional courses. While it is not known how many Muslims appeared for the entrance examinations of IIMs, they constituted only 1.3 per cent of the students on an all-India basis. The share of Muslims in MBA courses outside the IIMs was found to be one per cent, and in medical colleges, it was four per cent. Again, it is not known how many Muslims appear for the entrance examination for the Indian Institutes of Technology (IITs), but they constituted 1.7 per cent of undergraduate students, four per cent of postgraduate students, while the figure for Ph.D. courses was marginally better. In the premier colleges of Indian universities, including arts, commerce and science, only one out of 25 students in the undergraduate courses and one out of 50 in postgraduate courses was a Muslim with just a marginal presence in the science streams.

The low participation in higher education probably led to fewer job opportunities. This was borne out by the data presented in the Sachar Committee Report which stated that the Muslim participation in salaried jobs was poor — just about 13 per cent and these were mainly in casual labour. Even in urban areas, only 27 per cent of Muslims had regular work, while the figures were 40 per cent for SCs/STs and 36 per cent for OBCs. Only 24 per cent of Muslims were employed with the government, public sector and public/private sector, compared to 39 per cent and 30 per cent for SCs/STs and OBCs respectively. Muslims were employed more in their own enterprises or in the unorganised sectors, while 70 per cent of the women worked from their homes as compared to 51 per cent of other women workers.

The share of Muslims in the Civil Services and most departments of public sector undertakings did not exceed five per cent. They constituted only three per cent of the IAS, 1.3 per cent of the IFS and four per cent of the IPS. Even in the Indian Railways, their share was 4.5 per cent and that too at mostly lower levels of the hierarchy. Similarly, in the Posts and Telegraph Services, it was about five per cent. Just about 4.9 per cent of the candidates who appeared in the civil service examinations in 2003 and 2004 were Muslims—way below their share of population. They constituted just 3.7 per cent of the teaching faculty and 5.4 per cent of the non-teaching staff in universities, while the figures for SCs/STs were 7.4 per cent and 16.9 per cent respectively. The picture was even more dismal in Public Sector Banks, where their representation was a mere 2.2 per cent.

Desai and Kulkarni argued that greater opportunities for employment due to reservations for SCs/STs resulted in higher economic status, was motivating and enabled them to invest in their children's education. Since Muslims faced impediments in getting employment, they did not have the motivation to meet the challenge of improving their educational levels. The reason for the low participation of Muslims in both higher education and in jobs can, however, be traced to weak school education.

School Education

The Sachar Committee spent considerable time in evaluating the situation at the school level realising that it was the foundation for both higher education and employment. Without good schooling, there could be no access to either. According to the Census of 2001, only 65 per cent of Indians were literate with the literacy levels of males being higher than that of females and the levels in urban areas being higher than rural ones, the gap in both cases being about 20 per cent. The Muslim literacy rate was 59.1 per cent, that of SC/ST was 52.2 and of 'all others', 70.8 per cent. In the urban areas, the gap between Muslim literacy levels and the national average was 11 per cent and the gap between them and others including the SCs/STs was 15 per cent. Although the overall educational level in rural areas was lower, the gap between the categories was less. Compared to the 1960s, the gap between Muslims and 'all others' decreased to some extent in the urban areas, but remained the same in rural areas. While the literacy rates for SCs/STs, men and women had improved in urban and rural areas, Muslims were not been able to improve their educational status at the same pace.

The Sachar Committee pointed out that one cause of this could be that there were very few government primary schools in Muslim areas, and even fewer higher-level educational institutions. From those that existed, most were of a very low quality, with high teacher-pupil ratios. This was because Muslims found it difficult to get jobs as teachers in schools. Those who did get the jobs were allegedly badly treated. The main cause for the educational backwardness was possibly poverty. The children were required to earn for the family from a very early age, and even those who did go to school, could not cope without tuitions or parental support, resulting in drop-outs after a few years of schooling. Because of their perception of being discriminated against in getting jobs, Muslim families did not perceive any major gains from education. Difficulty in getting government jobs, even with certificates and degrees were brought up repeatedly, says the Report. The situation in the private sector was worse.

The 2001 Census provided statistics for the Mean Years of Schooling (MYS) for children aged 7–16, or those children who should have completed matriculation. It was found that the average Indian child went to school for only four years. In the case of Muslims, it was consistently lower at three years and four months, for both the urban and rural areas throughout the country. The mean years of schooling for Muslims were the lowest in West Bengal, Uttar Pradesh, Assam, Uttarakhand and Delhi; while in Kerala,

Bihar, Jharkhand, Karnataka, Maharashtra and Andhra Pradesh, they were higher than the SCs/STs.

The differentials in school education throughout the country were considerable in rural and urban areas, with the rural areas having the lowest levels. The Muslim attainment levels on the national level were only slightly higher than those of the SCs/STs, but considerably lower than the SCs/STs in the rural areas, primarily due to the abysmal levels of schooling of rural Muslim women. The high drop-out rate among Muslim girls, according to the findings of the Report, was not because Muslim families did not consider it important to educate their daughters, but primarily because of non-availability of schools within easy reach at lower educational levels, absence of hostels at higher levels, lack of female teachers and meagre availability of scholarships. At the national level, the numbers for Muslims getting education worsened as the level of education rose from primary to middle school to secondary school.

While 26 per cent of the over 17 years completed matriculation nationally, only 17 per cent of the Muslims did so. It was apparent that the increase in educational opportunities since Independence had not narrowed the gap between Muslims and the rest of the country. On the contrary, it widened consistently particularly among Muslim urban males and rural females; the gaps for SCs/STs however, reduced since the 1960s between both urban and rural males and females.

The main hurdle to cross was the primary level of schooling because after that the situation improves. Of the children enrolled in primary school, about 44 per cent of Muslim children, 39 per cent of SCs, 32 per cent of STs and 62 per cent of 'all others' were likely to complete that stage. After that the situation improved as the percentage of Muslim, SC and ST children completing middle school rose to 65 per cent as compared to 75 per cent for 'all others'. Roughly, 50 per cent of Muslim, SC and ST children completed secondary school compared to 62 per cent of 'all others'. About 34 per cent of 'all others', 26 per cent of Muslim and 23 per cent of SC and ST children made the transition from school to college.

The government set up Jawahar Navodaya Vidyalayas—residential 'pace setting' secondary schools—in the rural areas to provide high quality education to talented children. However, the percentage of Muslim children, particularly girls, who appeared for the entrance test and were selected was far lower than their share of the population. This was despite the fact that the examination was held in 21 languages including Urdu, and the education up to Class 10 was completely free.

In the 6–13 years age group, the share of students enrolled compared to the total population of all socio-religious categories was more or less the same, this gap widened at the higher education levels for SCs/STs, Muslims and OBCs with, in some cases, the SCs/STs overtaking the Muslims. This clearly indicated that while enrollment initiatives were working, action was needed to retain the students. The Sachar Committee detailed some steps to achieve this.

Madrasas and Maqtabs

The Sachar Report emphasised that although Muslims were aware of their educational backwardness, Madrasas and other private Muslim institutions often appeared to be the only choice available because of the paucity of schools and infrastructural facilities in areas of dense Muslim population. Most children across all the socio-religious categories studied in government or government-aided schools; about one-third attended private schools. About four per cent of Muslim children in the 7–19 age group studied in Madrasas which shows that it is wrong to say that Muslims prefer to send their children to Madrasas for religious education. Madrasas are not merely institutions of religious teaching. It is important to distinguish between Madrasas and Maqtabs.

Madrasas provide regular and/or religious education, except for the residential ones that provide solely religious education. Maqtabs are usually attached to a mosque and provide part-time religious education to children studying in mainstream schools, in order that they may learn Urdu and the Islamic scriptures as government schools do not teach Urdu adequately, and knowledge of this language is essential to read the Islamic scriptures. There were very few Urdu medium schools, and their state was abysmal. Karnataka, Maharashtra and Andhra Pradesh made better provisions for Urdu-medium schools, particularly at the primary level. In Karnataka, for example, the number of Urdu teachers in Urdu was substantial with women teachers predominant even at higher levels. This was important as Muslim families preferred to send their daughters to schools staffed by women. In general, particularly in the north, there was a dearth of Urdu-medium schools or schools that offered Urdu as an elective language, because the emphasis was on Sanskrit. The Report recommended that Urdu be offered as an elective language in areas with large Urdu-speaking populations.

Anwar Alam contested the language issue when he stated that Urdu was never the language of the Muslim masses, who generally spoke their regional languages.[8] It was only the elite Muslims in the Hindi heartland who promoted the language. However, it was the government's responsibility to provide education to the masses. While there had been considerable discussion on the modernisation of Madrasas, it was crucial to provide affordable, good quality, mainstream schools in the areas that lacked these. This proposition could not be refuted as under the Constitution, the government had to provide education up to the age of 14 to every child. However, minorities have a right to establish and maintain their own educational institutions under the Constitution and so it is equally incumbent upon the minority communities to establish and maintain quality institutions.

It must be mandatory for the government, the Report recommended, that an 'equivalence' be established between the two systems—the Madrasas and the mainstream education—so that a child's certificate from a Madrasa could have some equivalence in the latter. Madrasas needed to be affiliated to recognised education boards. For modernising Madrasas, basic infrastructure had to be made available to introduce modern, regular subjects into the curriculum, using modern methods of teaching, with good, well-qualified teachers who received adequate compensation. All these aspects had been ignored and the modern streams of the Madrasas had not been supervised or inspected as the Report stated. Even those who were in the Madrasas for religious training, needed to receive modern education to make them aware of secular learning and to bring them into the mainstream of contemporary life.

Firoz Bakht Ahmed felt that government intervention had to be meaningful and not mere sops.[9] Just earmarking funds for the modernisation of Madrasas was not enough and that did not exempt the government from its responsibility of providing mainstream educational facilities to the community. The responsibility for mainstream schooling lies on both the government and the community. As Bakht pointed out, the situation had become more complex because the community had also been misled by its fundamentalist leaders so that it had acquired a ghetto mentality. Even when schools were available, children were not sent thus making them develop an obscurantist and unstable outlook. In Bakht's opinion, even the minority status had harmed rather than helped the Muslims, generating a 'minority-majority' mindset that facilitated their 'ghettoisation'.

Education and Employment of Muslim OBCs

Among the backward classes, Muslim OBCs lagged behind all other OBCs, particularly in the rural areas, where there was significant lag in literacy. Almost 55 per cent of Muslim OBC children in the 6–12 age group did not attend school, which was the same figure for general Muslims, but was much higher than the 49 per cent for Hindu OBCs. In general, the education levels of Muslim OBCs across the education spectrum up to the graduate level and higher was lower than that of general Muslims, which in turn was lower than of Hindu OBCs. In universities, the general category Muslims and the OBC Muslims had only a notional representation.

The NSSO 61st Round showed that 9.2 per cent of Muslim OBCs were unemployed during 2004–05, while the figures were 7.5 per cent and 7.7 per cent for Hindu OBCs and general Muslims respectively. The figures were similar in urban and rural areas and for men and women. Similarly, their share of employment in the formal sector was much lower, at 3.5 per cent, compared to Muslims in the general and Hindu OBCs (7 per cent and 11.3 per cent respectively). More Muslim OBCs found employment in the private sector. Women, on the other hand, worked predominantly from their homes. In socio-religious categories, the Muslim OBC group was the largest number. In the public sector, for every 100 workers only one was a Muslim OBC, while three were from the general group and 11 were Hindu OBCs.

The Identity Problem

According to the Sachar Report, the lack of social, educational and economic development created feelings of insecurity, the extent of which varied in different geographic locations. There was a perception that the government was apathetic towards Muslims, especially during communal riots. This had resulted in many Muslim communities living in ghettos that they considered 'safe'. This affected women the most, and was a further impediment to their access to education, public transport and jobs, resulting in home-based work.

Differing opinions about the cause of insecurity point to the complexity of the situation. According to Anwar Alam, while the democratisation of other backward groups continued, the process had not only bypassed the Muslim community, there had also no internal democratisation resulting in a lack of social and educational reforms.[10] He blamed the Muslim leadership for this because they had not introduced any social reforms for the community since Independence and had exaggerated their threat perception increasing the insecurity and ghettoisation. Alam stated that Muslims were as heterogeneous as any other community, but the elite represented them as a homogeneous mass in order to demand reservations for the entire community, including themselves.

Seik Rahim Mondal analysed that since the vast majority of the middle classes opted for Pakistan during Partition, the Indian Muslim community lacked a strong middle class, which was a setback to the progress of the community.[11] Irfan Ahmad emphasised the need for land reforms within the community to empower the downtrodden.[12] Mondal appeared to agree with Anwar Alam, when he said that the Muslim leadership had neither bothered about the problems of Muslims nor had tried to take advantage of any programme aimed at their upliftment. They were more interested in bringing up emotive issues to keep themselves in leadership positions.

Affirmative Action So Far

Since Independence two commissions have been set up to ascertain the criteria to define a 'backward class', for purposes of remedial action. The first, the Kaka Kalelkar Commission, submitted its report in 1955 and was rejected for using caste and not economic criteria to identify backwardness. The second, the Mandal Commission submitted its report in 1980. It was accepted and partially implemented in 1991. While the Kaka Kalelkar Commission listed 2399 backward castes, with 837 as most backward, the Mandal Commission listed 3743 castes. The Mandal Commission further identified 'untouchables' converted to other religions and communities known by their occupations, whose Hindu counterparts were in the SC list. Thus, 82 groups of Muslim Arzals and Ajlafs were included in the OBC list. It is widely believed that the Arzals are converts from the 'untouchable' castes and since they continue with their traditional 'unclean' occupations, they continue to be ostracized. Despite this, they had not been included in the SC list of the Constitution. This was a reflection of an old colonial order of 1936, barring non-Hindus in the list prepared by the British. The Sachar Committee felt that the Arzals, being the worst off, should have been included in the SC list or at least in the most backward classes list.

Several states also had their own commissions, and these had their own separate lists of OBCs and More Backward Classes (MBCs), into which the Muslims had been added. Kerala has a 10–12 per cent reservation quota for jobs within the OBCs for Muslims. Kerala and Karnataka, further have the entire Muslim community in their states, barring the creamy layer in their OBC/MBC lists. About 95 per cent of the Muslims in Tamil Nadu are in the OBC list and almost the entire Muslim population of Bihar is in the MBC list.

Zoya Hasan maintained that although the Muslims were included in the OBC list, they were unable to get any actual benefit from this. She believed that a guaranteed percentage within the OBC quota for Muslims would help.[13] She argued that so far, the better off from the backward classes had secured considerable benefits while those at the bottom, including Muslims, continue to be marginalised.

A few Muslim OBC organisations were set up during the past decade, with the aim of including all backward communities into the OBC and SC lists. There was now a growing awareness that their problems were more social and economic than religious and an attempt was being made to forge bonds between Hindu, Christian, Buddhist and Muslim Dalits, which could well help a large number of Muslims to get out of their ghetto mindset. These organisations strongly resisted attempts at placing the entire community on the backward list.

What Can Be Done

The Sachar Committee Report in its findings revealed that although there was a general consensus that some action needed to be taken to address issues of backwardness within the Muslim community, there were significant differences of opinion within the community regarding the type of affirmative action the government needed to take:

- A majority believed that a separate quota for the reservation for Muslim OBCs would help uplift them, while others feared that it would have negative communal repercussions. Zoya Hasan agreed with the latter view.
- Some believed that good educational facilities and a non-discriminatory attitude would suffice.
- There were also differences as to who were entitled to reservations:
  - Dalit Muslims
  - The entire community
  - Based on some economic criteria
- Another view was that the Muslims be given an SC quota similar to that available to Neo-Buddhists and Mazhabi Sikhs.
- Others felt that the Muslim community should not receive a separate quota, but be part of the general OBC and SC quotas, based on their 'caste-like' categories. This latter opinion gained favour, as it was 'constitutionally tenable'. Several findings showed that some Muslim communities, follow the religion of Islam, but continue to practice the Hindu customs of the castes from which they were originally converted. The Dudekula Muslims of Andhra Pradesh and the Vangujjars, the nomadic buffalo keepers of the north and north-western Himalayan regions, are two examples.

According to Zoya Hasan, the use of religion as the criterion for selecting backward classes was incompatible with secularism and "threatened the national identity and cohesiveness of the State."[14] To use religion as a criterion for reservation required an Act of Parliament. This, according to Hasan, could create communal tension. Reservations under the SC category were set up primarily to provide social justice to the victims of the Hindu caste system. Since Muslims did not recognise caste, reservation could not be applied to them. Conversion to Islam and Christianity debarred Dalits from reservation. Further complications arose from differences within the community. The backward classes strongly objected to the entire community being declared backward, as they felt it would be to their detriment. The upper Muslim classes had already benefited from representation in government jobs, and the backward classes feared that the elite classes would swallow the entire benefits of reservation.

Firoz Bakht Ahmed appeared to share the apprehensions of the backward classes and felt that the Muslim leaders had no voice or utility.[15] They played vote-bank politics to gain political patronage, and it was their obscurantist attitude that kept the community backward. Hasan was of the view that a minimum percentage within the general OBC group being reserved for Muslims would be appropriate.[16] Seik Rahim Mondal agreed with this assessment. Hasan argues that while affirmative action for disadvantaged groups was a historic necessity, there was need to re-evaluate the concept of backwardness, to take into account the current realities of backwardness, by removing the caste concept, which was used to relieve institutionalised inequalities at an earlier stage.[17] It was time to look at other criteria of social stratification so that inequalities of class, gender and the disadvantaged of religious minorities were also appropriately addressed and social justice provided.

In two separate judgements (*Jacob* vs. *State of Kerala* and *P. Rajendra* vs. *State of Madras*), the Supreme Court noted that the place of habitation and occupation also needed to be taken into consideration for judging social backwardness, which was primarily the result of poverty. S.A.H. Moinuddin, however, argued for stating that ethnic identity and social background of a community as these were important parameters to determine backwardness, otherwise there was a danger that the politically articulate could grab the maximum advantage. What in effect was being said was that just like caste could not be the sole criterion for backwardness, religion also could not be the only factor in affirmative action.[18]

After the Sachar Committee

The Sachar Committee Report was challenged as a Public Interest Litigation Case by the Rashtriya Mukti Morcha.[19] Citing literacy rates in other Muslim states, the petitioners claimed that the educational backwardness of the Muslims was a worldwide phenomenon, and Indian Muslims, in fact, had higher literacy rates than those in countries such as Pakistan and Bangladesh. The challenge failed.

Two expert groups were formed following the recommendations of the Sachar Committee to establish an Equal Opportunities Commission. One was chaired by N.R. Madhava Menon to design an Equal Opportunities Commission and the other by Amitabh Kundu to design a Diversity Index to measure diversity in public spaces of education, health and housing.

The Kundu Committee points out that affirmative action is a set of positive anti-discriminatory policy measures to increase the presence of under-represented groups in various social spheres, particularly in preferred positions and levels in the society.[20] It cites Thomas Weisskoff who made a useful distinctive between two forms of Affirmative Action: preferential boosts and quotas. Preferential boosts imply implicit or explicit points given for being a member of the target group. The Diversity Index is an example of the preferential boost system. Both modes are employed internationally.

The Expert Group pointed out that affirmative action through quotas has produced uneven results. Through the diversity index, it would be possible to see clearly where a difference has been made and where more needs to be done. The Expert Group strongly felt that its deliberations should transcend the unidimensional division between religious majority and minorities and capture other dimensions of exclusion as well. It felt that it was necessary to bring together different kinds of exclusion into a common index which should be able to respond to the requirements of specific policies not necessarily confined to the minority-majority religious issues.

The Kundu Committee, points to the World Development Report 2006 (Equity and Development), which states that disparities among different sections of society arise owing to various factors such as caste, gender, schooling, work/occupation and sources of income generation. A diversity index based on such factors is needed because it is not enough to work out strategies for the underprivileged based on poverty alone. Poverty rates computed at the national or state levels have only limited utility as they are not much help in targeting policy towards the poor or those who need special assistance. To do that, poverty figures would be needed for district or even lower levels. The diversity index is an attempt to devise a quantitative measure to provide a working estimate of deprivation in specific areas which can be used for both inter-institutional comparisons and to assess patterns over time.

It is accepted that devising anti-discriminatory practices or identifying areas of discrimination requires deep understanding of social, historical and political environments, but statistical measures are vital for policy targeting. Although their use has been a contentious issue, accepts Mehra, experiences in the UK, France, the USA and Canada have amply demonstrated that they are useful in devising policy based on properly developed indicators, while reservations can be used in certain specific situations. But for a long-term solution for a systematic change, incentives and disincentives based on a Diversity Index could be more effective and hopefully more acceptable being less divisive than quotas. Every institution needs to develop a non-discriminatory and non-exclusionary framework and most constantly evolve norms and practices that ensure greater diversity over time.

Conclusion

In a plural society like India, the issue of reservation in the form of quotas for minorities has been a contentious one. Muslims form about 13 per cent of the population and are the largest religious group after the Hindus. Hindu-Muslim relations have often been clouded with distrust and the events of partition have left a mark. The Constitution has tried to allay some of the fears and mistrust by guaranteeing certain rights to minorities. However, social indicators show that a large part of the Muslim population lives in poverty and is socially and educationally backward. Within it, are certain groups listed among backward classes where the problems are of even greater magnitude. Such a situation needs to be remedied and recommendations have been made that point to remedial action. But this has to be done without alienating others and by ensuring that the benefits reach those who most need them. The problem is not dissimilar to the issues of affirmative action for the Hindu OBCs and SCs/STs. The recommendation of setting up an Equal Opportunities Commission to develop and implement secular indices of deprivation was wise and timely. However, it was not accepted by the Ministry of Human Resource Development.This is not a happy development as unless a secular deprivation index is drawn up and interventions done accordingly to reach the most deprived, irrespective of caste and religion, the already existing social divisions are likely to become intolerable, creating social unrest and even violence of increasing magnitude.

References

1. Engineer, Asghar Ali. 2003. *The Gujarat Carnage*, p. 293. New Delhi: Orient Longman.

2. Pandey, Bhrigu Nath. 2000. *Socio-legal Study of Cultural and Educational Rights of the Minorities*, p. 37. New Delhi: A.P.H. Publishing Corp.
3. Puri, Harish K. *The Scheduled Castes in the Sikh Community – A Historical Perspective*, http://theprg.files.wordpress.com/.../harish-puri-sel;o-scheduled-castes
4. *Ibid.*
5. The Report of the National Commission for Religious and Linguistic Minorities also known as Ranganath Misra Commission Report. 2007.
6. *K.P. Manu vs Chairman, Scrutiny Committee for Verification of Community Certificate*, Feb. 2015.
7. Rajinder Sachar, Committee Report, 2006. The discussion is based on the findings of the Report.
8. Alam, Anwar. 2003. "Democratisation of Indian Muslims", *Economic and Political Weekly*, November 15, 2003.
9. Ahmed, Firoz Bakht. 2008. "Keeping the Muslim Down", *Hindustan Times*, May 20, 2008.
10. Alam, Anwar. 2003. Op.cit.
11. Mondal, Seik Rahim. 2003. "Social Structure, OBCs and Muslims", *Economic and Political Weekly*, November 15, 2003.
12. Ahmad, Irfan. 2003. "A Different Jihad", *Economic and Political Weekly*, November 15, 2003.
13. Hasan, Zoya. "Reservation for Muslims", www.india-seminar.com/2005/549/549%20zoya%20hassan.htm
14. *Ibid.*
15. Ahmed, Firoz Bakht. 2008. Op. cit.
16. Hasan, Zoya. Op.cit.
17. Mondal, Seik Rahim. 2003. Op.cit.
18. Moinuddin, S.A.H. 2003. "Problems of Identification of Muslim OBCs in West Bengal", *Economic and Political Weekly*, November 15, 2003.
19. *Rashtriya Mukti Morcha vs. Union of India*, 2007.
20. Report of the Expert Group on Diversity Index, 2008.

10

Efficacy of Quotas and Alternatives

Introduction

Equity is sought in higher education in India through admissions done according to a rigid quota system for Scheduled Castes and Scheduled Tribes (SCs and STs), and for Other Backward Classes (OBCs) to the tune of 22.5 and 27 per cent respectively. However, little or no work has been done on the outcomes of access. That is, whether it is enough or even equitable to just concentrate on enrollment? Should there not be an equal emphasis on successful outcomes? There are practically no studies available on the outcomes at the tertiary education level. There is little or no tracking of students through their undergraduate careers to see how many succeed and therefore it is difficult to put measures into place to facilitate success. Often it is not possible to even do this as at the time of admission, the students' category is known but the results do not indicate it. So, the correlation between admission and outcome is difficult to assess.

An Effort at Outcomes

Being a faculty member in a college of Delhi University, I tried to analyse the outcomes for the SC and ST students, from the beginning of 1998 up to 2008, in an attempt to compare them with those for the general category. The findings are only indicative and imperfect because there is no systematic record keeping. Also, the system is complex and in the absence of proper tracking processes, it becomes difficult. For example, a student may be admitted to the more prestigious honours course in one of the social sciences, literatures or even the pure sciences, but if he/she gets 25 per cent or more up to 44 per cent in the first year, he/she is sent to the second year of the B.A. Programme. This means that the second-year class gets students from all other classes and subjects together with those who have been promoted from the first year of the B.A. Programme itself. The lateral entry students have to manage the first-year course themselves without any help from the institution. But if they were academically sound, they would not have faired so badly in their original course to begin with. Consequently, the second year sees a high dropout rate, failure or poor academic performance. This also affects those who originally belonged to the B.A. Programme making the entire class a disparate low-performing group, extremely difficult to motivate or teach.

A sampling was done for a period from 1998 admission year to 2005 as the results of the 2005 batch were declared in 2008. While all the candidates of the reserved category were looked at, a sampling was done for the students of the general category. In spite of imperfect tracking, there were certain basic statistics that emerged. The SC and ST students were divided into three streams—Science, Arts and Commerce. This was usual with all students. Then the numbers that graduated were compared to the number admitted and these were tabulated.

A number of students dropped out. This was not necessarily because of the inability to cope, especially in the science stream. It is a common phenomenon for students to drop-out in the first year in the sciences as the preferred courses are medicine and engineering rather than graduation in pure sciences. The results of the entrance for these courses often come out very close to the time or after the admissions to the university have been completed. Therefore, students take admission in the university but if they subsequently get a place in medicine or engineering, they leave. It may be noted that there is reservation in medicine and engineering as well. It is more difficult to explain why students drop-out in the Arts or Commerce stream.

Next, the percentage of students of the reserved category that passed was calculated after subtracting the dropout students from the total admitted. It was found to be generally in the range of 35–50 per cent in the Sciences and Commerce but much higher in the Arts stream. But if the overall pass percentage of the reserved candidates was compared to the overall pass percentage in college, it was low. One reason for this could be that there was usually a wide discrepancy in the school academic achievements of the students being admitted to the same class between the students of the general category and the reserved category, the latter having much lower marks than the former. And admission to the college being done according to the marks obtained in the Class 12, the last year in school. This would make it difficult for the students of the reserved category to cope. Also, there was no conscious classroom pedagogy being used that factored in this gulf.

A further analysis was done using the mean scores and correlative coefficients according to the Statistical Package for Social Science. A correlation was found between the mean marks in Class 12 and the mean final score in graduation both for the reserved category students and the general category students. Each of the three streams has been analysed separately. While investigating the students of SC/ST in Science stream, it was found that average score dropped down from 66.73 in Class 12 to 59.99 in under-graduation and the correlation between the marks in Class 12 and under-graduation was 0.53. Comparing it with the students of the general category, it was found that the mean score dropped from 83.44 in Class 12 to 69.74 in under-graduation and the correlation between Class 12 marks and under-graduation was 0.273. The correlation figure of the general category is less than that of students in the SC/ST category indicating a greater drop in performance of the students of the general category than that of the students of the reserved category. The main reason could be that the dropout/failure rate was high in SC/ST students and the pass percentage was more in students of the general category, but those SC/ST students who managed to pass, did quite well. In the students of the general category, although the pass percentage was very high, the academic achievement dropped compared to performance in school.

In the Arts stream, for SC/ST students, the mean score in Class 12 was 70.67 and it dropped to 49.82 in under-graduation, which was very steep. The correlation between the marks in Class 12 and under-graduation was -0.199. For the students of the general category, the average score in Class 12 was 79.21 and it dropped to 55.93. Also, the correlation between the marks in Class 12 and under-graduation was 0.436. It is seen that in the Arts stream, while the failure rate of the students of the reserved category is not as high as in the Science and Commerce streams, but the average academic performance deteriorates. This is also by and large true of the students of the general category although their performance is better than that of the students of the reserved category. One reason for this could be that most of SC/ST students come from Hindi medium and find it difficult to adjust with the majority of students who have studied in English medium schools.

Finally, coming to the Commerce stream, for the SC/ST students, the mean score in Class 12 was 70.66 and it dropped to 49.82 in under-graduation, which was quite a steep fall. Also, the correlation between marks in Class 12 and under-graduation was 0.169. For the students of the general category, the mean score for Class 12 was 86.945 and average score for under-graduation was 64.7138. The correlation between marks in

Class 12 and under-graduation was -0.348. Here again the dropout/failure rate was high among students of SC/ST category; but for those who did pass, the outcomes were better than for those in the general category. One reason for the poor performance of the students of the general category could be that most of them were looking at graduation as just an eligibility requirement for other courses.

Caste as an Indicator

Caste-based quotas and their expansion need to be evaluated in a systematic manner, which unfortunately has not been done. Professor Thorat's Nehru Memorial Lecture to the University of Mumbai in 2006 raised some vital issues of concern. He pointed out that although the reach of higher education had increased dramatically since Independence, it still left a lot to be desired at all levels of access, inclusiveness and quality.[1]

Thorat cites from three alternative methods used to estimate the extent of access to higher education: Gross Enrollment Ratio (GER), Net Enrollment Ratio (NER) and Enrollment of the Eligible Ratio (EER). GER measures access by taking the ratio of persons in all age groups enrolled in various programmes to total population in the age group of 18 to 23. EER measures the level of enrollment of those who complete the higher secondary level of education. Data on student enrollment is provided mainly through three sources: Selected Education Statistics (SES), National Sample Survey (NSS) and Population Census (PC).

Accurate data is a problem. For example, GER based on the Selected Educational Statistics (SES) was 8 per cent in 2000, but the National Sample Survey (NSS) and Population Census (PC) put it at 10 per cent and 14 per cent respectively. The differences were due to two reasons: SES did not take into account enrollment in unrecognised institutions and also some State governments did not report their enrollment annually. The NSS and PC reported higher percentages because their data were collected from households and hence may have included those who were doing diploma or training programmes such as computer training in unrecognised institutions. The PC data also did not distinguish between professional degree and diploma programmes.

Thorat studied disparities under seven heads: (1) rural and urban; (2) inter-State; (3) inter-caste; (4) inter-religion; (5) male-female; (6) occupation group; and (7) poor and non-poor. The disparities show that caste cannot be the only factor in ascertaining deprivation, although caste is an important factor in these indicators.

The inter-caste data of 2003–04 shows that the overall GER was about 13.22 per cent. However it was much lower for ST, SC and OBC—only 5 per cent, 7.5 per cent and 11.34 per cent, respectively compared to 24.89 per cent for others. Between SC/ST and OBC, the GER was higher for OBC; and between SC and ST, the GER was higher for SC by about 2.5 per cent point. Thus, the GER was the lowest for ST.

The Population Census figures revealed a similar disparity in GER. The general Hindu population had a GER of 15.57 per cent and for SC and ST, it was 8.39 per cent and 7.46 per cent respectively. The EER, however, revealed a different pattern. In 2003–2004, it was 54.4 per cent for ST, 57 per cent for SC, 54.8 per cent for OBC and 62.5 per cent for the other Hindu population. This shows that the general Hindu population had a higher EER compared to SC, ST and OBC but the difference among them was marginal. It indicates that once the school level had been crossed, there was greater convergence in the proportions that entered higher education. Hence, it was necessary to strengthen the system at the school level so that more people became eligible to enter higher education. The figures also show that based on GER, the OBCs had a higher enrollment rate compared to SC and ST; but after completing the higher secondary stage, a smaller proportion than the higher castes entered the higher education stream. This raises the question whether there could be other factors besides caste that influenced decision-making in this regard, for example, socio-economic factors.

Other Indicators Besides Caste

Thorat provided data on some other relevant factors besides caste and also pointed to the inter-linkages between caste and rural areas, occupation and location.

Disparities are evident between rural and urban areas. In 2003–2004, the GER for rural and urban areas showed a wide gap being 7.76 per cent and 27.20 per cent, respectively. Hence, the GER in urban areas was four times higher than rural areas. The Population Census figures of 8.99 per cent for rural areas and 24.52 per cent for urban areas in 2001 also indicate that the rural area enrollment was three times lower than the urban area. The EER worked out to 51.1 per cent for rural and to 66 per cent for urban areas showing the latter to be about 15 per cent higher.

There are wide inter-state variations. The GER at the aggregate level was 13 per cent but States like Nagaland (38.6 per cent), Goa (27.3 per cent), Kerala (24.2 per cent), Manipur (24.7 per cent), Himachal Pradesh (20.0 per cent) and Jammu and Kashmir, Tamil Nadu and

Puducherry (18 per cent) showed more than the national average. On the other hand, States like Tripura (3.2 per cent), Assam (6.6 per cent), Meghalaya (7.2 per cent), Chhattisgarh (7.6 per cent), Orissa (8.2 per cent), Jharkhand (10.3 per cent), West Bengal (9.7 per cent), Bihar (10 per cent), Sikkim (10.8 per cent) and Rajasthan (11 per cent) showed lower than the national average GER.

The EER is a useful indicator as it estimates the access to education to those who have completed the higher secondary stage. In 2003–04, 59 per cent of those who completed the higher secondary entered higher education. The ratio was much higher in Mizoram (87.1 per cent), Manipur (87.7 per cent), Nagaland (85.6 per cent), Jammu and Kashmir (76.6 per cent), and Kerala (70.6 per cent). By national comparison, the ratio was much lower in Tripura (37.8 per cent), Chhattisgarh (49.6 per cent), Orissa (50.2 per cent) and Arunachal Pradesh (53.5 per cent). In the rest of the States, it was around the national average of 59 per cent. This again indicates that it is imperative to strengthen access and retention at the school level. Merely expanding higher education is not likely to solve the problem of access at the level of higher education.

Access varies among the various religious groups as can be seen in the 2003–04 figures. The GER was the highest for Jains followed by Christians, Sikhs, Buddhists, Hindus and Muslims which stood at 57.43 per cent, 27.29 per cent, 15 per cent, 13.47 per cent and 8.19 per cent, respectively. The EER was similarly varied with Jains and Christians on the top, their EER being 74.7 per cent and 71.3 per cent respectively. Next came the Buddhists and Hindus, with about 60 per cent. The EER was low for Sikhs, at 52.8 per cent.

Gender impacts the access to higher education. It is lower for girls than for boys and this is more pronounced in rural areas. Significant male-female disparities also exist in EER. In 2003–04, the overall EER was 62.9 per cent for males and 54.1 per cent for females indicating that the girls were 9 per cent points lower than boys. The gender disparity was aggravated by caste and religion. For instance, in 2000 as against the overall average of 9.4 per cent for females, the GER for females in different categories was 2.4 per cent for ST followed by 4.7 per cent for SC, 7.6 per cent for OBC and 17.2 per cent for other females. In case of religious groups, the GER of Muslim females was 6.3 per cent compared to 10.8 per cent for Hindu and 12.7 per cent for Sikh/Buddhist females. If EER was taken, it was 50 per cent for SC/OBC females and 57 per cent for ST/other high caste females. At 48 per cent, it was the lowest for Muslim females compared to females belonging to other religions—54 per cent for

Hindu/ Buddhist females, 56 per cent for Sikhs, and about 69 per cent for Jain/ Christian females.

Poverty also creates disparities. In 1999–2000, the GER for the poor was 2.4 per cent as against 12.91 per cent for non-poor, the average being 10.10 per cent. Similar disparities were seen for the poor in rural and urban areas. The GER for poor and non-poor in rural areas was 1.30 per cent and 5.51 per cent compared to the poor and non-poor in urban areas — 7.12 per cent and 27.15 per cent, respectively. Poverty is also tied into caste and location, i.e. rural and urban areas. Among the poor, the GER was the lowest for ST and SC followed by OBC and others. The GER for the poor belonging to ST, SC, OBC and others was 1.55 per cent, 1.89 per cent, 2.30 per cent and 3.58 per cent, respectively. A similar pattern was observed for the poor in rural and urban areas. In rural areas, the GER was the lowest for ST — 1.11 per cent followed by 1.35 per cent for SC, 1.13 per cent for OBC, and 1.66 per cent for others. The overall GER in rural areas was 1.30 per cent. In urban areas, the GER for the urban poor was 3.86 per cent, 4.78 per cent, 5.10 per cent, and 7 per cent respectively for SC, ST, OBC and others – the average being 5.51 per cent. Among the non-poor, the GER for ST, SC and OBC was lower than for others. The GER for SC, ST, OBC and others was 6.68 per cent, 9.7 per cent, 8.69 per cent and 19.73 per cent, respectively. The all India average was 12.81 per cent.

Occupation is another factor, and can be clearly seen across occupation groups in rural and urban areas. In rural areas, the GER was five per cent, being generally higher for self-employed households engaged in farm and non-farm economic activities compared to 1.41 per cent for those who worked as farm wage labour and three per cent in non-farm wage labour activities. Similarly in urban areas, the GER was much higher for those engaged in business, regular salaried and other activities compared to casual labour. The GER was 28 per cent, 15.74 per cent and 3.21 per cent respectively for self-employed, regular salaried and casual wage labour. Thus, in both rural and urban areas, the enrollment of the casual wage labour was the lowest as compared to the self-employed and regular wage earner. The GER was particularly low for farm wage labour.

Occupation can be correlated to caste. The GER is generally low for wage labour and particularly low for SC/ST compared to other groups. For instance, while an overall level for wage labour in rural areas was 1.41 per cent, that of the ST, SC, OBC and others in this group was 0.67 per cent, 1.63 per cent, 1.16 per cent and 1.93 per cent respectively. In the urban areas, the GER for casual labour was 3.26 per cent at the overall level as against 1.53 per cent, 2.61 per cent, 3.34 per cent and 4.30 per cent for ST, SC, OBC and other wage labour.

Similar inter-caste differences are observed in the case of self-employed cultivators in rural and urban areas. The overall GER in rural areas for self-employed in agriculture was three per cent, 3.95 per cent, 4.21 per cent and 8.33 per cent for ST, SC, OBC and others, respectively as against an overall average of 5.64 per cent. The GER for self-employed in business in rural areas was 2.53 per cent, 3.77 per cent, 3.97 per cent and 7.73 per cent for ST, SC, OBC and others. In urban areas, the GER for self-employed among ST, SC, OBC and others worked out to 6.15 per cent, 7.37 per cent, 10.0 per cent and 22 per cent respectively. Among the self-employed and wage labour, enrollment was particularly low for the poor among them.

In the urban areas while the enrollment rate at overall level was 15.74 per cent, 28.10 per cent, 3.26 per cent, 50.15 per cent for self-employed, regular salaried, casual labour and other households respectively, it was 4.59 per cent, 0.6 per cent, 2.38 per cent and 14.39 per cent, respectively for poor households belonging to self-employed, regular salaried, casual labour and other households. In other words, the enrollment was lowest among the poor casual wage labour household in rural and urban areas. It works out to 0.86 per cent, 0.37 per cent and 2.38 per cent respectively for agriculture labour, other labour in rural areas and other labour in urban areas. It was particularly low among the same poor group for the ST/SC/OBC. The enrollment rate for agricultural labour for ST, SC and OBC was 0.9 per cent, 0.01 per cent and 0.93 per cent. Similarly, it was nil for ST and SC and only 0.52 per cent for OBC casual non-farm wage labour in rural areas.

All the above data show that in spite of the efforts of sixty years, the access of SCs and STs to higher education is low. Caste factors are undoubtedly important but equally important are other factors like occupation, gender, poverty and the disparity in the rural and urban areas of development. Caste also aggravates the deprivation caused by other factors. But what is vital is schooling, because there is a high dropout and failure rate at the school level with little or no alternative mechanism for remedial action. This again is higher for the weaker sections of society. Unless school education is strengthened, access to higher education cannot be improved.

School Education

Professor Dayanand Dongaonkar in the AIU occasional paper (2008) painted a grim picture of the state of school education both for the population in general and for the SCs and STs.[2] According to the Population Census 2001, the literacy rate is 65.38 per cent indicating that about 35 per cent of the population is still illiterate. According to the Population Census 2011, the literacy rate jumped to 73 per cent. However, the dropout rate was 27 per cent at the primary level and 41 per cent at the elementary level. Further, 13 per cent of students did not even transit from primary to upper primary level.[3] The dropout rates are even higher for SC, ST, OBC and Muslim populations.

The high dropout rate is worrying because it throws children out of the education system without providing a viable alternative of remedial action or skill development. School education therefore, obviously needs to be strengthened both for the general category and for the less privileged before better access can be provided in higher education. The approximate passing rate is about 45 per cent of those who appear in the 10th and 55 per cent of those who appear in the 12th. Therefore, a very large number of young students is being pushed out of the system with no alternative. Another vital issue is students' capacity to cope with higher education. This aspect has been completely overlooked. No studies are readily available on the challenges of diversity in classrooms, the pedagogical methodology required for effective teaching, and the actual current outcomes of access. Unless there are successful outcomes, mere access or enrolment is not enough as it does not benefit anyone.

Can Caste Be the Only Criterion for Affirmative Action?

Another pertinent question is whether group rights benefit all the members of the group. The question has been raised continuously in the case of OBCs with respect to jobs and is also being asked in the case of Scheduled Castes and Scheduled Tribes. The pivotal issue is whether, "caste can be taken as the sole criterion of backwardness." Amartya Sen points out that India has had a terrible tradition of social asymmetry, of which the caste system is only one. In fact, B.R. Ambedkar who chaired the committee that drafted India's Constitution indicated this when he said, "On January 26, 1950 we are going to enter into a life of contradictions. In politics, we will have equality and in social and economic life, we will have inequality."[4] But as Amartya Sen asserts, there is a connection between democracy and resistance to economic inequality because arguments and agitations provide a 'voice' to demand equality in different spheres of life. The nature of stratifications, according to Sen, is not because of a single factor but relates. Their understanding and amelioration depends on class, caste, gender and other barriers and depends on how well they are understood and engaged with politically and also on how much the communities participate in social action.[5]

The Indian Constitution itself provides for space to these issues in the democratic sphere. While the "fundamental rights", guarantee freedom of speech, association, equality before law and others, there are also Directive Principles that delineate a set of specific social and economic entitlements for the people and goals for the government. Democracy has created a lively debate and struggle pertaining to them so that they have been a basis for legal decisions by the Supreme Court on the one hand and of widespread popular agitation on the other. It has also brought the involvement of political leaders from disadvantaged classes and castes in Indian politics today.

Sen emphasises that class is not the only source of inequality and it has to be seen as part of a bigger picture that includes other divisive influences such as gender, caste, region, community, and so on. Class can accentuate these inequalities. The issue gets further complicated by what Sen calls, "friendly fire", borrowing a military term, which means that an army is hit by its own firing rather than by enemy shelling. That is why the actual impact of supportive public institutions and public policies has to be scrutinised constantly. Action taken has to be constantly adapted and evaluated open-mindedly rather than be implemented in a fixed, formulaic way. For example, differences of caste cause disparity, but the impact is much greater when the lower-caste families are also very poor. The trials of the Dalits or people from the other disadvantaged castes or of members of STs become magnified and severe by abject penury. Even the violence associated with caste-related conflicts involves more than just caste. The most impacted are the poor of that caste. Sen argues that this recognition does not make caste unimportant but only places it in a broader context in which not just caste but class is also factored in. He points to considerable evidence that affirmative action in favour of lower castes has tended to benefit the economically better off among them rather than those who have to bear the additional brunt of extreme poverty. For example, 'reserved' posts often go to relatively affluent members of disadvantaged castes. Therefore, for a policy of affirmative action to succeed not only does caste disadvantage have to be seen, but also the class background because that can make a substantial difference. Therefore, Sen is essentially arguing two things: that there are other sources of disparity apart from caste and class; and that while class disparities are important on their own, they are intensified by other forms of disparity.[6]

There are many different forms of deprivation such as poverty, illiteracy, political disempowerment, absence of healthcare, and others that can individually lead to different analytic results. There can be a strong temptation to see deprivation only in terms of poverty, but this can be quite misleading. All these factors can come together and lead to such severe deprivation that a big gulf is created between the comprehensive 'haves' from the comprehensive 'have-nots'. Yet often enough, as Sen points out, the same people are poor and illiterate, they work hard for minimal remuneration, are not influential in politics, lack social and economic opportunities, and are treated with brutal callousness by the police. This understanding and acceptance is necessary for effective affirmative action. Otherwise, the programmes for the disadvantaged can be cornered by those who have some vulnerability or deprivation but are certainly not the absolute underdogs of society. They may even end up worsening the deal for the real underdogs or those who are at the bottom layers of society and strengthening class divisions rather than weakening them. This is what Sen calls "friendly fire". It results in adding new barriers to the already existent ones. The very policies created to overcome the influence of class or caste may in actual have the opposite effect.

Intent of the Constituent Assembly

The question arises whether any other method can be used to take the benefits to those who really need it. At least two alternatives have been suggested. One is the use of purely economic criterion and the other to use diverse inputs to form a deprivation index as was done in JNU and later suggested by the Sachar Committee. Affirmative action based on economic criterion has been a persistent theme in the quota discourse in India. It was extensively debated in both the Indra Sawhney case (1993) and the Ashok Thakur case (2006). Justice Dalveer Bhandari in the Ashok Thakur case linked economic criterion to social backwardness while tracing the history of Article 15(4) of the Constitution. He pointed out that a careful analysis of the Constituent Assembly Debates revealed that the aim was to achieve a casteless and classless society for which socio-economic inequalities had to be urgently removed. Citing the Constitution Assembly Debates on Article 15(4), he said that Shri M.A. Ayyangar wanted to add 'economic' to ensure that the rich SEBCs did not receive special provisions. Shri Ayyangar said:

> I thought 'economic' might be added so that rich men may not take advantage of this provision. In my part of the country, there are the Nattukottai Chettiars who do not care to have English education but they are the richest of the lot, should there be a special reservation for them?[7]

He was satisfied that the term 'economic' was included in the term 'social'. Hence, the framers of the Constitution wanted to ensure that the richest of the (backward) lot would not benefit from the special provisions. Also, citing the Parliamentary Debates on the First Amendment Bill, Justice Dalveer Bhandari pointed out that the First Parliament too believed that, 'economic' was included in the 'social' portion of "socially and educationally backward". Prime Minister Nehru said:

> One of the main amendments or ideas put forward is in regard to the addition of the work 'economical'. Frankly, the argument put forward, with slight variation, I would accept, but my difficulty is that when we chose those particular words there, 'for the advancement of any socially and educationally backward classes, we chose them because they occur in Article 340 and we wanted to bring them bodily from there. Otherwise I would have had not the slightest objection to add economically.' But if I added 'economically', I would at the same time not make it a kind of cumulative thing but would say that a person who is lacking in any of these things should be helped. 'Socially' is a much wider word including many things and certainly including 'economically'. Therefore, I felt that 'socially and educationally' really cover the ground and at the same time you bring out a phrase used in another part of the Constitution in a slightly similar context.

Therefore, it was only because of the desire to achieve symmetry that the word 'economically' was not included. The question is whether the original framers intend to provide caste-based reservation only in jobs or also in education. Dalveer Bhandari argues that Article 15(4) was only added through the First Amendment and was a deviation from the goal of a casteless society. He points out that the original framers of the Constitution wrote prolifically and produced the world's longest Constitution in an attempt to remove as many doubts as possible. While they introduced a number of articles to reserve seats for various groups, they also imposed various limitations on reservation and these provided insights into the compromise they made between formal and substantial equality. Reservation was only provided for certain groups — SC, ST and BC— in certain areas like jobs in the government, seats in the Lok Sabha and Legislative Assemblies. Dr Ambedkar stated that, "The report of the Minorities Committee provided that all minorities should have two benefits or privileges, namely representation in the legislatures and representation in the services." Hence, additional benefits had to be added cautiously. In discussing draft Article 10 which found itself as Article 16(4) of the Constitution, Pandit Hriday Nath Kunzru observed:

> We are all aware that when the Report of the Minorities Committee was considered by the House, the entire House was anxious that

> reservations of whatever kind should be done away with as quickly as possible. Whatever protection might be considered necessary now, should be granted temporarily only so that the population of the country might become fully integrated, and no community or class might be tempted to claim special advantage for itself.

Instead of gradually removing reservations, the Parliament had gone the other way extending time limits and adding beneficiaries. Article 15(5) was just the latest example.

Justice Bhandari points out that while the original framers of the Constitution went out of their way to put SC/ST in the Parliament and State Assemblies and in government service, they did not reserve a single classroom seat. Instead, Article 29(2) prohibited caste-based discrimination in admissions, and Article 15(2) prohibited caste-based discrimination in general. Education was to remain reservation-free. When preferential treatment was given in regard to education, it was limited to educational grants and did not extend to reservations.

Rather than advocate for reservation, the original framers preferred free/compulsory education and scholarships. In the debate on Draft Article 294, Shri Brajeshwar Prasad noted that reservation in legislative bodies would fail to uplift SC/ST. Instead, he suggested that:

> It should be laid down clearly in express terms that free education shall be imparted to them...(and) for the tribals and Harijans provision must be made in the Constitution that free agricultural lands should be given to them. If we cannot give any one of these, I am quite clear in my own mind that by giving them a few seats here and there, their economic condition and their educational level will in no way be improved.[8]

In the Champakam Dorairajan (1951) case, the Union of India argued that Article 15(4), the First Amendment to the Constitution, reflects the intent of the original framers because it was passed by the same members that drafted the original Constitution. In the Parliamentary debates in 1951, Prime Minister Nehru argued in favour of amending the Constitution to overturn the judgement. This according to J. Bhandari[9] was a departure from the intent of the original framers who had drafted the original Constitution. Nehru displayed his awareness of this when he stated that Article 15(4) would give effect to, "what was really intended or should be intended." But what "should be intended" is always difficult to ascertain and so concludes Bhandari, Article 15(4) cannot be said to be the intent of the original framers.

Poverty as an Indicator of Social and Educational Backwardness

The issue of affirmative action can be seen in at least two ways: is it compensatory justice for past wrongs or is it distributive justice in the current scenario? Of course, past wrongs have had an undesirable impact on the present deprivation for certain sections but mere compensatory justice is simplistic and can progressively prove very divisive as time passes and the economic and developmental situation changes without adequately achieving what it seeks to do. The situation, as J. Kuldip Singh in the Indra Sawhney case points out, is far more complex, than what mere quotas can achieve.[10] He cites from Andre Beteille's book *The Backward Classes in Contemporary India* in which he argues that the problem of backward classes in India has been reduced largely to job reservation. However, their problems are too varied, large and acute for this to be done. Job reservation has not only done little to solve them, but has also diverted attention from the masses of Harijans and Adivasis who are too poor and lowly to even be able to avail themselves of the reserved job opportunities provided in their name. Job reservations, he argues, can only serve middle-class Harijans and Adivasis. The others, like the rest of the Indians, will remain outside it for the next several generations. Job reservation, says Beteille, is more a way of buying peace than of solving the age-old problems. Beteille makes a distinction between reservations for SCs, STs, and BCs. Reservations for SCs and STs, for all their limitations are directed basically towards the goal of greater overall equality. But reservations for OBCs and religious minorities, whatever may be their advantages, are really directed towards balance of power. The former, says Beteille, are in tune with the spirit of the Constitution, the latter must lead sooner or later to what Justice Gajendragadkar has called, "a fraud on the Constitution."

He added that protective discrimination in the shape of job reservations has to be programmed in a way that the most deserving of the BCs benefit and for this a means test could be devised. Backward classes can never be identified in a way that ensures that every member of that class is equally backward because there are bound to be disparities in the class itself. Some of its members may have individually crossed the barriers of backwardness but when identified with the class to which they belong they would come within the collectivity and be eligible for quotas. It can often be seen that there are some comparatively rich people in the backward class who may not have acquired any high level of education, but they move in society without being socially discriminated.

The members of the backward class, analyses Beteille, can be differentiated into superior and inferior. The discrimination that has been practised upon them by the superior class is in turn practiced by the affluent members of the backward class on the poorer members of the said class. The benefits of special privileges like job reservations inevitably go to the richer or more affluent sections of the backward classes; so, the poorer and the really backward sections among them keep getting poorer and more backward. Standards of deprivation and the extent of backwardness can only be put in place after looking at the lowest level of the backward class. The jobs are so few compared to the population of the backward classes that in any case it is difficult to give them adequate representation in the State services. Since it is necessary for the benefits of reservation to reach the poorest and the weakest section of the backward class, an economic ceiling to cut off the backward class to allow the benefit to reach the weakest section of the backward class is needed. Professor Beteille is pointing to the disjunct that takes place gradually between the levels of the individuals and of the group as a whole. Compensatory justice must gradually move towards distributive justice in order to benefit the most deprived individuals.

J. Kuldip Singh is in favour of using poverty as the dominant criterion for determining those who are socially and educationally backward. According to him, it is the main cause of all kinds of backwardness. A poor man is kept away from education and other societal benefits. Being caste neutral, poverty breeds social, economic and educational backwardness in any class so one can reasonably say that a person living below the poverty line is backward under Article 16(4).

Two reasons are advanced against using only the economic criterion:

1. Since social backwardness is a mandatory requirement under Article 16(4), only poverty cannot be an indicator for ascertaining backwardness under this article.
2. In this country, except for a small percentage of population, people are generally poor and hence they would all require reservation. This would defeat the purpose of reservation as reservation for all is really reservation for none.

J. Kuldip Singh has answered both the arguments. He thinks that the courts have erred in their reading of Articles 16(4) and 15(4). He points out that there is a distinction between them. The expression used in Article 16(4) is any "backward classes" and in Article 15(4), it is "socially and educationally backward classes". Hence, the scope of Article 16(4) cannot be limited by reading the expression "socially and educationally" used in Article 15(4). The object of Article 16(4) is to provide job reservations for those backward sections who have not found adequate representation in State service and in this context, the economic criterion is essentially relevant. In any case, any class of citizens living below the poverty line would come under "any backward class." Since poverty has a direct nexus to social backwardness, a rich person from a backward caste may or may not be socially backward, but a poor Brahmin struggling for his livelihood invariably suffers from social backwardness. The reality of present-day life, says J. Kuldip Singh, is that money confers social status on individuals. A poor person, however honest, has no social status, whereas a rich smuggler moves in high society. There are millions of people who belong to the so-called elite castes but are not only poor but even poorer than a very large proportion of the backward classes. It is a fallacy to think that a person though earning thousands or holding higher posts is still backward simply because he happens to belong to a particular caste or community, whereas millions of people living below the poverty line are forward because they were born in some other castes or communities. Poverty does not discriminate and binds all castes and religions in its common thread. Those who live in chronic-cramping poverty are socially backward *per se*. There are historical causes of poverty, but it is not possible to say that those who live under poverty conditions or below the poverty line are not socially backward. Hence, it would be doing "violence to the object, purpose and the language of Article 16(4) to say that the poor of the country are not eligible for job reservations." They cannot be denied their right simply because the claimants are very large in numbers.

J. Kuldip Singh points out that the numbers identified for reservation on caste basis are equally large. Mandal identified 52 per cent of the population as backward in addition to the 22 per cent of SCs and STs. Thus, in a way the demand is for reserving 74 per cent for the so-called backward classes. So it can hardly be said, says J. Kuldip Singh that 40 per cent of the poor can be denied job reservations. He then goes on to enumerate other indices that can be factored in like income, occupation, conditions of living such as slum dwellers, rural or urban and priorities can be worked out. It is high time, he feels that the dogmatic approach of making reservations in public services on the basis of caste as a symbol of backwardness is given up.

The Court is well aware of the difficulties of drawing lines as determining factors of backwardness. In the opinion of Pasayat and Thakker, the basis of exclusion should not be merely economic unless the economic advancement is so high that it necessarily means social advancement. Further, there are practical difficulties in imposing an income ceiling. It has to be such that it signifies social advancement. For example, an annual income of Rs 36,000 may not be much in metropolitan towns like

Delhi, Mumbai or Kolkata but would be a substantial income in rural India. The line that is to be drawn has to be a realistic one. Another question is whether such a line should be uniform for the entire country or for a given State or should it be different in rural and urban areas? Income from agriculture may be difficult to assess and therefore for agriculturists, the line may have to be drawn with reference to holding. Further, there are certain positions, the holding of which means social advancement as for example, the civil services.

The question really is, whether poverty indicators would be reliable enough to enable the truly needy to benefit. R.S. Deshpande and Amalendu Jyotishi maintain that the poor in India live largely in rural areas and are usually agricultural labourers by occupation. The density of labour is highest among the SCs and STs. The historical reason for this is that these groups of population, because of high stratification based on caste, were forced to remain at the lower rung of the economic hierarchy and had no occupational mobility. Poverty is largely concentrated in this group. The National Sample Survey data (1993–94) indicated that 52.17 per cent of SC population was below the poverty line and four per cent of STs were living even below the bare minimum threshold. The highest share of the poor is concentrated among households of agricultural labour and other labour households. Poverty is less in the households belonging to the category of other household occupations and self-employed in the non-agricultural sector.

Even though the majority of the poor are agricultural labourers, there are no clear policy programmes focusing specifically on them. Agricultural labourers belonging to SCs have also not been able to benefit from governmental policies because they are not organised and hence unable to plead their case. Even the Minimum Wages Act by which they could benefit somewhat is more on paper than in practice. There are very few facilities available in rural areas and they are even worse for SCs and STs. Only about five per cent of SCs and STs for example, have even proper toilet facilities. All factors point to an urgent need for larger investment towards development of infrastructure, especially for the weaker sections.

T.N. Srinivasan points out the inadequacies and uncertainties in determining poverty lines and consequently of the efforts to provide ameliorative measures for the weaker sections based on them.[11] Bibek Debroy, an economist has talked of multiple indicators to determine the segment of population that need to be helped. Caste cannot be the determinant.[12] He has pointed out that when the Courts imposed a ceiling of 50 per cent on reservations in 1963 in the Balaji Case (AIR 1963 SC 649), 50 per cent of India's population was actually below the poverty line. The National Sample Survey data shows a BPL figure of 27.5 per cent in 2004–05 according to one method and 21.8 per cent according to another. Hence, if we continue to harp on 50 per cent, Debroy feels that we fail to recognise that India has changed. There is a tendency to assume that all SCs, STs and OBCs, women, physically handicapped, ex-servicemen, those born from inter-caste marriages, dependents of armed forces personnel killed in action and Muslims are poor and so must benefit from quota reservations. The situation gets worse when caste is confused with class. The concept of caste-based quotas is based on two assumptions:

1. Everyone from backward castes is economically backward.
2. Everyone in a forward caste is economically forward even if he comes from the poorest areas of the country.

This is not borne out by data. For example, Orissa has 46.4 per cent population below the poverty line but the combined population of SCs/STs/OBCs based on NSS of 1999–2000 is 29 per cent. On the other hand, it is 66 per cent in Tamil Nadu, which is a more prosperous State.

Debroy argues that there is deprivation among the backward classes but it is of individuals and not of a group and so cannot be ascribed merely to a caste or geographical location. According to him, the mode of affirmative action can be debated but the more important issue is to identify the poor and poverty is not economic alone. Other indicators also need to be used such as, locations that lack any social or physical infrastructure worth the name. Other such collective elements can be factored in as suggested by scholars such as Purushottam Agrawal, Yogendra Yadav and Satish Deshpande as also by the Sachar Committee. The Planning Commission too has put forward thirteen parameters. Whatever method be used, says Debroy, the overall beneficiaries should not be more than 20 per cent for it to be truly beneficial. The index too cannot be too complicated. The UNDP, for example, has a simple human development index based on per capita income, education and health. Other alternate indices can be devised.[13]

The Diversity Index

Gender, poverty, caste, religion, region, occupation and habitation are some of the factors that reduce equality of opportunity and deny or reduce access. The Jawaharlal Nehru University devised a deprivation index which it uses in its admissions with a fair degree of success as the data of 2002–07 shows:[14]

Diverse Background and Regional Profile of JNU Students in Respect of the Last Five Years (2002–07) Admissions

Students Group	*Average of Last Five Years (per cent)*
Scheduled Castes	14.89
Scheduled Tribes	08.84
Other Backward Classes	>21.0
Minorities	>10.0
Differently-abled	02.79
Men	65.86
Women	34.14
Rural Background	35.87
Urban Background	64.12
Public School Background	27.21
Other School Background	72.77
Income below Rs 3000 p.m.	21.37
Income from Rs 3000 to 6000 p.m.	21.84
Income above Rs 6000 p.m.	56.77

Compiled by Prof. R.K. Kale, Professor in Life Sciences and Dean of Students, JNU from the JNU Annual Reports.

This was done to achieve a measure of social justice without compromising standards. The JNU students, says R.K. Kale, come from 28 States and 7 Union Territories. They have done their bachelors' degrees from more than 130 Indian universities/institutions/ boards. Another interesting feature is that only 27 per cent of the candidates had their schooling in public schools and 73 per cent came from municipal and non-public schools. While there was no mechanism available to count social groups such as minorities, according to a rough estimate more than 10 per cent of the students on campus were Muslims. If other minority religious groups were also included, the number of minority students would be even greater.

OBC candidates were drawn from the lists drawn up by the Government of India excluding the creamy layer and excluding income tax payers. Women OBC candidates were awarded ten deprivation points and the men five. The university recognised the rural and urban divide and realised that it has a significant cause of lack of access, equity, equality and quality because of the kind of education imparted in rural India. JNU undertook an extensive exercise to characterise and categorise all the districts in the country and group them State-wise. These were placed in different quartiles according to their backwardness. Deprivation points were awarded to all candidates including the OBCs, who had passed the qualifying entrance exam. Those coming from quartile one districts were given five points and those from quartile two, three points. Three parameters were used to place the districts in quartile one or two:

(i) Literates as percentage of total population after excluding the population of children from 0–6 years according to figures of Population Census 2001.

(ii) Non-agricultural workers as percentage of total workers according to census 2001.

(iii) Agricultural productivity per hectare averaged over 1997–98 and 1998–99.

The use of such indices resulted in 21 per cent OBC students being admitted from the non-creamy layer.

Conclusion

The case for affirmative action for disadvantaged groups can be made both on account of historical deprivation and for persistence of disparity and continuing discrimination. Dalits in India have historically suffered grave injustices, disparity, deprivation and discrimination. Compensatory policies can be designed for these historical wrongs, but over time they become highly contentious and gradually may not even reach the targeted groups. There is also evidence to suggest that the current economic and social systems perpetuate patterns of group-based disparities in all spheres of life, education, occupation/work, income/consumption and health indicators. This is seen in the access to schooling that the underprivileged have and their poor rates of success. A diversity index becomes a set of secular indices to target the most needy and devise policies accordingly. It can be more effective and more nuanced and also less contentious as it targets needy individuals rather than groups merely based on caste or religion. The Kundu Committee's recommendations were unfortunately not accepted by the Ministry of Human Resource Development without being given a chance to be debated and discussed in the public domain. The continued use of caste can lead to further divisions in a society getting progressively fragmented.

References

1. Thorat, Sukhdeo. "Higher Education in India: Emerging Issues Related to Access, Inclusiveness and Quality", www.ugc.ac.in/oldpdf/chair_sdt/chairman_nehru_lecture.pdf

2. Dongaonkar, Dayanand. "Missing Links in Education System in India", www.disc.in/Downloads/use of 20%20disc% 20 data/prof%20 Dayanand% 20Dongaonkal.pdf
3. Out of school children and dropout, a national emergency: UNICEF, *The Hindu*, April 13, 2013.
4. Ambedkar, Dr B.R. on Republic Day (26th January), openspace.org.in/node/ 822.
5. Sen, Amartya. 2005. *The Argumentative Indian: Writings on Indian History, Culture and Identity*. London and New York: Allan Lave.
6. *Ibid.*
7. Cited in *Ashok Thakur vs Union of India*, 2008 indiakanoon.org/doc/1219385.
8. Ashok Thakur Case, 2008. See also Constituent Assembly Debates on August 24, 1949, Part I, indiakanoon.org/doc/622068
9. Ashok Thakur Case.
10. *Indra Sawhney vs Union of India*, 16th Nov. 1998. indiankanoon.org/doc/ 1363234 Alternative Citations, AIR1993SC477, 1992 Supp.2 SCR 454.
11. Srinivasan, T.N. 2007. "Poverty Lines in India: Reflections after the Patna Conference", Vijaybhaskars.tripod.com/NIRD/pvlines.pdf
12. Debroy, Bibek. 2007. "Body Mass Politic", *Indian Express*, May 21, 2007.
13. *Ibid.*
14. Ray, Aswini K. "Reservation and Affirmative Action: The JNU Model," University News, Vol. XLIV, No. 49.

11

Access and Equity through Tertiary Education

In India, access to higher education is about 20 per cent, which is low. The dropout at the school level itself is very high, over 65 per cent. This shows that only a very small percentage of students have access to higher education. The dropout level and the failure rate even at the tertiary stage for those who do manage to enter college, indicate that for any meaningful access, the school education system must deliver. It is the real base for human resource. No changes in higher education will provide a satisfactory outcome unless the schooling improves. Pratham, a leading NGO in education, has pointed out in the tenth annual status of Education Report (ASER 2014) that was released on 13 January, 2015 revealed that for six years in a row, school enrollment in India was 96 per cent or above for the age group of 6–14 years and hence India was close to universal enrollment in this age group. The out-of-school children have remained in this age cohort at 3.3 per cent for the last three years. However, the learning outcomes still remain a grave cause of concern. About 25 per cent of class 8 students could not read a class 2 text. This implies that 75 per cent of class 8-level students can somehow manage to read a class 2-level text. In 2014, only one-fourth of all children in class 3 could read a class 2 text fluently and the numbers rose to half in class 5. Mathematics remains an area of concern. The situation is better than before but is still not adequate. Such outcomes mean that majority of the workforce in India lacks education. Further, they have to contend with an outdated system that involves rote learning rather than learning skills, understanding information and solving practical problems. Hence, the relevance of education at the tertiary level has also to be looked at.[1]

A large number of students are left out of the system. A study by Dr Sudhanshu Bhushan in 2004 divides the left-out students into three categories:[2] left out at the school level, pre-college level, and college level. In all these areas combined, there are about 30 million students with little or no alternatives. They need to have a well-developed tier of vocational education that links with school education on the one hand and higher education on the other. Vocational education is available in the form of Polytechnics, Industrial Training Institutes and, more recently, Community Colleges. However, all of them suffer from lack of resources and poor implementation.

The NSSO 61st Round states that while 70 per cent of the population completed primary education in the 18–22 age group, only six per cent completed a diploma course; and 97 per cent of the workforce in the country, in the 15–60 age group has no technical education. The inability of the system to provide continuation of education leads to fewer students going to the next levels of education, resulting in an inability to meet the needs of the job market, lower employability and an accumulation of people with low skills at the bottom of the job pyramid. Similar findings are seen in the Report on Condition of Work and Promotion of Livelihoods in the Unorganised Sector (2007). The average number of years of schooling of workers in the rural, unorganised non-agricultural sector was found to be 4.6 as compared to nine years in the organised sector, and for the unorganised agricultural sector it was 2.8. Mean years of schooling among casual workers in the unorganised non-agricultural sector was 3.5, thus denying workers access to jobs in the organised sector and confining them to casual labour.

With the commercialisation of agriculture, crop diversification and introduction of new technologies, education has become a key input even for the development and modernisation of agriculture and the welfare of the people dependent on it. Levels of illiteracy are such that it is almost impossible for them to assimilate new information on better agricultural practices.

Jayan Jose Thomas, commenting on the latest NSSO report pointed out that the generation of non-agricultural employment in India accelerated after the middle of the first decade of this century. At the same time, job creation has not kept pace with the rising supply of potential workers, especially females. With workers moving away from agriculture because of their rising educational attainments, this challenge will only grow bigger in the coming years, particularly in the rural areas. Unless economic growth revolves around employment, the country risks losing its demographic dividend.[3]

Why Access

Now, why should there be a focus on access to higher education when the school system obviously needs so much strengthening? Obviously because one of the aims of higher education is empowerment through economically productive employment. It has been argued in the case of Scheduled Caste/Scheduled Tribe (SC/ST) that even economic empowerment does not necessarily mean social empowerment. However, in simplistic terms, while empowerment can be social or economic, if one has to choose between the two, the latter is more important than the former. With economic empowerment, the social gradually follows or even if it doesn't, its effects are not so terribly debilitating. However, the existing system of higher education in India is not conducive to providing skills necessary for employment and a majority of Indian graduates are actually unemployable. The vocational sector of education is woefully lacking and the academic sector is not delivering the way it should. The problems have assumed serious proportions and there is an extreme urgency to introduce a skill or career orientation into tertiary education, which is available together with the academic stream and between which points of convergence can be created.

The Indian Labour Report 2007, by Team Lease Services states that while poverty is declining in India, inequality is rising and 57 per cent of Indian youth suffer from some form of skill deprivation. Corporate India cannot find skilled employees and much of the labour force is the 'working poor'. Despite the large human resource available in the country, employability remains a key challenge. Pressures on employment arise from several factors including shift in the demographics of the population, the inability of an ailing agricultural sector to support labour and an educational system that is not in sync with the requirements of business and industry. The inadequate interaction between the academics on the one hand and business and industry on the other results in a lack of focus on the skill development of individuals. The decision of most individuals to continue with education depends on their receiving adequate returns for the efforts made, and the current system does not enable them to do so, resulting in dropouts, under-trained and under-skilled labour. Globally, two approaches are followed to achieve better employability—educational reforms followed by a focus on lifelong learning opportunities.

Although the number of colleges and universities has mushroomed in the country, they lack the ability to impart career-oriented knowledge and training; curricula are outdated; there is little interaction between industry and educational institutes, and only about 10 per cent of the colleges show good academic achievement. The poor quality of colleges means that students passing out of them would earn low incomes or would be unable to find jobs relevant to the courses pursued by them. This is also one of the causes for the high levels of dropouts in higher education. When future prospects are not attractive, the better option appears to be to dropout, particularly for the deprived sections of society.

Further, there is a wide range of income divergence within the same stream depending on the quality of skills. Although higher education levels can help an individual reach the desired employment, sustainability depends on how well the skills are adapted and improved over time. It is thus the quality of the institute that imparts the education or training, which is the most important determinant of the income-earning potential. While the top institutes usually registered 100 per cent placements, the bottom ones barely managed 25 per cent. This was true for all streams of education in the country, emphasising the fact that good infrastructure, instruction and other inputs were essential to ensure high standards of education, liberal or vocational, and this was lacking in the majority of educational institutes.

The Half Yearly edition of Team Lease Employment Outlook Report for October, 2014–March, 2015, also shows that employers need newer and more sophisticated skills while aspirations of candidates for cutting-edge careers was also increasing. The gap that separates the two consists of institutional inadequacies that empower candidates with technological and market-focused capabilities. Employers are also placing more emphasis on soft skills and team and collaborative skills, together with technological tools that would lead an employee to fit into the organisation.

Resistance to Vocational Education

There has been resistance among students to vocational education in India because of the perception that it is meant for those who are not good at academics. But with the opening up of the economy, the demand for specialised skills has gone up manifold. To meet this demand, the focus on vocational education has to be directed at the school level. It may be argued that vocational education was attempted earlier and the endeavour failed. It is necessary to analyse why this happened. One on-going reason is that if a student opts for a vocational subject at the school level, he or she has no opportunity to pursue this or an allied subject at the tertiary level. In colleges and universities, no credit is given for the vocational subject studied at the school level and so it actually becomes a disadvantage to do so. Also, at the time that vocationalisation was attempted in India, the economy did not have the capacity to absorb skilled human resources at different levels that it has now and the demand can only grow. Another drawback is that a person in the vocational stream has little or no opportunity to rejoin the academic stream at any point in his/her life without starting totally afresh. In other words, no credit is given for either the vocational knowledge or the work experience acquired.

While universities may prepare engineers, scientists, industrialists and social leaders of a country, a second-tier educational level is essential to produce the middle-level technologists who can manage and maintain the industrial infrastructure. Without such an educated and technical workforce, there can be no progress. Steps were taken during the early 1980s to introduce Application-oriented Courses (AOCs) within the framework of the graduate courses and in the 1990s, several self-financing institutions sprang up with the approval of universities and State government to run job-oriented programmes in fields such as electronic, computer science, accountancy, food science, hospital and hotel management and others, which have been popular with students. The University Grants Commission also introduced vocational courses as part of the three-year bachelor's degree courses. The curriculum was restructured to integrate the vocational angle. Add-on courses oriented towards skill development were also allowed outside the timetable.

This appears to be confused thinking as academic colleges are not oriented towards vocational education and do not have the wherewithal to do so. Heads of academic educational institutions have difficulty in identifying industries for practical application work and funding agencies to finance the training. There is still a considerable gap in what the industry wants and colleges are able to provide. The country needs different levels at the tertiary education system so that a bouquet of options is available. This will bridge the gap between what the students are taught and the demands of the workforce. It will also provide opportunities for training to the large unskilled workforce available in India. There is also a backlog of school dropouts who are over the school age of sixteen and work as unskilled workers. According to an ILO report, 95 per cent of the Indian workforce has no marketable skills. This vast need for productive skills cannot be achieved only through the formal sector especially if it is as rigid as it tends to be in India. A parallel informal, flexible system is also required to identify and develop local talent for local needs.

Industrial Training Institutes

Vocational and technical training as a means of empowerment is not a new idea. It has been recommended and tried much earlier but with limited success. Technical and vocational training was considered very important for the underprivileged and marginalised groups to improve their productivity, particularly as they were usually first-generation learners. Traditionally too, they had been engaged in skilled and semi-skilled work and were likely to perform better in those areas. Also, there were more opportunities for their employment in the newly-established industries where jobs were reserved for them. The major vocational institutions imparting training for middle-level technical personnel were polytechnics, industrial training institutes, junior technical schools, crafts and handicrafts schools, and other industrial and technical schools.

The Secondary Education Commission, in 1953,[4] had recommended the setting up of technical schools, as separate institutes or as part of existing institutes, in industrial areas, which would work in collaboration with industries. When the Commission reviewed the situation in 1964–66, it found a shortfall of middle-level technical personnel and recommended an increase of part-time and full-time vocational and professional courses at the lower secondary level and after Class 12. It also reported that semi-skilled and skilled workers were primarily trained in the ITIs, while technicians were trained in polytechnic. A doubling of ITIs was recommended. Most importantly, it was recommended that the courses should allow for students to move to the academic stream. This, however, has never happened and there are no enabling structures or systems to date.

Further, the Working Group on Technical and Vocational Education recommended in 1978 that the ratio between graduates and technicians should be 1:2, but the output ratio dropped to 1:1.[5] The main reason for this was that students belonging to different backgrounds found it difficult to adjust, facilities were not fully utilised, there was shortage of operating funds and lack of motivation in both teachers and students. The Working Group emphasised that it was necessary to consolidate, diversify and improve quality in existing institutions before attempting further expansion. The Sixth Five-Year Plan, 1980–85 made similar recommendations, and also stressed that ITIs had to be revamped to orient them towards self-employment.

The thinking persisted well into the 1980s that technical and vocational training was especially useful for the SCs and STs, the most disempowered sections of society as it could provide skills for job opportunities that were continuously expanding. A study of five States on,'Scheduled Castes and Scheduled Tribes in Industrial Training Institutes' was conducted by the National Institute for Educational Planning and Administration (NIEPA) in the early 1980s. The study indicated that while the utilisation of the facilities in the ITIs was good for SCs, there was a considerable gap in the case of STs, even in the special ITIs set up in tribal areas, that were well-equipped, but lacked motivated personnel. Their enrollment rates were far below those of other groups and much less than their proportion in the population, with large-scale State-wise variations, despite reservations. Several studies showed that the reserved quota was seldom fully utilised, mainly because the number of qualified students was inadequate. This was particularly true for the STs. One solution recommended was to make district-wise reservations rather than course-wise. Wastage in terms of failures and dropouts is high. Most ex-trainees work as apprentices and self-employment was minimal. Further, the waiting time to get a job was higher for SCs/STs as compared to others and the special incentives for them were found to be inadequate and the implementation of schemes was defective.

Polytechnics

Polytechnics were set up to build up the technical education system and there are about three hundred institutes, which had an annual intake of around 30,000 students. About 70 per cent of the polytechnics were run by State governments and the rest by private agencies or autonomous bodies. The institutes have three-year and two-year full-time courses and sandwich courses. However, because the machinery for systematic evaluation of their work and progress was inadequate, there was little feedback on performance.

A National Expert Committee, Chaired by S.S. Kalbag,[6] was set up in 1987 to appraise the status of community polytechnics in the country. It stated that for the balanced development of the country, human resource for all sectors, both the organised and the unorganised, had to be prepared by the technical education system. The All India Council for Technical Education recommended in as early as 1978 that a few select polytechnics that had shown initiative in promoting interaction with the rural community at large and had the necessary capacity to undertake rural development work, could be used as focal points to promote transfer of technology to the rural sector and make contributions to rural development. These polytechnics were designated as Community Polytechnics.

Community Polytechnics were to make a socio-economic technical survey of adjoining villages to determine the needs of the people. They were then to develop human resource and training through a wide variety of trade courses, non-formal training programmes, and entrepreneurial development programmes. Further, they were to facilitate technology transfer to rural areas and provide technical support service to ensure the sustenance of rural technologies. They were to also assist local entrepreneurs in various aspects of enterprise building by disseminating information, creating awareness about various developmental schemes and by applying science and technology to find solutions for specific problems.

These efforts however, met with limited success because of the inadequate implementation. There was little attempt to integrate the curricular activities of regular and community polytechnics. Scant attention was paid to costing in most of the projects undertaken by them. In some cases, the training courses organised for rural youth did not reflect the skill and potential of the polytechnic either in content or in methodology. This was further aggravated by a weak information system that limited technology transfer. Besides, since the entire institution was not involved in this activity, the efforts did not have the expected multiplier effect. It was therefore felt that the whole scheme needed to be reoriented. The main objective of the polytechnics had to be to develop the human resource in the rural areas through the development of technical skills. A scientific methodology needed to be used to identify the opportunities in the economic environment of the region and exploit them. This required that the polytechnics as a whole had to raise the science and technology level of their own staff and students by solving rural problems. This meant that Community Polytechnics needed to be strengthened and guided in the selection of projects so that they could perform more effectively as agents of change in the rural areas.

Since the level of technology in village society was low, polytechnics could be very useful in rural transformation. They could select a village institution, preferably a secondary school, to act as its village extension arm, where they could build training facilities for multi-skill programmes relevant to the village environment or of educational significance. Trainers could be developed from amongst the village youth including school teachers within the village centre and all training had to be multi-skilled, oriented towards self-employment. In addition, students had to be given the ability to read, write, communicate and also acquire some computational skills.

Little progress was made as was evident from the experience of a team from the Community Colleges for International Development (CCID) that visited India in the late 1980s to explore the possibilities of collaboration between the community colleges in the USA and the polytechnics of India. The CCID is a consortium of colleges that aims to pursue formal higher education with economic development, and take up skill development in developing countries. It found a severe mismatch between the industry's requirements and the skills learnt at polytechnics because of the lacuna in planning and implementation. There was limited specialisation and very little interaction between the polytechnics and the industry. The equipment was obsolete, faculty development was poor, and teachers had no incentive to make use of the Technical Teachers' Training Institute (TTTI) established in the country. The faculty did not keep abreast with the latest changing technologies within the local industries.

The team recommended that the present and future employment skills, knowledge and abilities required by industry had to be identified for curricula development and purchase of relevant equipment. Faculty had to be constantly upgraded and needed to maintain close contacts with industry so that obsolescence could be continuously taken care of in all areas such as, curriculum, equipment and pedagogy.

A Special Committee for Reorganisation and Development of Polytechnic Education was set up in 1991.[7] It agreed with most of these comments and recommendations of the CCID, accepting that even earlier there had been serious criticism of polytechnic education in the country by educationists, industrialists, professional bodies and employers. It had been pointed out that the diploma courses in polytechnics were mostly theoretical. Being a poor imitation of degree courses, they did not serve the purpose of training middle-level technical personnel. There was little attempt at specialisation and the industry linkages were weak. Also, faculty development and better academic infrastructure was required.

A survey of industries indicated that while diploma holders remained unemployed, a significant proportion of technicians' positions went to persons without formal qualifications but with job experience at the craftsman level. Students of polytechnics did not and could not fit directly into job situations in industry because of insufficient application orientation to the education and training imparted by polytechnics. The Committee found that the academic organisation and control did not permit flexibility and freedom to experiment and innovate in collaboration with the industry. Autonomy for polytechnics was essential to allow for innovations in curricula and pedagogy and for establishing meaningful industry linkages. Where this had been allowed, the quality of the institutions had improved.

Skills for Progress

Lacking effective skill development institutions, several private initiatives were being taken to meet the ever-expanding job requirements of the country. For example, Skills for Progress (SKIP), an all India association of private technical and vocational training institutions that collaborates with the Community Colleges for International Development

(CCID), USA. CCID and SKIP have been working on programmes focussing on curriculum and workforce development, communications and electronic education resources. The programmes aim at capacity building of institutions to stay relevant to the changing needs of vocational and technical training so as to enhance employability of the students.

Skill Development Initiative of the Confederation of Indian Industry (CII)

The Confederation of Indian Industry (CII) took the Skills Development Initiative in 2004, to provide social inclusiveness and bring the marginalised sections of society into the mainstream economy through empowerment by skill development. The main features of the initiative were its localised and need-based approach, practical hands-on experience, training and testing, accessibility, quality, cost-effectiveness and centralised certification. Under this initiative:

- Most training facilities as well as trainers function for 8–10 hours per weekday and they can be used for the remaining periods of time to save costs.
- Geographical areas and target groups are identified, following which the relevant skills—localised and marketable—that need to be developed are identified.
- The curricula are worked out in collaboration with the local industries.
- Panchayats and other local bodies are also consulted.
- Trainees are selected on the basis of their motivation and abilities and the programmes are flexible in scheduling.
- Constant monitoring and assessments of trainees are undertaken and unsuccessful candidates can reappear for assessments and can even join another batch for additional training.
- Certification is important as it indicates a certain minimum standard acceptable to industry throughout the country to allow for mobility of workers.

The India Skills Report 2014 by CII states that although India will have about 0.8 billion people in the working age group by 2020, if corrective steps are not taken, there would be a skill gap of 75–80 per cent across industry sectors. There will be people but with skills that the corporates do not need and jobs for which the right fit is not available. While the economic impact of this vicious cycle can be estimates, the social impact of having a powerhouse of educated yet frustrated youth is unimaginable.[8]

Weaknesses Pointed out by the Working Group on Higher Education—Eleventh Five-Year Plan

The Eleventh Five-Year Plan, known as the Education Plan because of its emphasis on education also accepts that there are several systemic challenges posed by tertiary education in India. It recognises that there is an abundance of talent in the country, which is mostly un-nurtured. There is lack of flexibility in the system leading to a mismatch between school and employment hours. Knowledge resources are not easily available and there are inadequate opportunities to use even what is there. The quality of teaching is questionable and there is a gap between the demand and supply of knowledge and skills together with lack of collaborative learning. There is little or no personalised monitoring and long-term tracking of learning, skill upgradation and performance. And finally, the situation is aggravated by a growing digital divide. Most of these issues are not new.

Changes were introduced in the Indian system that led to the creation of new types of institutions but the implementation left a lot to be desired. For example, when vocational/technical education was to be introduced, the 10+2+3 system was formulated, with the intention of bifurcating students to academic or vocational/technical education at the + 2 stage. Industrial Training Institutes (ITIs) and polytechnics were created, but subsequently very little attention was paid to the way these operate. The UGC also formulated a scheme in the 1990s to introduce B.A. (vocational) in which one vocational subject is taught together with other academic subjects. The lack of faculty and proper academic and physical infrastructure, however, did not allow it to take off successfully. Consequently, there has been no appreciable shift of students to the vocational streams in the existing institutes nor has the education impacted the students or the economy. An attempt was made to rectify both access to education and to strengthen vocational education in the Eleventh Five-Year Plan.

Open and Distance Learning (ODL)

The Eleventh Five-Year Plan envisaged increasing the enrollment from 11 to 20 per cent by 2012. The goal was to reach 30 per cent enrollment by the end of the Twelfth Five-Year Plan. One of the strategies was to strengthen the open and distance learning system that provides higher education to about 25 per cent of learners. The Eleventh Plan expected this figure to increase to 40 per cent providing quality education and training to a large learner population, by using ICT to create access and opportunities through the length and breadth of the country. The learner profile included the employed and the unemployed, those seeking to upgrade skills and knowledge while working, and the disadvantaged and the marginalised rural youth. The system developed a wide delivery network.

The National Open University, which is also the nodal institution for distance learning programming in the country, is the Indira Gandhi National Open University (IGNOU). It was established in 1985 to promote distance learning. It has widened access to higher education by adopting integrated multimedia instructions increasing its reach considerably through the use of Gyan Darshan, an educational TV channel and Gyan Vani, FM channels. It has a delivery network of 53 regional centres, 1,400 study centres and about 25,000 counsellors providing learner support. It has 28 FM radio stations and 6 TV channels, including three interactive channels. It has been given the responsibility to develop an additional 15 FM radio stations.

The focus of Open Distance Learning during the Eleventh Plan period was on professional, vocational, and career-oriented programmes at certificate, diploma and degree levels, concentrating on skill development, vocational training and community development programmes. Skill development has so far been underdeveloped, but two-way interactive platforms like EDUSAT have created a vast potential for short-term training and there has been a shift from enrichment programmes towards curriculum-based learning programmes. The system however, needs inputs in terms of research, innovations, development of resource material and dedicated networks for efficient delivery and system upgradation.

The Twelfth Plan states that Open and Distance Learning will be used to widen access and significantly expand capacity in a cost-effective and flexible manner. IGNOU, State and Open Universities and other institutions of distance education would be supported and increased to expand access, particularly for those beyond the normal schooling age. Such programmes would be regularly evaluated so that curricula and pedagogical changes can be made on an ongoing basis. There has been a growing concern about the quality of online and distance education programme and hence it is proposed to strengthen the regulatory oversight. Traditional institutions would be encouraged to offer part of their curriculum online so as to promote blended learning and provide students more choices, while keeping costs low. This would also enable them to reach out to more students and non-traditional learners.

Emphasis on Skill Development

The Eleventh Five-Year Plan had favoured a comprehensive National Skill Development Mission. As a result, a "Coordinated Action on Skill Development" with a three-tier institutional structure was established in

2008. It consisted of a PM's National Council; National Skill Development Coordination Board (NSDCB), and a National Skill Development Corporation (NSDC). The Prime Minister's National Council of Skill Development was to lay out the policy, the direction in the form of "Core Principles", and a vision to create 500 million skilled people by 2022 through skill systems having a high degree of inclusivity. Individual States also came up with plans and policies to face the challenge of skill development. The National Skill Development Coordination Board (NSDCB) under the aegis of the Planning Commission was to coordinate all these activities. The NSDC geared itself for preparing comprehensive action plans and activities that would promote Public Private Partnerships (PPP) models of financing skill development. The increasing emphasis on skill development and the government's seriousness on the subject were evident from the fact that in May 2014, a new Ministry was created for Skill Development and Entrepreneurship. The immediate mandate of the new Ministry was to ensure that India meets the target of skilling and up-skilling 500 million people in India by 2022. This is the first time that a separate ministry for skill development has been created.

Higher Education and Community Colleges

Apart from enhancing the distance learning system of education, the Eleventh Five-Year Plan's Working Group on Higher Education recommended the setting up of community colleges. It recognised that there were significant disparities in the GER for rural and urban areas, being 5.58 per cent and 21.74 per cent respectively in 2000, as per Census figures. The growth of higher education needed to be viewed from both the supply and the demand side. From the supply side, it needed to be ascertained that those who have passed the senior secondary level and were eligible to join higher education, had access to it. At the same time, higher education not only needed to grow but also needed to diversify to meet the growing needs of the economy and society. This meant that higher education should have backward linkages with school education and forward linkages with the economy to supply the relevant human resource along with well-qualified teachers for the education sector itself. For this to happen, the content of higher education needed continuity with the earlier levels of education. Care had to be taken to ensure that students did not take up courses and subjects, in an *ad hoc* manner as that would lead to wastage; at the same time, the system had to be flexible enough to enable them to choose their courses according to their own talents and inclinations.

The Eleventh Five-Year Plan accepted community colleges as an alternative system of education to help the poor, the tribal population and women to find gainful employment in collaboration with local industry, business and the community. The importance of community colleges was that they could provide education for a livelihood; and eliminate exclusion from the formal system. They could also reduce the mismatch between education and employment and thus be an important means of reducing poverty, unemployment, under-employment, un-employability and dropouts. The Plan stated that community colleges had the unique record of empowering the socially, economically and educationally backward sections of society during the past ten years wherever they have been started.

The Working Group on the Eleventh Plan recommended the national recognition of the Community College system; and the vertical mobility of the Community College student through open and conventional universities with a three-tier system of diploma, associate degree and degree. Community colleges needed to be set up in educationally backward regions to correct regional imbalances in higher education with emphasis on the development of soft skills. Central placement cells could be set up in collaboration with the Confederation of Indian Industry and Chambers of Commerce. The reach of community colleges could be further strengthened through distance learning for those students who were unable to commute to college or stay in hostels.

The Twelfth Plan promises to place special emphasis on skill-based programmes in higher education. A framework for setting up community colleges based on the North American is to be developed. This has been endorsed in principle by the Central Advisory Body on Education.

Community Colleges

The Community College or the people's college as developed in the US could well be adapted to the Indian system of education to offer quality education, with technical and vocational training, in order to create competent career-oriented individuals.

American community colleges are designed as comprehensive institutions combining liberal arts, vocational, technical and adult education. They have two-year duration courses and students accumulate credits that are transferable to colleges of higher education. A majority of students complete the first two years of junior college at such institutions. They have an open-door policy that enables almost anyone seeking higher education or the enhancement of vocational and technical skills to enrol. Today, in the Indian system, barring open universities and schools, and those offering correspondence courses, this is difficult, if not impossible.

Community colleges can be linked to specific universities and colleges so that credits gained in them can be used to enter mainstream higher education. Typically, students of community colleges would be older to 'traditional' students, would not have parental financial support and would most likely be part-time students, who are holding down jobs. Additionally, community colleges can work in partnership with business organisations, thereby ensuring that skills are kept up-to-date and meet the requirements of the job market. Courses could include agriculture, engineering technologies, communications, healthcare, office occupations, computers, data processing, trade, tourism, hospitality and others. These could be part-time or full-time; short duration courses of 10–15 weeks, or long ones of up to two years.

Community colleges link education with technical and vocational training, developing skills in the emerging or sunrise industries. They conform to some concepts enunciated in the National Policy of Education of India such as open access, continuing education and vocational training. These have a better chance of success in the current environment than before because there is a growing trend to reject 'liberal' higher education, which is seen as elitist and to view higher education as a source for trained human resource. The technological explosion has created a need for highly educated theoretical scientists and experts in the service and other industries, supported by a strong structure of technicians and middle-level staff. Community colleges also provide motivational programmes and help disadvantaged students to develop self-esteem together with realistic career options. They are locally controlled and are responsive to the needs of the local community, industry and business. Their aim is to provide students with relevant, quality job skills instituted in consultation with local industry and business. Teachers work in industry and industry too provides teachers from its personnel. Finally, community colleges act as cultural and intellectual centres for the entire community and as catalysts in development.

These are all important aspects in the Indian context, with its vast range of cultural and linguistic diversity, differing educational requirements and economic development. An educational institution located in a particular region, responsive to regional needs and aspirations would mean better, low-cost education, resulting in improved economic development opportunities for the people.

There are three types of courses that such colleges can offer which could suit Indian requirements:

- First, vocational and technical courses.

- Second, a two-year programme that prepares students for transfer to a three-year bachelor's degree in science, arts or commerce at a traditional college.
- Third, a remedial programme that brings students up to the required levels in reading, writing, mathematics and communication so that they can pursue further education. This is eminently suited to the Indian environment, with a large number of first-generation learners, who do not have home support for their studies and lag behind, frequently resulting in dropouts; those who have already dropped out of the education system, and could have even reverted to illiteracy; and adults who may not have had an opportunity to study.

It has been proved beyond doubt that several Indian children are not academically prepared to compete for entrance to institutions of higher education. This applies to a diverse body of students but especially to many who have had low quality schooling. These are usually the poor and other marginalised sections of society. On several occasions, it has been seen that these students are unable to cope with the courses they have entered. This is where remedial colleges, with an open-door policy would bring significant benefits; even though it means that the period of study may increase. For this, however, the government needs to show sincere commitment and provide the required resources.

Since these institutions would all have a general education component, students who originally joined a vocational or remedial course, have the opportunity to prepare for higher college courses, if they come up to the required standards. Courses could be designed to give diplomas, certificates, and, as in the case of the US, associate degrees, that could equal a certain number of credits, enabling entrance to traditional universities. These could be designed for skill upgradation in collaboration with industrial houses, or for the development of new skills, particularly in the 'sunrise industries'. Therefore, the philosophy of a community college is an institution that provides transfer to higher education and prepares a student for an occupation. Being locally based and supported by the community, it is expected to link the aspirations of the community through an education that provides employment or higher education. It accommodates over-achievers and under-achievers.

Fulfilling the Constitutional Provisions of Access, Equity and Relevance in Higher Education

Community colleges appear to be the ideal solution to fulfil the constitutional provisions of access, equity and relevance in higher education as they give an opportunity to all those seeking tertiary education but are unable to qualify for admission to a university. They provide the much-needed skills for employment while simultaneously facilitating lateral entry into academic courses. As the community itself is involved in the colleges, there is a greater commitment to their success. It also enables links with industry and this minimises obsolescence in curricula.

Many existing institutions can be transformed to suit the educational requirements of the communities they serve. If the community college programme of two-year duration provides comprehensive education to students, it opens opportunities for those aspiring to higher degrees and graduation, to step into the traditional formal universities and colleges. At present, those students who opt for vocational/technical training at the +2 stage have no opportunity to move to universities at any stage in their lives. Therefore, the Indian educational institutions at the lower levels of higher education need to be transformed to be more receptive to local community needs, while providing adequate comprehensive education and maintaining links with formal higher education institutions and bodies. The latter has to also develop flexible structures to accommodate those coming from the vocational stream.

Community colleges are needed where there are an adequate number of school pass-outs to make use of them and where such facilities are not available. These can be both in urban and rural areas. In rural areas, which are remote and backward, community colleges could immediately provide the much-needed access. Urban areas have a perennial shortage of educational institutions and community colleges could share some of that pressure. Of course, it would help if within a reasonable distance there were large-scale industries and businesses, which would enable adequate number of learners to get absorbed within the area. Where facilities such as polytechnics, and arts and science colleges are available but are not being properly utilised, these can be converted, partially or wholly to community colleges. Of course, communities have to be aware of and amenable to supporting such ventures.

References

1. Img.arercentre.org/docs/publications/ASER%20Reports/ASER%202014/National %20PPTs/aser2014indiaenglish.pdf

2. Bhushan, Sudhanshu and Kauser Wizarat. *Alternative and Innovative Forms of Higher Education of Left Out Youth*, New Delhi: NUEPA (Unpublished).

3. Thomas, Jayan Jose. 2014. The Demographic Challenge and Employment Growth in India, *Economic and Political Weekly*, Feb. 8, 2014, 49: 6.

4. www.kkhsou.in/main/education/secondary_education.html
5. Kolhatkar, M.R. 1997. *Educational Planning and National Development: Some Crucial Aspects*, New Delhi: MD Publications.
6. www.teindia.nic.in/mhrd/50yrsedu/g/T/HB/OTHB07.htm
7. Saha Samir Kumar and Sangita Ghosh, "Commissions and Committees on Technical Education in Independent India: An Appraisal," *Indian Journal of History of Science*, 47.1 (2012), 109-136.

   (www.insa.nic.in/writeraddata/uploadpiles/IJHS/VOl47_1_6_sksaha.pdf).
8. https://wheebox.com/whebox/resources/Indiaskills Report.pdf.

   See also India Skills Report 2015; http://wheebox.com/india-skills-report-2015.htm

Part - III

12

Education and the Widening of Consciousness

The aim of education is two-fold: collective and individual. At the collective level, the aim is to make an individual into a good citizen, that is, a person with harmonious relationship with other members of the community, a person useful to society, and one who fulfils his or her obligations as a citizen. At the individual level, the student expects an educational institution to help him or her to develop a strong and healthy body, build his or her character, attain self-mastery and supply opportunities to discover and realise natural abilities.[1]

Both expectations are justified but it is necessary to understand the relationship between the individual and society and that the aspirations of the two need to be mutually harmonised. The human mind tends to emphasise one or the other and the current dominant thought is that individual interest must be subordinated to societal interest. Therefore, the collective aim of education has overshadowed the individual aim and the chief challenge facing educators is how to fit the individual to the demands of society.

The needs of society are determined by what society thinks it requires at that point of time. For example, at the time of war, society may require defence personnel, scientists for arms industries, traders in arms and ammunition, defence strategists, and others. Such societal aims are usually determined by the perceptions of the ruling class. If there are powerful patrons of culture, society will produce artists of all kinds. If industrialisation is taking place, then the need will be for engineers and technicians.

There are less obvious societal influences on individuals. For example, if competition is a cherished value of society, a person may be thrown into the corporate jungle after completing higher education primarily on his own resources and with whatever help he can get from family and friends. This is also because a paradigm shift has taken place from hereditary trades to the freedom of choice for the individual. The price for it is greater insecurity and consequent mental tension.

Again, money has come to play a vital role in modern society. For example, in a technologically-driven society, the greater the investment in research and development, the greater the number of scientific discoveries and inventions translating into increased productivity and creation of wealth. In such a society, money becomes an indispensable condition of material achievement and the benchmark of success. The same money also becomes a corrupting agent because it is not always the most honest and capable who get the greatest share of it but often the clever and the crafty.

Education is supposed to give the intellectual elite for society and mould it through them but, in actual fact, systems of education and society influence each other. Since modern education is also a means of upward mobility in society, it leads to a race for marketable degrees rather to for real knowledge and much less to wisdom.[2]

Developments in the Twentieth Century

The twentieth century belonged to the West. Events and movements that started mainly in the West from around the fifteenth century with the Renaissance culminated in the twentieth century. The seventeenth century brought the idea of progress through Enlightenment and for the next two centuries, Europe became a scene of intense intellectual activity in the field of education and culture. Keen interest developed in the applied sciences as humankind tried to break free from tradition, convention and prejudice. The Age of Enlightenment and Reason brought a great sense of optimism and paved the way for the Industrial Revolution. In between came the upheavals of the American Independence, the French Revolution and the subsequent Napoleonic wars. With the Industrial Revolution, technology was harnessed to the production of economic wealth and material prosperity. Wealth and the means of its production became the focus of study for the first time. Science and technology made nature subservient to man and money was enthroned replacing human values. However, the pursuit and accumulation of wealth led to the terrible exploitation of man by man. This became the first cause of disillusionment in the agenda of progress as intense hostility developed between the workers and the employers.

Other disillusionments were to follow. Science had claimed the pursuit of truth as its ideal. It was seen as the chief tool of progress; not just material progress but also of moral progress. The belief was that as men acquired more knowledge, they would become wiser and consequently more impartial and just. The subsequent course of events belied this faith. Liberty, equality and fraternity, the great ideals of the French Revolution that aroused so much enthusiasm, proved to be hollow words as events unfolded. Democratic institutions that men fought to build and died for also proved to be so imperfect that often they ended up supporting greater authoritarianism and corruption than the ones they replaced.

The truth of science in itself got limited to only that knowledge, which was gained through the senses. By dismissing possibilities of any higher form or source of knowledge, utility replaced truth as the object of science. This is not a value judgement as this point of view in itself proved very useful in helping the human mind to get rid of irrational beliefs and blind superstitions. It led to a marked advance in the economic sphere, raising standards of living, improving healthcare, and ameliorating conditions of work. Far-reaching societal changes came about like the abolition of slavery and child labour, dismantling colonialism, protection of the rights of workers leading to improvement in their social status, emancipation of women, better healthcare services, elimination of famines and starvation deaths and increase in longevity.[3]

However, two other things also took place:

- Different nations arrived at different levels of material prosperity for historical and sociological reasons and within each of them, too, there were marked inequalities.
- No amount of material progress and social engineering could prevent the two major world wars, which caused massive destruction; not to speak of regional wars that continue and never ever having come to a halt.

Interconnectedness and Technology

However, from the very places where material progress and collective societal wealth seemed to have reached its peak, subtle signs of change have also begun to emerge. There is growing realisation that we are all interconnected. This has been a consequence of breakthroughs in technology and rapid transport and communication that have made the world a global village by creating a global network. Actions in one part of the world have repercussions on people, places and events in other parts. Further, mass communication and satellite technologies have all ensured that now there are no more secrets. All movements, whether environmental or human, can be mapped and recorded.

The realisation that our actions do not take place in isolation but have far-reaching implications has led to several grassroots movements through non-governmental organisations, social activism and propagation of practices such as the recycling of waste, tapping of alternative energy sources, holistic medicine and others. We are just beginning to comprehend that we cannot confine ourselves to the narrow spheres of our own personal identities or even of the identities of family and immediate community. We need to expand our vision to not only include the nation but the entire humanity and also non-beings in nature. If we are all so interconnected, existence cannot be a ladder of hierarchies but rather of networks, interrelationships and connectedness requiring an ability to see eternity in a grain of sand.

A telling example given by Thich Nhat Hanh is a case in point. A sheet of paper combines the universe. It has clouds that bring rain that nourishes the tree, which is cut to make the paper. It therefore has the air, the water, the sunlight, the soil, the seed, the work of the logger who made it into paper, the elements of the implements used and of those who made them, and all that went into its production, and so on. The list is endless and leads to the embracing of the entire universe. When such a perception dawns, the nature of awareness or consciousness is also bound to change. It makes us realise that we have the potential to evolve to higher levels of consciousness that embrace all creation rather than the narrow immediate one from where we usually function. Also, we understand that things have different significances and meanings for different people according to the levels of their consciousness. Hence, there is no one single objective truth but many truths and we have the potential of finding greater meaning and significance in our milieu and thus in our own lives according to the level of our consciousness.[4]

Bertrand Russell analysed the far-reaching effects of modern knowledge on the growth of our mental life that influences our way of thinking, willing and feeling. The three are interconnected because knowledge has given us the kind of power that was perhaps unimaginable before and has made us capable of both great good and great bad. We have, on the one hand, created weapons of mass destruction such as the nuclear bombs but we have also, on the other hand, made medicines that can affect miraculous cures.

We can mould life on earth or put an end to it because science has vastly extended human power. We have the power to control the weather, cause drought and flood, change the tides, raise levels of the sea, and alter climates. Every increase in knowledge has meant an increase in man's capacity to act. Science and technology have ensured that good men can do more good and bad men more bad than our ancestors could have dreamt as possible. As Russell has pointed out that hitherto man had been unable to do too much harm because of his ignorance and his inefficiency but at the basic level, unless moulded by civilisation and educational influences, he is a ferocious animal. As in the past, tyrants and bigots have pursued horrifying objectives and if the working of the mind is not transformed, human beings will continue to do so with even worse consequences. We will perish as the dinosaurs did in spite of once being the lords of creation because now those objectives can be followed more efficiently, completely, and ruthlessly due to the increased power that enhanced knowledge has put in our hands.[5]

Russell emphasises that religion has always taught that it is our duty to love our neighbour and to desire the happiness for others rather than their misery, but active men have paid little attention to this. However, the kindly feelings towards others advocated by religion will have to become an indispensable condition of survival.

As Russell has stated, "Hitherto, although we have been told on Sundays to love our neighbour, we have been told on weekdays to hate him, and there are six times as many weekdays as Sundays. Hitherto, the harm that we could do to our neighbour by hating him was limited by our incompetence, but in the new world upon which we are entering there will be no such limit, and the indulgence of hatred can only land to disaster."[6] Today, the interdependence in the world is becoming as close as that which exists between the cells of a body. In a human body, for example, the hands cannot be in conflict with the feet and the stomach cannot be at war with the liver. What one eats nourishes every part of the body but the mouth does not say why it should take so much trouble for the entire body. We will similarly have to realise that it is in our enlightened self-interest to forgo short-term gains to achieve long-term goals. Therefore, feelings of welfare towards the whole society will have to become necessary for human beings to accomplish what they wish to enjoy. Man is capable of wisdom that synthesises knowledge, will, and feeling rather than seeing them as mutually exclusive.

Knowledge and the power that it brings needs to influence feelings because it is feelings that decide what an individual will do with power. Russell indicates that feelings too, have evolved through the struggle for existence. As humankind formed itself into a society, it grew from an individual to a family, to tribes, nations, and federations. It got divided into two large groups with two opposite systems of morality — one for dealing with one's own social group; and the other for dealing with outsiders.

It came to be considered as 'moral' to support members of one's group while waging wars against the other was justified. The fame of many 'so called' heroes of history rests on their role in helping their own group to kill other people's group and to steal from them. Hence, history till recently has been read chiefly as a chronology of wars. This whole conditioning has now become disadvantageous. Previously, when a tribe killed another tribe and occupied its lands, it acquired greater prosperity and lived more comfortably. But now the consequences are the opposite. Two nations that cooperate are more likely to achieve economic prosperity than those who compete. However, the faith in competition continues as we are conditioned from the past and cannot make our emotions grow at the same rate as our skills. We can see that in a technically-developed world, what is done in one region has enormous effects in other regions but as long as we limit ourselves to feeling only for our own region conflicts will continue because we will go on acting in our narrow self-interest, unmindful of the consequences on others in spite of knowing intellectually that the world is interconnected.

The Skills Required

Some skills can be seen as fundamental in spite of changing requirements of capacity building such as the ability to read and write, proficiency in mathematics, an understanding of scientific thought and theory, and a historical consciousness. But even these get redefined with technological advances. Today, knowledge can be accessed through sources not known before from simple classrooms to a thousand different sites on the computer screen. In fact, so much information is now available that sorting, evaluating and judging it has become a critical. The other side to it is that learning institutions have lost their primacy as sources of information. According to Albert Einstein, "It is not so very important for a person to learn facts. For that he does not really need a college. He can learn them from books. The value of an education in a liberal arts college is not the learning of many facts but the training of the mind to think something that cannot be learned from textbooks."[7]

There are three strands in learning: to be competent, to be engaged and to be ethical. Competence embraces development of skills, a critical capacity to think, ability to identify problems and suggest solutions. But what is competence itself? It is redefined continuously from one generation to another according to the changing conditions of the world, advances in science and technology and the general rise in human expectations.

By engagement is meant the capacity of knowledge to change society. While personal growth and fulfilment may be the fundamental objects of learning, human beings are social creatures and so they naturally look outwards. The change that we seek to bring about is usually concerned with improving living standards but that can only be one aim of education and not the most fundamental one. Today, under all the glitz, there is a genuine sense of searching. The older verities have lost their hold and a society that is essentially rootless and ephemeral lacks the structure to build a meaningful life. This accounts for the rebirth of very structured and conservative movements. It is a sign of the spiritual emptiness that people feel. They are searching for greater clarity and security.

The desire for good and the search for truth are real and active components of every human life. Hence, morality is not to add something to human beings but the act of coming to consciousness and education is the vehicle to create conditions for consciousness. Educational institutions must devise means to produce not just technologically competent individuals, but also ethical beings. J. Krishnamurti has attempted to sketch what should be the aim of educational institutions. In the context of the two schools, one at Rishi Valley and the other at Rajghat, J. Krishnamurti, talks of what he thinks is the fundamental function of education and hence of a learning organisation. Most educational institutions all over the world produce specialists–technicians, scientists, educators and the like. However, these specialists are not capable of meeting the enormously complex challenge of life although they are supposed to provide leadership. The problem is that they are all responding to immediate problems while simultaneously a long-term view of the challenges has to also be taken. The function of education is to bring about a mind that can go beyond the immediate. As J. Krishnamurti points out, "The real issue is to find out how to live in a world that is so compulsively authoritarian; so brutal and tyrannical, not only in the immediate relationship but in social relationships, how to live in such a world with the extraordinary capacity to meet its demands and also to be free. I feel education of the right kind should cultivate the mind not to fall into grooves of habit, but to have a mind that is extraordinarily alive; not with knowledge, not with experience but alive. Because often the more knowledge one has, the less alert the brain is."[8]

Learning therefore is not the same as acquisition of knowledge because that amounts to only gathering information and storing it up. Since education around the world is merely concerned with the acquisition of knowledge, the mind, overloaded with information becomes dull and ceases to learn. The question then arises whether it is possible to develop a mind that simultaneously acquires the knowledge needed to live but also constantly learns. This can only happen when education concerns itself with the totality of life and not just with responses to immediate challenges. A person who lives only in the immediate lives a superficial and rather empty life that he tries to fill up with more and more wealth, material possessions, over indulgence in food and drink, clothes, sex and power.[9]

The question is, what kind of individuals do we want our educational institutions to shape? As Krishnamurti points out, "If we concentrate very much on examinations, on technological information, on making the child clever and proficient in acquiring knowledge, while we neglect the other side, then the child will grow up into a one-sided human being. When we talk about a total human being, we mean not only a human being with inward understanding, with a capacity to explore, to examine his inward being, his inward state and the capacity of going beyond it, but also someone who is good in what he does outwardly. The two must go together. That is the real issue in education to see that when the child leaves the school, he is well-established in goodness, both outwardly and inwardly."[10]

Acquiring Knowledge

The question arises how are we to acquire a higher consciousness and awareness and whether formal institutions of higher learning are equipped to bring this about. Universities lay a great emphasis on the development of the mind but there is no clarity on what exactly is meant by the mind. As Sri Aurobindo has pointed out, the word is used indiscriminately to cover, "the whole consciousness for man is a mental being and mentalises everything" but actually the mind is that "part of the nature that has to do with cognition and intelligence with ideas, with mental or thought perceptions, the reaction of thoughts to things, with the truly mental movements and formations, mental vision and will, etc. that are a part of (a person's) intelligence."[11]

As Tony Buzan has pointed out, the mind has five major functions:

- ***Receiving:*** It receives the impressions and perceptions taken in by the senses.
- ***Holding:*** This is the ability to store information and to recall it when required.
- ***Analysing:*** This is a part of the pattern of recognition and information processing.
- ***Outputting:*** This is any creative act or communication including thinking, analysing, writing, painting and others.
- ***Controlling:*** This refers to all mental and physical functions.

These five functions reinforce each other. For example, it is easier to receive data if one is interested and motivated and if the receiving process is compatible with brain functions. If the information is received efficiently, it is easier to hold and analyse it. Conversely, if efficient holding and analysis takes place, the ability to receive information increases. Analysis is a complex array of information-processing tasks that requires an ability to hold the information that has been received. The quality of analysis is affected by the ability to receive and hold information.

The three functions of receiving, holding, and analysing converge into the fourth of outputting or articulating through speech, gesture, writing, painting or any other form of creating or express. The fifth category, 'controlling' refers to the brain's general monitoring of all mental and physical functions including general health, attitude and environmental conditions. Therefore, the mind is the faculty through which we seek knowledge, expressing it to the extent it is comprehended and then formulate action based on it. However, it is a scientifically proven fact that we all use a very small portion of our mind. Therefore, in spite of all the knowledge placed in front of it, it only remains an instrument with possibilities, faculties that are latent but which can be developed.[12]

One central area of concern for educational institutions must then be how to widen the mind, overcome rigidities, preconceived ideas concepts, and points of view, so that one can learn to consider everything from as many points of view as possible.

Since training of the mind is at the heart of educational institutions, they must devise methods of making individuals capable of meeting the challenges of the times through adjustment, adaptation, and accountability. It is not merely a question of reacting to constant changes by making minor adjustments while essentially maintaining the status quo because that would only obscure the sense of what we are, who we are, and what we might become.

One of the imperative tasks of education then, must be to re-tool our thinking, to being about the transformation of consciousness; a paradigm shift in the mind from seeing ourselves as separate from the world to perceiving ourselves as an integral part of the whole. This would widen our consciousness to understand the interdependence of multiple factors in events. It would change our view of the world from a hierarchical one to a system of interconnected networks and make us realise that in any given event, since so many interlinked factors are involved, outcomes are always indeterminate and unpredictable.

We are not living in a world that is 'given' to us in its entirety like a book leaving us free to open any chapter that we choose. It is a world being constantly created, emerging and evolving towards something more integrated and complex here and now and not in some distant future that we can complacently ignore as being of no consequence to us. Hence, the systems we create and teach in a learning institution have to be open rather than closed ones because the latter are bound to decay, while the former have an inherent possibility of evolving into states of increasing complexity and order. Since this feature applies to all aspects of the universe and to all living things including human beings and organisations, such an approach tends to lead to harmony of action rather than to contradictions.

Expanding Mental Consciousness

Sri Aurobindo suggested that evolution offers human beings the possibility of development towards higher levels of consciousness — to a more integrated and whole personality and opening to a fuller humanity. Humankind is not the end point of development, but only a step along the way. Ken Wilber, on whom Sri Aurobindo is a significant influence among other thinkers, suggests that our task is to shift beyond our present limited rationality to a wider integrated rationality or to a 'vision logic' that helps us to hold various rational perspectives together at once and reconcile seemingly incompatible notions. It is this vision logic, according to Wilber, that helps us to prepare for the challenges of a global network. In the field of education, it means designing novel processes and programmes that can be created on the spot, out of events, dialogues and relationships of that moment; that is, developing the creative spirit rather than working on preconceived notions and prearranged solutions through rigid institutional frameworks.

Bertrand Russell asserts that according to astronomers the physical universe is continually expanding. Everything that is near us is moving away and the more further objects are receding even farther. Now, whether this scientific theory of an expanding physical universe continues to be accepted or not, there is no doubt that the mental universe will have to expand to comprehend the cosmos as is now revealed by science. We have to stretch our imaginations both in space and time to an extent unknown before. This can be bewilderingly painful to many because it makes them feel that they and their preoccupation are puny and insignificant in this cosmic theatre. In an effort to make us understand the magnitude of space that our imagination must encompass, Russell lists a few figures. The nearest fixed star is about twenty-five million millions miles away. The Milky Way, the system nearest to us, has about three hundred thousand million stars and there are many million assemblages like the Milky Way. The distance between each of these is such that it takes about two million years for light to traverse. The sun weighs about two billion billion billion tons and the Milky Way weighs about a hundred and sixty thousand million times as much as the sun. Also, while there is so much matter, immensely large part of the universe is "empty" or very nearly so. The mind has to stretch to its utmost capacity to even begin to understand this vastness.

A similar stretching of our thoughts is necessary with respect to time as has been shown by geology and palaeontology. The dating of fossils and sedimentary and igneous rocks proves them to be much older than we had previously imagined. Astronomy constantly pushing forth fresh discoveries about the origin of the solar system and of the nebulae. With the most powerful existing telescopes, we can see objects from which light has taken five hundred million years to reach.

A moment's thought about this cosmic theatre fills us with awe but after the first reaction is over, the rational mind realises that there is no great quality necessarily connected with size. The physical size of the man's brain is small but its vastness is to be measured by the size and complexity of the universe or other issues that he can grasp in thought and imagination. However, as per Russell, the mind of the astronomer should grow step by step with his knowledge of the universe not just in the intellectual aspect but also in his will and feeling, because if the intellect becomes cosmic but feeling and will remain parochial, a disharmony would be produced which would be disastrous. That is, in effect, wisdom must grow. Wisdom can be said to be a harmony of knowledge, will and feeling, which does not come with the mere growth of knowledge.[13]

When a child is born, his world is tiny, bound by what is apparent to his senses in the immediate present. Gradually, as knowledge grows, this limitation recedes. Memory and experience make what is past and what is distant gradually more vivid in the life of the growing child. As his knowledge grows, the universe of experience expands in terms of time and space. But his life will always remain full of contradictions and his capacity to act will remain limited unless his feelings harmonise with his thoughts and enable him to act wisely, which can be safely said to be synonymous with what Russell calls 'acting ethically':

> We are beset in our daily lives by fret and worry and frustrations. We find ourselves too readily pinned down to thoughts of what seem obstructive in our immediate environment. But it is possible, and authentic wise men have proved that it is possible, to live in so large a world that the vexations of daily life come to feel trivial and that the

purposes which stir our deeper emotions take on something of the immensity of our cosmic contemplations. Some can achieve this in a greater degree, some only in a lesser, but all who care to do so can achieve this in some degree and, in so far as they succeed in this, they will win a kind of peace which will leave activity impeded but not turbulent.[14]

Such a state of mind is one of wisdom and the world needs it as it has never needed it before. If humankind can acquire it, it can bring the greatest measure of happiness and well-being with the new powers that knowledge has brought, otherwise there can be irretrievable disaster. Therefore, learning organisations need to devise modes by which the great potential of human nature is encouraged to seek the highest. Although the capacity to learn lies at the heart of humanity, it cannot just happen. It is a difficult and demanding task and has to be systemically constructed.

Achieving Transformation

Sri Aurobindo and the Mother, who did a lot of work on education have given us some practical guidance on how to achieve this personal transformation and then use it towards the growth of institutions and organisations thus moving from the individual to the collective and creating a symbiotic relationship between the two. As the Mother points out, when the imagination expands and consciousness widens, tension evaporates and action can be done in a calm frame of mind. "The easiest way", she says, "is to identify yourself with something vast. For instance, when you feel that you are shut up in a completely narrow and limited thought, will, consciousness, when you feel as though you were in a shell, then if you begin thinking about something very vast, as for example, the immensity of the waters of an ocean, and if really you can think of this ocean and how it stretches out far, far, far, far in all directions, like this...how, compared with you, it is so far, so far that you cannot see the other shore, you cannot reach its end anywhere, neither behind or in front nor to the right or left...it is wide, wide, wide, wide...you think of this and then you feel that you are floating on this sea, like that, and that there are no limits.....this is very easy. Then you can widen your consciousness a little."[15]

Most difficulties arise because of the ego, which makes us react from a narrow personal position to circumstances, events and people around us. But if as a first stage we can create the sense of widening ourselves a kind of unfolding of ourselves, then whatever holds and strangles us, making us suffer or paralyses our movements also begins to gradually unfold and become diffused as if it has been exposed to the light rather than being packed away within. When one can attempt to mentally let go or relax, that is, unfold one's mind to allow higher influences to enter, the problem inevitably dissolves as the ego preventing the solution from emerging, dissolves.

This is, as the Mother points out, much easier than struggling against the difficulty with one's thought because if one begins to discuss with one's own self, one finds that there are arguments both for and against and both are so convincing that it is quite impossible to get out of the inconclusive debate within without a higher light. By allowing the mind to widen and receive the possibilities of different solutions, one does not struggle against the difficulties, nor does one try to convince oneself but allows a solution to emerge. It is somewhat like what Keats meant by 'negative capability'.[16]

Again, when we find ourselves hurt and disheartened, the feelings can be overcome by bringing about a shift in attitude, perception, or point of view. As the Mother says:

> There is a way also of trying to identify yourself with all things upon earth. For example, when you have a small narrow vision of something and are hurt by others' vision and point of view, you must begin by shifting your consciousness, try to put it in others, and try gradually to identify yourself with all the different ways of thinking of all others. This a little more…how shall I put it?….dangerous. Because to identify oneself with the thought and will of others means to identify oneself with a heap of stupidities…and bad wills, and this may bring consequences, which are not very good. But still, some people do this more easily. For instance, when they are in disagreement with someone, in order to widen their consciousness they try to put themselves in the place of the other and see the thing not from their own point of view but from the point of view of the other. This widens the consciousness, though not as much as by the first ways I spoke about, which are quite innocent. They don't do you any harm, they do you much good. They make you very peaceful.[17]

Thich Nhat Hanh has also given us a meditation, which is a useful tool in problem solving and is used in many Buddhist monasteries for the training of the mind. In any conflicting situation, it is necessary for the mind to comprehend both points of view. In the example that he gives of a river and a swimmer, a student is asked to first give the point of view of the swimmer in the river. However, after a while, he is asked to articulate the feelings of the river in which the swimmer is swimming. This makes the mind supple and flexible and is likely to lead to an understanding through which a solution is possible.[18]

As the Mother points out, "all contradictories can be transformed into complements, but for that one must discover a higher idea that will be able to harmonise them. It is good to consider all problems from all possible standpoints to avoid partiality and exclusiveness, but if the thought is to be active and creative, it must, in each case, be the natural and logical synthesis of all the points of view taken in. And if you are to make to the totality of your thoughts, a dynamic and constructive force, you must take great care as to the choice of the central idea of your mental synthesis; for upon that will depend the value of your synthesis."[19]

She gives a useful exercise for problem solving:

> ...there is an exercise which gives great suppleness and elevation to the thought. It is as follows: a clearly formulated thesis is set; against it is opposed its antithesis, formulated with the same precision. Then by careful reflection the problem must be widened or transcended until a synthesis is found which unites the two contraries in a large, higher and more comprehensive idea.[20]

Acquiring this suppleness of mind and techniques of problem solving is absolutely essential for living in communities because human beings as we have seen, have to work in collectivities rather than in isolation. Living in a community we see perceptions of ourselves are reflected back to us. It is easy to dismiss these, especially the negative images, but we must learn to accept these and try to see and hear even when we want to reject them. When we work in a community, our shared experiences allow us to clarify our thinking, open ourselves to critical ideas, increase our awareness of others and uncover our values and beliefs, that is, our self-knowledge increases through community. Thus, experience is enhanced when we respect diversity. Listening carefully and learning from our differences broadens our point of view. Besides, listening creates a community because we then notice not only those needs and understandings that are fully formed, but also participate in the formation of new needs and understandings. In this way, mutual learning and growth takes place.

Role of Educational Institutions

Educational institutions must not only develop the technological proficiency in a student, but must also uncover the deeper layers of his mind. A human being whose inner development is neglected while making him a perfect professional, does not just grow into that but is also jealous, angry, frustrated, in despair and ambitious. Hence, there is always disorder in society. It may create a great society in which there is immense material wealth and social equality but a great society need not necessarily be a good society. A good society implies order that is not merely external like trains running on time or mail efficiently delivered. The order has to be an inner one. Therefore, both technology and the inner life of a human being must be simultaneously and equally developed. There can be no separation between these two as we have presently done in our educational institutions. The educational institutions must aim to bring them together. Krishnamurti says, "If there is proper education, the student will not treat them as two separate fields. He will be able to move in both as one movement.....In making himself technologically perfect, he will also make himself a worthwhile human being."[21]

An ethical person recognises the great potential for good in human life and so tries to cultivate it. It means having profound respect for others, which leaves no room for attitudes such as, racism and exploitation. It is also opposed to dogma and inflexible moral positions. It leads to a realisation that sexual preferences, ethnic identity, gender, learning and physical differences have to be accommodated with dignity because when we reject them, we not only sacrifice the dignity of those rejected but of all. We have to always remember that we are not islands unto ourselves but that we form a part of the great fabric of human activity. Our deepest personal needs remain unmet if we do not rise above our narrow concerns and biases and seek the good of others.

Somehow we feel compelled to suppress with great force the inner feeling and voice that reminds us from time to time that our true task is some kind of mystical evolution. Why do we do this? Perhaps because to acknowledge it would render most of our political gyrations, battles on grounds of religious dogma and financial manoeuvring not only counter-productive but also trivial. Today, this quest for the ultimate meaning has broken the bound of rationalist movement as is evident from the amazingly large number of books and magazines on the theme of personal and social change. The desire for meaning in life and fulfilment is growing to be a part of something that is greater than just us. We seek these answers although we know that the reality will not become perfectly clear to us and that our questions will remain unanswered. However, we still embark on the quest because we are convinced that even our striving makes us grow as human beings.

Many view the concentration on inner growth and development as egocentric and self-centred but there are others who recognise the moral idea that behind this commitment, it is a redefinition of what is a better or higher mode of life, not in terms of what we materially desire or need but in terms of what we ought to desire for our own freedom and happiness. For many, this ideal involves a pursuit of meaning; for others, it is the need to become authentic, i.e. to define ourselves as true to one's own originality. It is only through authenticity that we become better equipped to create harmony in ourselves and in others. Paradoxical though it may sound, personal change leads to social change because those who undergo personal change, bring their ideas and vision into the mainstream of society.

The Task Ahead

The challenge before learning institutions is to how reshape our thinking: recreate our organisations and how to redefine the way we work within the universities and thus the mode of our functioning outside in society. The organisations can only reshape themselves through a shared vision among their members, an invitation to them to engage in a dialogue among themselves and with those outside the organisation. The three cornerstones for an organisation to change itself could be aspiration, conversation, and conceptualisation. Aspiration takes into account the personal vision of the individuals and tries to create a shared vision for the institution. This can only be done by a process of conversation or dialogue through which individuals attempt to draw out into the open their internalised assumptions and subject them to the scrutiny of others and of their ownselves. These processes are carried out within a context of systems thinking — looking at relationships and interdependence of the parts of the organisation. For example, if we adopt a systems orientation, we might ask ourselves who is an expert or a specialist. We may realise that such rapid changes are taking place in knowledge, the problems and issues are increasingly complex and there is a diversity of expertise available among individuals and groups. We may then, instead of relying on one individual or discipline, adopt a more interdisciplinary and multidisciplinary approach. Also, we may realise that we have to employ new combinations of resources and knowledge orientations to deal with issues. Another approach would be to take a longer-term perspective that gives less importance to immediate pay-offs and more to multiple benefits in the future.

If we really do have a capacity to develop psychologically towards greater integration, consciousness and wholeness, it means we have the capacity to develop not just horizontally as in the expansion of knowledge and skills but also vertically as in the evolution and transcendence of ourselves, our perspectives and world views. Vertical education for transcendence and integration moves beyond horizontal expansion, and through its challenges and support of growth and development, promotes those processes integration and transformation.

In institutions of higher education, there is considerable experience in addressing development along the horizontal plane but very little on how to develop along the vertical plane. Universities have not had issues to spirituality, transformation and transcendence on their agenda. Educators themselves are not ready to accept that spiritual strivings and personal transformation are part of the challenge of higher education. Many see it as self-indulgence or are wary of supporting moral ideas outside their sphere of work. Also, in the age of computation and measurable outcomes, education that attends to personal transformation, is at odds with education that promotes observable knowledgeable skills. The successful programmes on the vertical plane would require adult educators who themselves are on the development path of the transformation of the self. However, themes of meaning, spirituality and human consciousness need to be given a place. Students often have well-worked out career-related goals, but the inner dissatisfaction and groping arise out of a need to know more about and develop their ownselves. Educators tend to get too involved in extrinsic aspects of motivation and miss the intrinsic goal, which is to foster human qualities that would contribute to the functioning of the whole integrated personality. Hence, a more central place needs to be given to self-development and consciousness studies in higher education through forums, courses, conferences, symposia and study groups. Another important task is to create opportunities for self-reflection. It is important to be consciously self-reflective, aware of the way our organs register information and how we can direct and control our experiences. A brief moment occurs, if we can train ourselves to be aware of it, between the stimulus and our response to it, which can be used for self-reflection. With self-reflection, we begin to write our own programme for action. It is to be proactive in a very specific way because then we stop reacting, get a moment to reflect on our own action, and figure out whether we are contributing to our own problems. If educational institutions can teach us to view ourselves to become witnesses to our own thoughts and actions and to have the honesty and courage to act dispassionately, apart from making us technological proficient, they will impact society in a way so as to create a better and more humane world for all to live in. They would then have attained their true goal.

References

1. Pavitra (P.B. Saint-Miltaira), 1961. Reprint 1996. *Education and the Aim of Human Life*, Pondicherry: Sri Aurobindo International Centre of Education; p.1.

2. *Ibid.*, pp. 5-7.
3. *Ibid.*, pp. 12-13.
4. Thich Nhat Hanh, 1997. Reprint 1999, *Being Peace*, Delhi: Full Circle, pp. 45-47.
5. Russell, Bertrand. "The Expanding Mental Universe – 1", http://joynote.wordpress.com/2009/02/26/the expanding-mental-universe-1-betrand-russell/

   See also, parts 2 and 3 of "The Expanding Mental Universe."
6. Russell, Bertrand. "The Expanding Mental Universe – 2", http://joynote.wordpress.com/2009/02/26/the expanding of mental universe – 2-bertrand russell/

   Russell, Bertrand. "Knowledge and Wisdom", www.personal.kant.edu/rmuhamma/philosophy/RB Writings/knowledge AND wis.hton
7. "An Interview with Albert Einstein on Science Careers", by Dalbart, blogs.sciencemsg.org/sciencecareers/2011/01/an-interview-wi-html
8. *Ibid.*
9. *Ibid.*
10. Krishnamurti, J. "On Education", Chapter 2, www.jkrishnamurti.org/krishnamurti-teachings/view-text.php? Tid=chid=207.
11. SABCL, Vol. 2, Letters on Yoga, p.1. Sri Aurobindo, Letter on Yoga, Sri Aurobindo Birth Centenary Library (Pondicherry: Sri Aurobindo Ashram, 1970) Vol. 22, pp. 320-321.
12. Buzan Tony with Barry Buzan. 1994. *The Mind Map Book: How to use Radiant Thinking to Maximize your Brain's untapped Potential.* Thanks to net.com/mind_Map_Book-info.html.
13. . Russell, Bertrand. "The Expanding Mental Universe – 1", http://joynote.wordpress.com/2009/02/26 the expanding-mental-=universe-1-bertrand-russell/

   Russell, Bertrand. "The Expanding Mental Universe – 2", http://joynote.wordpress.com/2009/02/26/theexpanding-mental-universe – 2 – bertrand-russell/
14. Russell, Bertrand. "The Expanding Mental Universe – 3", http://joynote.wordpress.com/2009/02/27/the-expanding mental universe - 3 – bertrand – russell/
15. The Mother, 1954. *Collected Works*, Vol. 6, 29 September 1954.
16. Keats, John. 2002. Dec. 21, 1817, *John Keats: Selected Letters*, Oxford University Press.
17. The Mother, 1954. *Collected Works*, Op.cit.
18. The Mother, 1976. Reprint 1999, "Mental Education", *On Education*, Pondicherry: Sri Aurobindo Ashram, p. 26.
19. Thich Nhat Hanh, *Being Peace*, pp. 74-79. Op.cit.
20. The Mother, 1976. Reprint.1999. "The Science of Living", *On Education*, Pondicherry: Sri Aurobindo Ashram, p. 5.
21. Krishnamurti, J. "On Education", www.jkrishnamurti.org/krishnamurti - teachings/view-text.php? Tid=43+chid=297+w=+s= text

13

Swami Vivekananda's Views on Education

Introduction

By the nineteenth century, when great men like Ramakrishna Paramahamsa and Swami Vivekananda came on the scene, India as a nation had perhaps reached the lowest point in its decline. One of the evident areas of degeneration was education. With British administration gaining control, the indigenous education system was destroyed without anything to replace it. This led to mass ignorance and illiteracy. Where a new system was put in place, it destroyed indigenous languages, knowledge systems, and culture and replaced it with something alien that removed the students emotionally from their roots, created alienation and bred an intense sense of inferiority amongst them about their own cultural heritage and traditions. It is ironical that almost sixty-eight years after the country's independence the demand for English language is so palpably strong, not as the learning of an additional language required as an international *lingua franca*, but as the medium of instruction. Inextricably linked with language is the culture of the people which in turn, is connected with the individual's rootedness in the soil of the country. The elite, who were educated in the new education system lost their moorings in India and aped the West in all aspects of their lives, holding their own people in contempt. They became part of the bureaucracy in British India and became the head of governance structures in post-independence India. They propagated the western norms blindly, which led to the masses to also aspire to them blindly. The hallmark of education became the ability to speak English and to live a westernised lifestyle. Macaulay succeeded beyond his wildest dreams.

Decline of Indigenous Education

In this context, it would be useful to examine the state of education before the British administrative control of India and what led to its downfall. As Mahatma Gandhi pointed out in his lecture delivered to the Royal Institute of International Affairs on 20th October, 1931:

> I say without fear of my figures being challenged successfully that today India is more illiterate than it was fifty or be hundred years ago because the British administrators when they came to India, instead of taking hold of things as they were "began" to root them out. "They scratched the soil…and left the root like that and the beautiful tree perished."[1]

Some seminal work on this has been done by Dharampal in *The Beautiful Tree.*

The reasons for the decline and disappearance of indigenous schools have been pointed out by the British officers themselves. These have been cited by Dharampal. A.D. Campbell, the Collector of Bellary, in his report to the Government of Madras, dated 17.8.1823 said,

> I am sorry to state that this is ascribable to the gradual but general impoverishment of the country. The means of the manufacturing classes have been, of late years, greatly diminished by the introduction of our own European manufactures, in lieu of the Indian cotton fabrics. The removal of many of our troops, from our own territories to the distant frontiers of our newly subsidised allies, has also of late years, affected the demand for grain. The transfer of the capital of the country, from the native governments and their officers who liberally expended it in India, to Europeans, restricted by law from employing it even temporarily in India and daily drawing it from the land has likewise tended to this effect…The greater part of the middle and lower classes of people are now unable to defray the expenses incident upon the education of their offspring, while their necessities require the assistance of the children as soon as their tender limbs are capable of the smallest labour. Of the 533 institutions for education now existing in this district, I am ashamed to say, not one now derives any support from the state.[2]

Similar state of affairs has been noted by Adam, a Baptist missionary who came to Bengal in 1818, as also by Leitner who was for some time the Principal of Government College at Lahore and Acting Director Public Instruction, Punjab in 1882, among others. The people were impoverished because of the colonial exploitation of the economy and so could not support education, as they had done earlier. Not only that, they were unable to send their children to school as poverty compelled them to put every working hand to work as early as possible, even at a very tender age. Hence, children were put to work as soon as they could to bring in some income to the family. Besides, wherever the British put an education system into place, it was very expensive and beyond the reach of the common man. It was also very alienating. Adam says:

> In the report of 1st July 1835, mention is made of an English school at Bauleah, the capital of this district, but no information was then possessed respecting it...The school was established in July 1833 and placed under the care of an English teacher receiving eighty rupees per month, with an assistant receiving twenty rupees and Bengali teacher receiving eight rupees. The English teacher in addition to his salary had a bungalow built for him at a cost of eight hundred rupees which he occupied rent-free; and a school house was built at an expense of one thousand and two hundred rupees. With economical repairs and proper care, both the houses might last fifteen years. The expense of books, pens, papers, ink, and a sweeper to keep the school house clean, was estimated on an average at twelve rupees per month. The current monthly expenditure thus amounted to one hundred and twenty rupees.[3]

And Ananda K. Coomaraswamy speaks about the products of the new education as early as 1908:

> Speak, to the ordinary graduate of an Indian University— he will hasten to display his knowledge of Shakespeare; talk to him of religious philosophy — you find that he is an atheist of the crude type common in Europe a generation ago, and that not only has he no religion but he is as lacking in Philosophy as the average Englishman; talk to him of Indian music — he will produce a gramophone or a harmonium, and inflict upon you one or both; talk to him of Indian dress or jewellery — he will tell you that they are uncivilised and barbaric; talk to him of Indian art — it is news to him that such a thing exists; ask him to translate for you a letter written in his own mother tongue— he does not know it. He is indeed a stranger in his own land.[4]

As Dharampal points out, the consequences of uprooting Indian education and replacing it by an alien rootless system not only led to the obliteration of literacy and knowledge, but also destroyed the social balance.[5] It is no wonder that education formed a part of the rationalist agenda articulated by the most ardent nationalists of the time such as, Swami Vivekananda, Sri Aurobindo, Mahatma Gandhi or Gurudev Rabindranath Tagore.

Manifesting the Perfection Within

What was Swami Vivekananda's vision of education? What did it mean to him? What was the purpose of education?

"Education" said Swami Vivekananda, "is the manifestation of the perfection already in man."[6] All knowledge then is nothing but what a person discovers or unveils by taking the cover off his own soul, which is a mine of infinite knowledge. Lest we think that he is only talking of matters spiritual, the example that Vivekananda gives is of Newton and his discovery of the force of gravity. Gravity, as he says, was not something lying in the corner waiting to be discovered by Newton. Its recognition was already in his mind. Newton only observed an external phenomenon and came to a conclusion by rearranging all the previous links of thought to uncover a new link, the law of gravitation. "All knowledge and all powers are within."[7]

This implies that no one can really teach another. Each of us has to teach himself or herself. The external teacher only offers the suggestion, which arouses the internal teacher to work to understand things. Just as the small seed has the potential to give rise to a large banyan tree, the mind has immense potential to grasp and create the most complex of things. A child cannot be taught just as a plant cannot be taught to grow. Only conditions can be created to protect and nourish the plant so that it may grow. And it is not only teachers who have to realise that children can only learn and grow at their own pace, the parents too have to give their children free scope for growth otherwise they become stunted. As Swami Vivekananda puts it, "If you do not allow one to become a lion, one will become a fox."[8] Liberty is a prerequisite to growth. No one, not even parents, can work out someone else's salvation. They cannot presume to know everything and — most of all, take charge of someone else's spirit, even of their own children.

Education is not to stuff the brain with information that remains undigested and runs riot throughout an individual's life. Education, to use Swami Vivekananda's words is, "Life-building, man-making, character-making."[9] Learning the ideas of others by rote and that too in a foreign language that one does not really understand, is not education. In any case, what does such an education equip one for? A clerkship? To become a civil servant, lawyer, or any other profession? But does such an education teach the common mass of people how to equip themselves for the struggle of life? For Vivekananda, the end of all education and all training is man-making, to make a person grow and be able to meet the challenges of life with equanimity. It must above all, develop the strength of character and mind to face the ups and downs of life.

Formation of Character

The character of any man is but the aggregate of his tendencies, the sum total of the bend of his mind as these evolve in his journey. It is impacted by the challenges that life presents to him. Part of our energy is used in preserving our bodies. Beyond that, every particle of our energy is being used to influence others. In the same way,we are being influenced by them. As we experience pain and pleasure, they leave an imprint on us and mould our character. We are what our thoughts make us. Words are secondary to thoughts. Thoughts live and travel by themselves and through words. If a person has good thoughts, his speech will be good and he will do good work. Good work motivates a person to do even better. Similarly, bad thoughts lead to bad actions and these too have a way of multiplying. Great occasions and great crises arouse a person to great actions. But only that person is truly great whose character remains great at all times even in adversity and irrespective of where he is.

Both good and evil mould character; but at the end of the day, pain and adversity are greater teachers than happiness. If we study the great characters that the world has produced, it was adversity that taught them more than happiness and wealth. The blows of life bring out the inner fire more than praise. Buffeted by storms, when hope seems lost, the light within gleams. Help does not come from outside but from within. And it gives courage and strength to undo or deal with the mistakes made.

Therefore, the ideal education and training is to develop strength within, and thus pave the way for the growth of man. An internally strong person is a dynamo of power who, when he is ready, can do anything and everything he likes. And yet time is spent in education on polishing the outside and neglecting the inner core. Philosophers and religious teachers who may not seem very sophisticated have succeeded in moving nations and countries. This is because they do not touch only the intellect, they touch the very being of a person.

Developing the Personality

How can such a personality be developed? The science of yoga claims that it has uncovered laws that develop this personality and by proper attention to those laws and methods, each one can grow and strengthen his personality. This strengthening of personality is needed by everybody — householder, rich, poor, women, men of business, spiritual man or whoever else. These are laws much finer than the physical laws. According to Vivekananda,

> There are no such realities as a physical world, a mental world; a spiritual world whatever is, is one. Let us say, it is a sort of tapering existence, the thickest part is here, it tapers and becomes finer and finer; the finest is what we call spirit; the grossest, the body. And just as it is here, in the microcosm, it is exactly the same in the macrocosm.

> This universe of ours is exactly like that; it is the gross external thickness, and it tapers into something finer and finer until it becomes God.[10]

And the greatest power is lodged in the fine, not in the coarse. For example, muscles have great power but it is the fine nerves that give the muscles their power. If one of these tiny nerves is cut off, the muscle loses its power. And the nerves derive their power from something finer; that is thought. Often we can see the movement of the muscle but are unaware of the movement of the mind, or thought that made the muscle move because it is so subtle that we may not even be conscious of it. Therefore, control of thought is self-mastery.

How can thought be controlled? The aim of the practice must be to control even the fine movement of thought because only then thought can be controlled at the root; even before it has become thought, and so necessarily before it has become action. When this mastery is gained, it becomes possible to control the whole existence. If we can find a method by which we can analyse, investigate, understand and finally grapple with the finer powers, the finer causes, then it is possible to have control over ourselves. And the man who has control over his own mind assuredly can control every other mind. "That is why" says Vivekananda, "purity and morality have been always the object of religion; a pure, moral man has control of himself. And all minds are the same, different parts of one Mind. He who knows one lump of clay has known all the clay in the universe. He who knows and controls his own mind knows the secret of every mind and has power over every mind."[11]

Attaining Knowledge

How does one attain knowledge? There is only one way and that is developing the art of concentration. From the illiterate to the yogi, all have to use concentration to attain knowledge. The chemist needs concentration in his laboratory as does the astronomer as he peers in his telescope. The professor, the student and the workman, all need concentration. A man polishing shoes will do them better if he concentrates, just as a cook will make better food when he concentrates. Even someone only interested in making money will be more successful if he concentrates, as will be the one worshipping God if his mind does not wander. As Vivekananda points out, the main difference between men and animals is that while human beings can concentrate, animals can't. Animals are trained through repetition followed by predictable outcomes, while human beings learn through their power of concentration. The attention of the highest evolved man is not diverted by any distraction while the lowest man is easily distracted.

All success in any field depends on concentration. The question is how to develop concentration? The practice of meditation leads to concentration. The two essential ingredients to successful learning are concentration and detachment. What is detachment? It is the ability of the mind to step back and see a situation objectively without personal involvement, without even a trace of self-interest into it. Once the instrument or mind is perfected, it can collect facts at will.

The Teacher and the Taught

There are certain conditions necessary for learning. The qualities of both the teacher and taught are important. For the students purity of character, a real thirst for knowledge, and perseverance are essential. Purity in thought, speech and action builds a strong moral fibre and prevents distractions from the path of seeking knowledge. As for thirst for knowledge, it is an old law that we get whatever we want or seek. None of us can get other than what we fix our hearts upon. As Vivekananda says, "There must be a continuous struggle, a constant fight, an unremitting grappling with our lower nature, till the higher want is actually felt and victory is achieved. It is not a question of one or two days, of years, or of lives; the struggle may have to go on for hundreds of lifetimes. The success sometimes may come immediately but we must be ready to wait patiently even for what may look like an infinite length of time. The student who sets out with such a spirit of perseverance will surely find success at last."[12]

In regard to the teacher, whether he knows the scriptures of all religions or not, is not as relevant as his having imbibed the spirit of the scriptures. "The whole world reads the Bible, the Vedas and the Koran but they are all only words, syntax, etymology, philology, the dry bones of religion. The teacher who deals too much in words and allows the mind to be carried away by the force of the words loses the spirit."[13] It is the knowledge of the spirit that lies behind the scriptures that alone constitutes the true teacher. The second condition is that the teacher like the taught must have purity of character.

Why should we look into the character and personality of a teacher? It is because truth cannot be acquired for oneself, or for imparting to others, without the purity of heart and soul. It is the teacher's character that imparts value to his words. The function of the teacher is not a mere classroom transaction. It goes far beyond. It is the transference of something from the teacher to the taught, which is not mere stimulation of existing intellectual faculties in the taught. Something real and appreciable comes from the teacher and goes to the taught. Therefore, the teacher must be pure. The third condition is in regard to the motive. The prime motive of a teacher cannot be money or quest for name or fame. He must work out of love. The rest is subsidiary. Teaching is not simply a profession; it is a passion, a love of learning, a love for the student and for humanity. It is a spiritual force that can only be transmitted through love. Any selfish motive, such as the desire for gain or name, will immediately destroy the conveying medium.

Educating the Masses

For Swami Vivekananda, the great national sin of India was the neglect of the masses and that, for him, was the cause of her downfall. No amount of politics, he felt, would be of any avail until the masses in India are once more well-educated, well-fed and well-cared for. One yardstick for the advancement of a nation is the proportion of education and intelligence that has spread among the masses. The chief cause of India's ruin has been the monopolising of the whole education of the land by a handful of people. The only service that one can do for the people of this country, therefore, is to give them education and to develop their individuality. Their eyes have to be opened to what is going on in the world around them, and then they will work out their own salvation. As Vivekananda repeatedly says, every man, every woman and similarly every nation has to work out his own salvation. People have to understand and be convinced of that they can do it and are not inferior to anybody. This is the only help they require and then the rest will inevitably follow.

Education, which will teach people to become self-reliant and self-sufficient, has to be imparted in the language of the people, that is, in the vernacular. Once they understand the importance of such an education, they will get the information themselves. But something more is essential, and this is culture. Swami Vivekananda emphasises the importance of culture. "Give them culture", he says for "Until you can give them that, there can be no permanence in the raised condition of the masses."[14] The majority of people have been so engrossed in their struggle for existence, that they have had no time or opportunity for the awakening of knowledge. They have worked so long like machines and the clever educated section of society has taken advantage of them for so long, appropriating the substantial part of the fruits of their labour, that they have had no time, inclination or means to inculcate the fine aspects of life through culture. But times have changed. The poor wailing masses are gradually realising their exploitation and uniting against it. The upper classes will not be able to repress the lower. In their own self-interest, it will become imperative for the higher classes to help the lower to get their legitimate rights.

To spread education among the masses, three things are necessary. The first is to feel from the heart because intellect or reason goes only a few steps and then stops. But inspiration comes through the heart and love opens impossible gates. The second is to go beyond talk and to try and find a solution. In the path of that solution, there will be many impediments, including from one's family, community and others. These test one's steadfastness. The third is work. While one feels and knows the solution, the only way to ameliorate the situation is to work.

Conclusion

Hence, according to Swami Vivekananda, the decline of India was inextricably connected with the decline of education and the rendering of the masses into ignorance. The indigenous system was dismantled by the British without replacing it with anything viable. The Indian economy became a 'colonial' one, exploiting the people for the aggrandisement of the coloniser. What came into being by way of education was beyond the means of the impoverished masses and alienating for those who could afford it. Two aspects of education were very important for Swami Vivekananda — purity of thought and of purpose both in the teacher and taught. He saw education as a means of uplifting the masses but in a way that made them self-reliant and able to withstand any hardship while improving their own lot and serving the nation.

References

1. Dharampal, 2000. Collected Writings,Vol. III, Reprint 2007, p. 6. *The Beautiful Tree: Indigenous Indian Education in the Eighteenth Century*,Goa: Other India Press in association with SIDH.
2. *Ibid.*, p. 192.
3. Di Bona, Joseph (ed.), 1983. *One Teacher, One School: The Adam Reports on Indigenous Education in 19th Century India*, Biblia Impex, New Delhi. Cited in PPST Bulletins, "Indian Education in the Early 19th Century – A Survey" http://ppstbulletins.blogspot.in/2011/10/indian-education-in-early-19th-centurya.html.
4. Dharampal, Op.cit. *The Beautiful Tree*, p. 64.
5. *Ibid.*, pp. 61-63, p. 86.
6. *The Complete Works of Swami Vivekananda,* Vol. 4, p. 358. "Lectures & Discourses", What We Believe In: Letter written to Singaravelu Mudaliar from Chicago, US, 3rd March 1894, Advaita Ashrama, Madras.
7. *The Complete Works of Swami Vivekananda*, Vol.1, "Vedanta and Privilege", p. 422.

   See also, *Education: Compiled from the Speeches and Writings of Swami Vivekananda,* Compiled and edited by T. S. Avinashilingam, Coimbatore: Sri Ramakrishna Mission Vidyalaya, 1943 (Many ideas in this essay have been taken from this compilation.).

See also, Romain Rolland, *Life of Vivekananda and the Universal Gospel*, Kolkata: Advaita Ashram, March 2010.

8. *The Complete Works of Swami Vivekananda*, Vol. 7, p. 22.
9. *The Complete Works of Swami Vivekananda*, Vol. 3, p. 170.

   See also, Swami Lokeswarananda (ed.), *My India: The India Eternal*, Calcutta: Ramakrishna Mission Institute of Culture, pp. 1-2.
10. *The Complete Works of Swami Vivekananda*, Vol. 2, "The Powers of the Mind", Delivered at Los Angeles, California, Jan. 8, 1900.
11. *Ibid.* See the discussion in T. S. Avinashilingam, Compiled and edited, *Education & Swami Vivekananda*. Madras: Sri Ramakrishna Nath, 1943.
12. *The Complete Works of Swami Vivekananda*, Vol. 3, "Bhakti Yoga", pp. 48-49.
13. *Ibid.*
14. *The Complete Works of Swami Vivekananda*, Vol. 3, Lectures from Colombo to Almora, "The Future of India", p. 29.

14

Aim of Higher Education: An Aurobindonian Paradigm

Introduction

The first question that we need to ask is, why should any individual be educated at all? One possible answer could be, for the progress of society. What is progress? It is the constant effort to improve human conditions. The Mother[1] tells us that two tendencies are seen here:

> ...which seem to be contrary but which ought to complement each other so that progress may be achieved. The first advocates a collective reorganisation, something which could lead to the effective unity of mankind. The other declares that all progress is made first by the individual and insists that the individual should be given the conditions in which he can progress freely. Both are equally true and necessary, and our effort should be directed along with these lines at once. For collective progress and individual progress are interdependent. Before the individual can take a leap forward, at least a little of the preceding progress must have been realised in the collectivity. A way must therefore be found so that these two types of progress may proceed side by side.

As an answer to this urgent need, Sri Aurobindo conceived the scheme of his international university.[2] But what is the aim of this progress? Sri Aurobindo points out:

> Modern society has discovered a new principle of survival, progress, but the aim of that progress it has never discovered, — unless the aim is always more knowledge, more equipment, convenience and comfort, more enjoyment, a greater and still greater complexity of the social economy, a more and more cumbrously opulent life. But these things must lead in the end where the old led, for they are only the same things on a larger scale; they lead in a circle, that is to say, nowhere,

> they do not escape from the cycle of birth, growth, decay and death, they do not really find the secret of self-prolongation by constant self-renewal which is the principle of immortality, but only seem for a moment to find it by the illusion of a series of experiments each of which ends in disappointment. That so far has been the nature of modern progress. Only in its new turn inwards, towards a greater subjectivity now only beginning, is there a better hope; for by that turning it may discover that the real truth of man is to be found in his soul.[3]

This is not to bring back the religions of the old societies in a new garb and terminology. For them, the individual's quest for salvation was a release from the burden of life on earth. Sri Aurobindo's progress is evolution on earth itself, the possibility of a divine life in a divine body. "Human society itself never seized on the discovery of the soul as a means for the discovery of the law of its own being or on a knowledge of the soul's true nature and need and its fulfilment as the right way of terrestrial perfection."[4] This implies that a complete change of outlook for the whole society has to be constructed around the human soul and its need to evolve towards a higher consciousness, thereby the consciousness of the society.

Aim of Higher Education

Collective and Individual

Higher education must necessarily have two broad aims: "A collective aspect and an…individual aspect."[5] The collective aspect requires, as Pavitra (P.B. Saint-Hilaire) points out that an individual is a good citizen when he or she has harmonious relations with other members of the community, is useful to society, and fulfils his or her obligations to society. The individual aspect demands that through education, he or she develops a strong and healthy body, builds up character, attains self-mastery and gets opportunities to discover and develop natural abilities harmoniously. Both aspirations are justified. The individual and society can grow together helping each other but such harmony has rarely been achieved because the mind, with an imperfect vision of things, always tends to emphasise one over the other.[6]

The collective aspect of education is the societal aim and, as Pavitra points out, it has overshadowed the individual aim:

- The problem of education becomes almost exclusively: how to fit the individual to the need of society?
- This is evidenced by the change we witness in the education programmes in answer to the growing demand for scientists, engineers and technicians, and by the numerous institutions that are created to satisfy this demand.

> By the need of society is meant that society thinks it requires. Temporary necessities may arise (war, new discoveries, geographical or political changes) which may for some time reflect themselves on education. But it is clear that the formulated requirements of any society, as far as education is concerned, depend on the aim of human life as it is conceived largely by the ruling class at the time. It may be general culture and adornment of life — artists of all sorts will be encouraged and become the favourites of the princes. It may be military aggrandisement and adventure — then soldiers and sailors will be needed. It may be industrialisation as a means towards material wellbeing — the need will be for engineers and technicians.[7]

Higher Education in India

The foundations of higher education in India were laid by Macaulay who had a twofold aim: one, to produce cheap clerical labour to serve the needs of the colonial empire; second, to create a class of people who would perpetuate the legacy of the empire by looking down upon their own, cultural values and upholding those of the British ruling class. Amilcar Cabral, a revolutionary thinker (born in 1924 at Bafatá in Guinea-Bissau and murdered in 1973) pointed out that the experience of colonial domination shows that the coloniser provokes and develops the cultural alienation of a part of the population by the so-called assimilation of indigenous elites distancing them from the popular masses. As a result, a section of the people assimilate the colonisers mentality, considers itself culturally superior to its own people and looks down upon their cultural values.[8] This is the situation of the majority of colonised intellectuals and their position is consolidated by increase in social privileges.

The University system set up by the colonisers for their own ends has ironically been expanded and strengthened rather than being dismantled in independent India. From twenty universities and five hundred colleges at the time of independence, there has been a manifold increase in the number of colleges. As of March 31, 2014, there are 666 universities and 39,671 colleges. Over 23 million students are enrolled in these institutions. Approximately 85.12 per cent of all college and university students are in undergraduate courses, 12.55 per cent are at the Master's level and a very small proportion, i.e. 0.9 per cent in research. Only 1.68 per cent students are enrolled in diploma or certificate courses. Of all the undergraduate and postgraduate students, 89.49 per cent and 73.61 per cent respectively, are in affiliated colleges while the remaining are in the universities and their constituent colleges. In the case of diploma/certificate course, too, university departments and university colleges have an edge over affiliated colleges. Since the majority of students are in colleges, the foundations of higher education are laid there and their functioning has far-reaching implications. Of the undergraduate students, the highest number, about 86.7 per cent, is pursuing liberal arts and 1.76 per cent is pursuing commerce in colleges of uneven standards. The colonial system of education is mechanically churning out unemployable graduates with poor skills and little development of mind or personality.[9]

Why has this happened? Because no sincere thought has been given to what was sought to be achieved through higher education. Even before independence, Sri Aurobindo had voiced the disillusionment and explained its cause:

> All that appears to be almost unanimously agreed on is that teaching in the existing schools and universities has been bad in kind and in addition denationalising, degrading, and impoverishing to the national mind, soul and character because it is overshadowed by a foreign hand and foreign in aim, method, substance and spirit.[10]

At the time of independence, India lacked every kind of material prosperity. There was an immense desire to catch up with Western standards of living as soon as possible. Factories and dams were hailed as the new temples of India. In the predominance of the external, the internal was neglected. Disregard of individual growth by the education system must inevitably lead to failure even in the collective or societal aims sought to be achieved. As Sri Aurobindo tells us:

> There are three things which have to be taken into account in a true and living education, the man, the individual in his commonness and in his uniqueness, the nation or people and universal humanity. It follows that alone will be a true and living education which helps to bring out to full advantage, makes ready for the full purpose and scope of human life all that is in the individual man, and which at the same time helps him to enter into his right relation with the life, mind and soul of the people to which he belongs and with that great total life, mind and soul of humanity of which he himself is a unit and his people or nation a living, a separate and yet inseparable member.[11]

Thus, the education of the individual is very important because the individual is the building block of society, of the nation, and of humanity. However, to individual aspirations have to be balanced by societal good.

The education of an individual is not a matter of stuffing his mind with facts. As Nolini Kanta Gupta points out:

> The word 'education' literally means, "to bring out." Plato pointed to the same truth when he said that education is remembrance.

> You remember what is imbedded or secreted within, you bring to the light, the light of your physical mind, what you have within, what you already possess in your being and inner consciousness. Acquisition is not education.
>
> True education is growth of consciousness. It is consciousness that carries the light and the power of light.[12]

Consciousness is the substratum of all existence. According to Sri Aurobindo:

> All that exists or can exist in this or any other universe can be rendered into terms of consciousness; there is nothing that cannot be known. This knowing need not always be a mental knowledge. For the greater part of existence is either above or below the mind, and mind can know only indirectly what is above or what below it. But the one true and complete way of knowing is by direct knowledge.[13]

Although the mind is usually the chief concern of the educator, since so much knowledge is outside the pale of the mind, all parts of a human being need to be developed in order to experience direct knowledge. Such an education, which takes into account the entire complexity of man's nature is 'integral education'. Integral education recognises the relationship between the individual and the collective as neither can be denied. Sri Aurobindo says:

> In Europe and India, respectively, the negation of the materialist and the refusal of the ascetic have sought to assert themselves as the sole truth and to dominate the conception of life. In India, if the result has been a great heaping up of the treasurers of the spirit — or of some of them — it has also been a great bankruptcy of life; in Europe, the fullness of riches and the triumphant mastery of this world's powers and possessions have progressed towards an equal bankruptcy in the things of the spirit. Nor has the intellect, which sought the solution of all problems in the one term of matter, found satisfaction in the answer that it has received.[14]

Integral education seeks unity between the two and hence seeks to develop:

> Five principal aspects relating to five principal activities of the human being; the physical, the vital, the mental, the psychic and the spiritual. Usually these phases of education succeed each other in a chronological order following the growth of the individual. This, however, does not mean that one should replace the other but that all must continue, completing each other, till the end of life.[15]

Each of these parts has been defined and has its own law of growth and fulfilment. The spirit remains unchanged as it is beyond space and time both as we try to educate the other parts of our being. The Mother says:

> We shall perceive that the truth we seek is made up of four major aspects: Love, knowledge, power and beauty. These four attributes of the truth will spontaneously express themselves in our being. The psychic will be the vehicle of true and pure live, the mind that of infallible knowledge, the vital will manifest an invincible power and strength and the body will be the expression of a perfect beauty and a perfect harmony.[16]

Education of the Parts of the Being

The question then arises, how are these parts of the being to be educated. While detailed guidelines have been given, the underlying process is one of self-awareness, of becoming conscious and aspiring to perfection. According to Sri Aurobindo:

> Consciousness is made up of two elements, awareness of self and things and forces and conscious power. Awareness is the first thing necessary, you have to be aware of things necessary, you have to be aware of things in the right consciousness, in the right way, seeing them in their truth; but awareness by itself is not enough. There must be a Will and a Force that make the consciousness effective. Somebody may have the full consciousness of what has to be changed, and what has to go and what has to come in its place, but for want of a right awareness may be unable to apply it in the right way at the right time.[17]

Thus, two things are essential for true education: Awareness and will. "To work for your perfection, the first step is to become conscious of yourself, of the different parts of your being and their respective activities. You must learn to distinguish these different parts one from another, so that you may become clearly aware of the origin of the movements that occur in you, the many impulses, reaction and conflicting wills that drive you to action. It is an assiduous study which demands perseverance and sincerity. For man's nature, especially his mental nature, has a spontaneous tendency to give a favourable explanation for everything he thinks, feels, says and does. It is only be observing these movements with great care, by bringing them, as it were, before the tribunal of our highest ideal, with a sincere will to submit to its judgement, that we can hope to form in ourselves a discernment that never errs."[18]

Once there is honest self-awareness, the will has to be strengthened to make a sustained effort: the will can be activated and developed just as the muscles can by methodical and progressive exercise. As the Mother says:

> You must not shrink from demanding the maximum effort of your will even for a thing that seems of no importance, for it is through effort that its capacity grows, gradually acquiring the power to apply itself even to the most difficult things. What you have decided to do, you must do, whatever the cost, even if you have to renew your effort over and over again any number of times in order to do it. You will be strengthened by the effort and you will only have to choose with discernment the goal to which you will apply it.[19]

Such an approach can be applied to all fields of study. For example, a student of commerce will have to apply his or her honest awareness to how well he or she knows the subject or must acknowledge if it is only facile cramming for the examination. If it is the latter, then he or she must use personal will to truly understand the subject no matter how much effort it requires and make it a part of personal knowledge. This the student must do even if the cramming by itself can ensure the required marks.

The Role of the Teacher and the Three Principles of Teaching

Integral education, then, is really a synthesis of two approaches towards education: the traditional spiritual one and the modern rational one. The teacher in this system does not lay down the law but works as a facilitator. As Sri Aurobindo says:

> The wise Teacher will not seek to impose himself or his opinions on the passive acceptance of the receptive mind; he will throw in only what is productive and sure as a seed which will grow under the divine fostering within. He will seek to awaken much more than to instruct; he will aim at the growth of the faculties and the experiences by a natural process and free expansion. He will give a method as an aid, as a utilisable device, not as an imperative formula or a fixed routine and he will be on his guard against any turning of the means into a limitation, against the mechanising process.[20]

Thus, a teacher is not an instructor who has to be passively and unquestioningly followed. In integral education, teaching becomes a shared adventure, a participatory process. This is in keeping with the three principles of teaching enumerated by Sri Aurobindo:

> The first principle of true teaching is that nothing can be taught. The teacher is not an instructor or task-master, he is a helper and a guide. His business is to suggest and not to improve. He does not actually

> train the pupil's mind, he only shows him how to perfect his instruments of knowledge and helps and encourages him in the process. He does not impart knowledge to him, he shows him how to acquire knowledge for himself. He does not call forth the knowledge that is within; he only shows him where it lies and how it can be habituated to rise to the surface.[21]

The second principle is that the mind has to be consulted in its own growth. The idea of hammering the child into the shape desired by the parent or teacher is barbarous and ignorant superstition. It is the child himself or herself who must be induced to expand in accordance with his or her own nature. There can be no greater error than for the parent to arrange beforehand that the child shall develop particular qualities, capacities, ideas, virtues, or be prepared for a prearranged career. To force the nature to abandon its own *dharma* (path of evolution) and tendencies (*samskara*), is to do it permanent harm, mutilate its growth, and deface its perfection. It is selfish tyranny over a human soul and a wound to the nation: which loses the benefit of the best that a man could have given it and is forced to accept instead, something imperfect and artificial, second-rate, perfunctory, and common. Everyone has in him or her something divine, something personal, a chance of perfection and strength in however small a sphere, which God offers to take or refuse. The task is to find it, develop it, and use it. The chief aim of education should be to help the growing soul to draw out that in itself which is best and make it perfect for a noble use.

The third principle of education is to work from the near to the far, from that 'which is' to that 'which shall be'. The basis of a man's nature is almost always, in addition to his soul's past, his heredity, his surroundings, his nationality, his country, the soil from which he draws sustenance, the air which he breathes, the sights, sounds, habits to which he is accustomed. They mould him not the less powerfully because insensibly, and from that we must begin. We must not take up the nature by the roots from the earth in which it must grow or surround the mind with images and ideas of a life which is alien to that in which it must physically move. A free and natural growth is the condition of genuine development. The past is our foundation, the present our material, the future our aim and summit.

Setting Up a Centre for Higher Education

The challenge that arises is how these principles of integral education can be translated into structures of an institution of higher education. It is not possible to outline all the contours of such an institution but some indications can be given. The physical structure of the institution itself would have to be aesthetic — embodying the aspiration for cleanliness, order and beauty. The pivotal role would that be of the teachers. In addition to academic excellence, they would need to develop some essential qualities, as the Mother says:

> Teachers who are not perfectly calm, who do not have an endurance that never fails, and a quietude which nothing can disturb, who have no self-respect — those who are like that will get nowhere......One must have a perfect attitude to be able to exact a perfect attitude from the students. You cannot ask anyone to do what you don't do yourself. That is a rule.
>
> Those who succeed as teachers here — I don't mean an outer, artificial and superficial success, but becoming truly good teachers — this means that they are capable of making an inner progress of impersonalisation, of eliminating their egoism, controlling their movements, capable of a clear sightedness, an understanding of others and never failing patience.[22]

Thus, the institution must provide structures to enable both outward and inward growth of teachers.The teachers must necessarily work with students. The admission of students cannot be done on the basis of marks alone. While academic criteria will have to be met, they will also have to be tested at the time of admission for qualities of self-awareness, reflection, sincerity and aspiration for truth, perfection and excellence, the best that can be achieved through true honesty of purpose and will.

Again, the very study of subjects will have a different orientation. The aim cannot be mere marks but a true understanding of the subject. If the mind has to be consulted in its own progress, the system will allow the student to explore various areas of study before adopting one. Emphasis on project work, written work, experiential techniques will facilitate exploration of the subject and experiential learning. The examination system will need to be flexible in both time and mode to encourage true understanding rather than rote work.

Programmes would need to be developed to teach concentration, positive thinking and values, the simultaneous habit of meticulous observation and analysis combined with the enthusiasm of aspiring to new ideas. Meditation and self-awareness courses would have to become part of a student's training.

The subjects of study in such institution will of course, have to be determined according to what the institution wishes to specialise in but always remembering the needs of the individual student. It might be useful to examine the various systems of university education prevalent in different countries of the world such as the UK, USA, France, Germany, Singapore and China but the system should be evolved keeping the needs of students in India in mind. Any system that is not of "truly national character" will not move towards its highest aspirations. Since the term "national character" is so fraught with controversy, it is worthwhile to see what Sri Aurobindo means by it:

> Man has not been seen by the thought of India as a living body developed by physical nature which has evolved certain vital propensities, an ego, a mind and a reason, an animal of the genus homo and in our case of the species *homo indicus*, whose whole life and education must be turned towards a satisfaction of these propensities under the government of a trained mind and reason and for the best advantage of the personal and the national ego. It has not been either the turn of her mind to regard man pre-eminently as a reasoning animals, or let us say, widening. The familiar definition, a thinking, feeling and willing natural existence, a mental son of physical nature and his education as a culture of the mental capacities, or to define him as a political, social and economic being and his education as a training that will fit him to be an efficient, productive and well disciplined member of the society and the state. All these are no doubt aspects of the human being and she has given them a considerable prominence subject to her large vision, but they are outward things, parts of the instrumentation of his mind, life and action, not the whole of the real man.
>
> India has seen always in man the individual a soul, a portion of the Divinity enwrapped in mind and body, a conscious manifestation in nature of the universal self and spirit. Always she has distinguished and cultivated in him a mental, an intellectual, an ethical, dynamic and practical, an aesthetic and hedonistic, a vital and physical being, but all these have been seen as powers of a soul that manifests through them and grows with their growth, and yet they are not all the soul, because at the summit of its ascent it arises to something greater than them all, into a spiritual being, and it is in this that she has found the supreme manifestation of the soul of man and his ultimate divine manhood, his paramartha and the highest purusartha. And similarly India has not understood by the nation or people an organised state or an armed and efficient community well prepared for the struggle of life and putting all at the service of the national ego, — that is only the disguise of the national ego — that is only the disguise of iron armour which masks and encumbers the national Purusha, — but a great

communal soul and life that has appeared in the whole and has manifested a nature of its own and a law of that nature, a Swabhava and Swadharma, and embodied it in its intellectual, aesthetic, ethical, dynamic, social and political forms and culture. And equally them our cultural conception of humanity must be in accordance with her ancient vision of the universal manifesting in the human race, evolving through life and mind but with a high ultimate spiritual aim, it must the idea of the spirit, the soul of humanity advancing through struggle and concert towards oneness, increasing its experience and maintaining a needed diversity through the varied culture and life motives of its many peoples, searching for perfection through the development of the powers of the individual and his progress towards a diviner being and life, but feeling out too though more slowly after a similar perfectibility in the life of the race.[23]

Conclusion

Real education is the working of the spirit in the mind and body of both the individual and the nation. Education must serve collective as well as individual aims but without losing sight of the spiritual movement in both. As P.B. Saint-Hilaire points out, "Education will embrace all knowledge in its scope, but will make the whole trend and aim and the permeating spirit not merely worldly efficiency, but self-developing and self-finding. It will pursue physical and psychical science not in order merely to know the world and nature in her processes and to use them for material human ends, but to know through and in an under and overall things the Divine in the world and the ways of the spirit in its masks and behind them."[24]

References

1. The Mother, born Mirra Alfassa in Paris on 21 February 1878, whom Sri Aurobindo entrusted, since November 1926, with the full material and spiritual charge of the Sri Aurobindo Ashram in Pondicherry. Under her guidance, for nearly fifty years, the Ashram grew into a large, many-faceted spiritual community. In 1952 she established Sri Aurobindo International Centre of Education, and in 1968 an international township, Auroville.
2. The Mother, 1974, 1st edition; 2nd revised edition 1996. An International University Centre, "Education of the Future", *Integral Education Series*, Pondicherry: Sri Aurobindo Society, pp. 1-2.
3. Sri Aurobindo, Sri Aurobindo Birth Centenary Library (SABCL), Vol. 15, p. 210, cited by Pavitra (P.B. Saint-Hilaire), *Education and the Aim of Human Life*, 1961, 1st edition; Reprint 1996. Pondicherry: Sri Aurobindo International Centre of Education, p. 37.

4. *Ibid.*, p. 37.
5. *Ibid.*, p. 4.
6. *Ibid.*
7. *Ibid.*, pp. 4-5.
8. Amilcar Cabral was a revolutionary thinker, who was born in 1924 at Bafatá in Guinea-Bissau and murdered in 1973.

   Cabral, "National Liberation and Culture", The Eduardo Mondlane Memorial Lecture delivered at Syracuse University, New York, 20th February, 1970, Return to the Source, (New York, Africa Information Service, ed. 1980), pp. 47-48.
9. University Grants Commission, Annual Report, 2013-14, New Delhi.
10. Sri Aurobindo, 1956, 1st edition; Reprint 1997. "A Preface on National Education", *Sri Aurobindo & the Mother on Education*, Pondicherry: Sri Aurobindo Ashram, pp. 5-6.
11. *Ibid.*, pp. 13-14.
12. Gupta, "Education as the Growth of Consciousness", 1976, 1st edition; 1993, 2nd edition. *Evolution and Earthly Destiny*, Pondicherry: Sri Aurobindo International Centre of Education, p. 197.
13. Sri Aurobindo, 1955, 1st edition; Reprint 1998, *A Practical Guide to Integral Yoga*, Pondicherry: Sri Aurobindo Ashram, p. 173.
14. Sri Aurobindo Birth Centenary Library (SABCL),Vol. 18, p. 9, Cited in *A Divine Life Manifesto: An Integral Education for a Divine Life*, 1995. Jhunjhunu, Rajasthan: Sri Aurobindo Divine Life Education Centre, p. 8.
15. *Collected Works of the Mother*, Vol. 12, p. 9. Cited in Pavitra *Education and the Aim of Human Life*, Pondicherry: Sri Aurobindo International Centre of Education, p. 52.
16. *Ibid.*, Vol. 12, pp. 8, 53.
17. Sri Aurobindo Birth Centenary Library, Vol. 22, p. 238. Cited in *A Divine Life Manifesto.* Op. cit., p. 72.
18. *Collected Works of the Mother*, Vol. 12, p. 3, cited in *A Divine Life Manifesto*, Op. cit., pp. 72-73.
19. *Ibid.* Vol. 12, pp. 22., 73.
20. Sri Aurobindo Birth Centenary Library, Vol. 2, pp. 60-61, Cited in *A Divine Life Manifesto*, Op.cit., p. 211.
21. *Ibid.*, Vol. 17, pp. 204-205, Cited in *A Divine Life Manifesto*, Op.cit., pp. 224-225.
22. *Collected Works of the Mother*, Vol. 12, pp. 353-54. Cited in *A Divine Life Manifesto*, Op.cit., p. 228.
23. *Sri Aurobindo, "A Preface on National Education, 2" Sri Aurobindo Birth Centenary Library,* Vol. 17, Pondicherry: Sri Aurobindo Ashram, 1972, p. 406.
24. Pavitra (P.B. Saint-Hilaire), *Education and the Aim of Human Life*, Op.cit., p. 39.

15

Education and Pandit Madan Mohan Malaviya

The Background

Education was a contested site during the Indian independence movement. Many nationalists involved with the independence movement tried to articulate what would be appropriate to the India genius. The seeds of nationalisation can be traced back to the 1857 Uprising and its aftermath. It was a period of turmoil. While the Uprising may have been seen as a 'mutiny' by many in the British Parliament and English writers, Disraeli, speaking in the House of Commons on July 27, 1857, was quite clear that it, "Was a national revolt and not a military mutiny," recalls Tara Chand in *History of the Freedom Movement in India* (Vol. II). He also points out that Justin McCarthy had said:

> The fact was that throughout the greater part of the north and northwest of the great Indian Peninsula, there was a rebellion of the native races against English power. It was not by any means a merely military mutiny. It was a combination of military grievances, national hatred and religious fanaticism against the English occupation of India. The native princes and native soldiers were in it. The Mohammedan and the Hindu forgot their old religious antipathies to join against the Christian.[1]

So, the seed of nationalism was planted at that time itself. Post-1857, the British Empire got firmly established as India came under the direct rule of the British Crown in 1858 but the counter-movement, the determination to be an independent country in spite of the 1857 defeat, got strengthened.

The events of 1857, however, left a scar. After the Uprising had been quelled, there erupted a heightened religious consciousness that was divisive.

Schisms developed not only between Hindus, Muslims, and Christians but also among the orthodox Hindus, the Arya Samajis, and the Jains. The British contempt for Indians, for their religion and culture did not help matters. Apart from the missionary propaganda, many civil and military officers too seemed to behave like evangelists. For example, Rev. M. Edmond issued a circular letter from Calcutta in which he stated:

> The time appears to have come when earnest consideration should be given to the subject, whether or not all men should embrace the same religion. Railways, steam vessels and the electric telegraph are rapidly uniting all the people of the earth. Christian is the only religion, which claims to have come from god by way of direct revelation. This is the only religion, which can confer happiness in the world and in the other world whose conditions are revealed by it. It is our wish to see the churches filled with Indians, where not only foreigners but the people of the country also will proclaim regularly the good news of the Christian gospel and where men and women will be required to seek repentance from their sins and to prepare themselves for meeting god; and where children will be taught morality and truth.[2]

Such an attitude tended to be counter-productive as it led to the desire to defend Hinduism and to strengthen it, especially among the educated Hindus. It brought together like-minded influential leaders of Indian society who thought of setting up institutions that could rise above narrow sectarian interests, serve the cause of nation building and provide education on the lines of *Sanatana Dharma* while combining it with the best in western scientific methods. This, they felt, would provide "a broad liberation of mind and religious spirit" and this was the thought and vision that lay behind Pt. Madan Mohan Malaviya establishing Banaras Hindu University, which he founded seeking the help of not only prominent people but all people in society.

Preoccupation with Education

By 1890, organisations such as the Arya Samaj, the Ramakrishna Mission and the Theosophists had heightened their activities. These movements made such good progress that a National Conference was held in 1900 in Delhi under the presidency of the Maharaja of Darbhanga. The aim was to unite the various Hindu organisations and this led to the formation of the Bharata Dharma Mahamandala in 1902 with Pandit Din Dayal Sharma as its Secretary.

It is notable that education was one of the important objectives of the Bharat Dharma Mahamandala because of the serious apprehensions caused by the proselytising activities of the missionaries especially through the mode of education. The stated objects of the Mahamandala were to:

- Promote Hindu religious education in accordance with the *Sanatana Dharma* to diffuse the knowledge of the Vedas, Smritis, Puranas and other Hindu Shastras and to introduce, in the light of such knowledge, useful reforms into Hindu life and society;
- Promote and enrich Sanskrit and Hindi literatures in all the branches;
- Introduce such useful reforms as may be warranted by the Shastras in the management of the Hindu charitable and religious institutions and *tirthas*, that is, sacred places;
- Establish, affiliate and control Branch Sabhas in different parts of India;
- Support the existing Hindu colleges, schools, libraries and publishing establishments and found new ones in consonance with the object of the association.

This period also saw an increase in commercial activities, and with it came, "the extension of the means of communication and transport, large increase in India's foreign trade and modernisation of India's economy...." India was drawn into international trade and was seen as an important trading unit. European-like business organisations came into being and profits rose benefiting the rich businessmen.

Poverty, Industrial Growth and Importance of Education

However, amidst this progress, the country went through a series of calamities and millions died for sheer want of food. The unsatisfactory financial position of the government resulted in heavier taxation, the decline of Indian handicrafts, and lack of employment opportunities. This, with the dominance of the Europeans in civil and military services caused great discontent, which became a major cause for arousing opposition to British rule. Tara Chand concludes:

> The analysis of the economy of India leads inevitably to the conclusion that basically the poverty of India was the consequence of foreign rule — the system of administration introduced by the British in India. It followed that no improvement in the economic conditions of the people could be expected in the character of the government. It was necessary, therefore, to agitate for a change in government, or the introduction of a representative and democratic system, for the transfer of political power from the British to Indian hands. Important and

> urgent as the economic questions were, their solution depended upon the attainment of self-rule by India.[3]

Pandit Malaviya felt the pain of India's poverty and pauperisation under British rule keenly. He described the position of the country in the following words in his speech as President, Indian National Congress, at the Lahore Session of 1909:

> The national income is low and therefore the national prosperity is low. People are dying with plague and malaria. Famines are claiming a large toll and people are unprosperous and unhappy. That is the condition of the country. On the other hand, you find that this is the country most richly endowed with natural resources. It is the country whose people are not lacking in intelligence and industry, and living most simple life. They are not addicted to crime as some of the most advanced countries are. Can there be anything more sad and disappointing than to find the people as still in such unfortunate condition that this country should be lie so low in the scale of nation? And if this is so what is our duty for the motherland?[4]

Malaviya advocated the promotion of technical education and indigenous industries as a remedy for India poverty.

The victory of Japan over Russia in 1905 in the first great war of the twentieth century over Manchuria and Korea, arising out of the rival imperial ambitions of the two nations also encouraged Indian nationalists to think that the Japanese had succeeded because of their economic power and their high degree of scientific technical ability. This gave birth to economic nationalism and strengthened the Swadeshi Movement originally initiated by the boycott campaign in Bengal. It not only became a political weapon, but also led to the development of small-scale industries all over the country. Under the urge of this economic nationalism, large sums were raised for sending students abroad for technical education. It is therefore, particularly understandable why leaders such as Swami Vivekananda, Rabindranath Tagore and Madan Mohan Malaviya, all admired Japan and wanted to incorporate in India's vision for her future, Japan's way of combining art and utility, its emphasis on technical education and its aesthetics. With the fusion of political and economic demands, the trading classes who had remained largely aloof from politics began to align themselves with the political class.

The First World War opened up further opportunities in India for industrial development and by the end of it, the government had to yield to public pressure and appoint an Industrial Commission to recommend how Indian industries could be best financed and developed. When the legislatures were enlarged in the post-war period and more power was placed in the hands of the trading classes, demands were made in the name of economic nationalism, which met with a degree of success that helped Indian industry.

Many leading Indian trading and business families began to adopt the British modes of commerce and exploit the new opportunities. With this, the colonial society provided mechanisms to rise socially. These became especially important for the aspiring new class of government officials, urban professionals, businessmen and publicists. The most efficient, which spanned both colonial and indigenous arenas of public domain, was philanthropy and patronage of charitable, educational and religious institutions. This class contributed to medical and educational philanthropy and supported public libraries, the latter being a new addition to the colonial state's educational agenda.

In a period of rapid modernisation when the religious identity was in the process of being negotiated, reformulated and asserted, the institution of caste was rediscovered and several associations were formed on that basis. This was in tune with the rising culture of the formation of associations, a natural outcome of networks formed through philanthropic, trading and professional activities. These were also invested with moral messages and so emphasised social service and reformist activities. Agendas of community uplift had a clearly patriotic thrust and were seen eventually as a means to uplift the Indian nation at large. In the modern public arena, caste affiliation came to be portrayed as, "an expression of citizenship and spiritually informed nationality which had the potential to fulfil and regenerate the modern Hindu."[5]

The culture of forming associations also saw a proliferation of debating clubs, scientific institutes and literary or reformist societies. With its focus on education, literature, and social reform, this new form of organised indigenous agency grew out of, and catered to, the need of the educated Indian elite to debate the implications of colonial rule and participate in the process of modernisation of the Indian. There were intersections of both synergy and conflict between various sections of people whether they were rising professionals, small-scale house owners, old service communities, religious grouping, merchants and others. Each of them attempted to establish local areas of influence. Gradually, the grip of the influential old *rais* (elite, rich) families over the social life of the city weakened and professional men and publicists began to replace them gradually as intermediaries with the local authorities. An outbreak of 'communal' tension between 1909 and 1917 provides an insight into the shifts in local influence and power. While the members of the old *rais* families and some powerful new traders continued to play an important role in the maintenance of peace, professional men and publicists were found taking a much more active part. For example, during the outbreaks of 1917 and after, active lawyer-politicians such as Purushottam Das Tandon and Madan Mohan Malaviya, consulted with the authorities and arranged bodies of conciliation.[6]

Macaulay, Modernisation and Education

Throughout this turbulent period of struggle for independence when there was a strong desire to ameliorate a lot of people, national leaders were constantly preoccupied with the kind of education that needed to be given in India if the country was to be freed and made prosperous. Thomas Macaulay laid the foundations of higher education in India and he had a two-fold aim:

- Produce cheap clerical labour to serve the needs of the colonial empire.
- Create a class of people who would perpetuate the legacy of the empire by looking down upon their own, cultural values and upholding those of the British ruling class.

As Amilcar Cabral pointed out, the experience of colonial domination showed that the coloniser provoked and encouraged the cultural alienation of a part of the population by the so-called assimilation of indigenous elites, distancing them from the popular masses.[7] As a result, a section of the people assimilated the colonisers' mentality, considering itself culturally superior to its own people and looking down upon their cultural values. This was the situation of the majority of colonised intellectuals and their position was consolidated by increase in social privileges.

The University system that was set up by the colonisers for their own ends was ironically been expanded and strengthened in independent India rather than being adapted to meet the requirements of a newly emerging nation. Why did this happen? Because no sincere thought was given to what was sought to be achieved through higher education. There was a turmoil of ideas, and perhaps our minds were too conditioned by the West and its institutions while being critical of our own heritage, with some justification as these had degenerated for a variety of reasons, to be able to achieve clarity of purpose and base for our educational institutions on our own heritage.

Indian civilisation and culture met the European at a time of social disintegration and political anarchy. It was the evening of the past from which a new age had to start and the impact of the West with its new ideas and, in many respects, opposite civilisational values provided a challenge. While it created a sense of great inferiority with regard to their tradition and heritage in Indians, it simultaneously forced them to take a hard look at it, reassess it and to come to terms with it. In the process, education became a dominant theme in the minds of many national leaders who attempted to make connections between the past and the modern knowledge and ideas coming from the West.

The question arises as to what the modernist agenda was and what form it took in India because of the European contact and British rule. The British highlighted the weaknesses of the traditional social order of the Indians; they inferiorised their culture, epistemology and even the people as a race. This provoked a reaction on two planes. On one, the traditional order was found inadequate to meet the challenges of Western modernity. On the second, the cultural hegemonisation by the colonial state was found unacceptable as it bred an anxiety about the survival of tradition itself hence the debates on tradition and modernity.

For most, 'modern' became associated with 'western' and all the debates took place from the point of view of how to come to terms with modernisation and westernisation and the vision of progress and economic prosperity. What was 'western' provided the model and showed the way. It came to be believed that change could only be brought about in the 'western' way; that the only possible route and finally acceptable model was the 'western' one. The total acceptance of this model of modernisation created the relationship of the teacher and the taught between the West and the East. The idea turned into a conviction that to become modern, people must learn the knowledge system of the West, its lifestyle, and behaviour patterns. In effect, the East must become the mirror image of the West. Britain used this not only to strengthen British colonialism but also to project Indians as incapable of self-rule, and the white man's burden being to civilise India. Pt. Madan Mohan Malaviya was perhaps the first to combine the scientific modern western thought with the Indian heritage of philosophy and other learning. Before he enunciated his vision for the Banaras Hindu University and then worked tirelessly to establish it, he was preceded by some of the best minds articulating their vision for education in independent India.

Indian Thinking on Education

The contact with the West brought its difficulties but it shook India out of its complacency. The first generation of intellectuals arose with their western education. They were intensely patriotic and impatient to see a transformed India, modernised completely in body, mind and spirit. But they realised that colonial education was not the answer. Sri Aurobindo voicing his disillusionment with it said:

> All that appears to be almost unanimously agreed on is that the teaching in the existing schools and universities has been bad in kind and in addition denationalising, degrading and impoverishing to the national mind, soul and character because it is overshadowed by a foreign hand and foreign in aim, method, substance and spirit.[8]

Swami Vivekananda saw education as a "man-making" process. His ideas were moored in Vedanta as he emphasised the need to awaken man to his spiritual self through education. The evil of present-day education for him was that it had no definite goal to pursue and hence the teacher himself was floundering. But education was a means of arousing an individual to the awareness of the true Self. The soul or the spirit, however, could not be developed in isolation from the body and mind. Therefore harmonious development of the body, mind and soul was required. It is not "the amount of information that is put in your brain and runs riot there, undigested all your life." It is a process by which character is formed, strength of mind is increased and intellect sharpened; as a result of which one can stand on one's own feet. While he advocated the use of the mother tongue as the right medium of instruction, he also prescribed the learning of English and Sanskrit. English was necessary for mastering Western science and technology, Sanskrit led one into the depths of our vast store of classics. In his scheme of education, Swami Vivekananda included all those studies that were necessary for the all-round development of the body, mind, and soul of the individual. These can be brought under the broad heads of physical culture, aesthetics, classics, language, religion, science and technology. According to Swamiji, the culture of India has its roots in her spiritual values. The time-tested values are to be imbibed in the thoughts and lives of the students through the study of the epics and scriptures such as Ramayana, Mahabharata, Bhagavad Gita, Vedas and Upanishads. This will keep the perennial flow of our spiritual values into the world culture.

Rabindranath Tagore also was completely unhappy with the colonial education that had been established in India. He said,

> For us, modern education is relevant only to turning our clerks, lawyers, doctors, magistrates and policemen......This education has not reached the farmer, the oil grinder, nor the potter. No other education society has been struck with such disaster...If ever a truly Indian university is

> established, it must from the very beginning implement India's own knowledge of economics, agriculture, health, medicine and of all other everyday science from the surrounding villages. Then alone can the school or university become the centre of the country's way of living. This school must practice agriculture, dairying and weaving using the best modern methods...I have proposed to call this school Visva Bharati.[9]

Tagore tried to grapple with the question of what Indian Education should be:

> What would truly be Indian education? We must try to understand how Indian genius expressed itself. Unless we try to put these together and discover the integrating factors behind these diverse streams of thought and make them a subject of study at our universities, we would only be borrowing knowledge from abroad. The natural habitat for knowledge is where it is produced. The main task of universities is to produce knowledge, its dissemination is its secondary function. We must invite those intellectuals and scholars to our universities who are engaged in research, invention or creative activity.[10]

While nations sought primarily to give their citizens a means of livelihood through education, Tagore believed that there was a more important aim —that of personal fulfilment and self-improvement. It was important to borrow knowledge and experience from abroad, but not to use them as the foundation for Indian education. Even so, if there was one European quality which Indian university students needed to acquire, it was "the desire to know, to find out about the laws of nature and to use them for the betterment of the conditions of human beings." It was fully realised that science and its applications in the form of technology had led to the power and prosperity of Western countries. Unless India acquired the knowledge of science and technology through its universities and schools, poverty and powerlessness would continue. To transform life and make it richer, healthier and more educated, it was imperative to accept technology and science. But Tagore wanted science to be taught along with India's own philosophical and spiritual knowledge at Indian universities.

As far as Mohandas Karamchand Gandhi was concerned, "No one rejected colonial education as sharply and as completely as Gandhi did, nor did anyone else put forward an alternative as radical as the one he proposed,"[11] to use Krishna Kumar's words. Education for him not only moulded the new generation, but also reflected a society's fundamental assumptions about itself and the individuals which compose it. He himself had been a beneficiary of Western education and while in South Africa, urged people to take advantage of it. But gradually he became opposed to English education as he saw it as an instrument of subjugation of the people of India. His experience in the freedom struggle and the fact that all official, legal, and commercial interaction had to be in English, which divided the elite from the masses, the ruler from the ruled, thus disempowering the vast majority of the people, made him firmly believe that education should be in the native tongue. He did not blame the British for imposing English because he saw that it was logical for them to mould Indians into their ways of thinking and living as this was a way of consolidating the Empire. Indians were to blame as they had accepted this situation.

To remedy the situation, Mahatma Gandhi turned the education system on its head through his concept of 'basic education' when he insisted that craft had to be at the core of learning. Hence, students had to be educated in the production processes involved in craft such as spinning, weaving, leather work, pottery, metal work, basket-making and book-binding, that had up to now been the monopoly of specific caste groups in the lowest stratum of the traditional social hierarchy. This was in contrast to India's own tradition of education as well as the colonial education system that emphasised skills such as literacy and acquisition of knowledge, which was the stronghold of the upper castes. Giving primacy to craft meant empowering the child belonging to the lowest stratum of society. It was a way of restructuring opportunities and bringing about societal transformation.[12]

Pt. Madan Mohan Malaviya and Banaras Hindu University

Banaras Hindu University was Madan Mohan Malaviya's attempt to give shape to what he thought would be education appropriate for an emerging independent nation. The idea of the university was born out of his deep love for Hindu culture and its spiritual ideas but the scheme for the university was drawn up through discussions with his friends and with the cooperation of Mrs Annie Besant, the Maharajadhiraj of Darbhanga, and the Maharaja of Banaras. The Banaras Hindu University Bill was introduced in the Imperial Legislative Council on March 22, 1915. For the University, Pt. Madan Mohan Malaviya singlehandedly and untiringly raised funds. Apart from the individuals he knew, Malaviya went to the Maharajas of the States of Jodhpur, Kashmir and others who motivated their citizens to help in the cause. The idea of founding a Hindu University at Banaras won support from the entire country, from the rich and poor alike. As has been said in *Visionary of Modern India: Madan Mohan Malaviya*, Mahatma Gandhi acknowledged that there was no greater "beggar than Pandit Madan Mohan Malaviyaji on the face of the earth. He has never begged for himself;

by the grace of God he has never been in want, but he became a voluntary beggar for causes he has made his own, and God has always filled his bowl in an overflowing measure."[13] He called Pandit Malaviya the "Prince of Beggars."[14] The Maharajas of Darbhanga, Bikaner and many other states not only donated funds, but also accompanied him during his fund-collection tours. A Sadhu gave him his *chadar*, a beggar gave a rupee, a poor eighty-year-old-widow a few rupees, a mail runner 2 annas, a herdsman 8 annas, poor *chapras*is, *patwar*is and *madar*is (peons, land supervisors and street performers) their salaries. That made him also the "Beggar of the beggars!"[15]

Since the huge amount collected had come largely from Hindus, he was instrumental in limiting the membership of the university count to Hindus, which lay him open to the charge of communalism. He defended himself by saying, "The Hindus who might make benefactions in favour of the institution should feel satisfied that their charity would be administered by men who will be in religious sympathy with them." In the Senate, which was the academic body of the university, he pointed out, one-fourth of the members might be non-Hindus so that the cooperation of non-Hindus in the ordering of the academic activity of the university was assured.

The importance that he attached to the economic development of the country made Pt. Madan Mohan Malaviya combine the teaching of science and technology with that of religion. The Colleges of Agriculture, Engineering, Mining, Metallurgy and Geology, the Ayurvedic College and an Allopathic Hospital, which was named after Pandit Sunder Lal, the first Vice-Chancellor of the University, were started soon after the University was established. This made the Hindu University pre-eminent among the then existing Indian universities.

Parmanand Singh and Sunita Singh have analysed the philosophy of Pt. Madan Mohan Malaviya's educational vision.[16] He initially wanted the proposed university to promote the study of Hindu Shastras and Sanskrit literature generally as a means of preserving and popularising, for the benefit of Hindus in particular and of the world at large, the best thought and culture of the Hindus, and all that was good and great in the ancient civilisation of India; to promote learning and research generally in the arts and science in all branches; to advance and diffuse such scientific, technical and professional knowledge combined with the necessary practical training as is best calculated to help in promoting indigenous industries, in developing the material resources of the country; and to promote the building of the character in youth by religion and ethics as an integral part of education. So, these objectives show Pandit Madan Mohan Malaviya's vision of higher education. On the one side, it was to reflect the Vedas, the Upanishads, all of India's ancient scriptures and texts; and on other side, reflect science, technology, and the integration of medical, engineering, agriculture and technical education.

He dreamt of a new kind of curriculum taught by a new kind of school for a self-reliant society. To attain this end, he provided the tentative patterns of vocational studies in which cultivation of initiative and self-help were the dominant objectives. The idea was to create an appropriate education system that could meet the urgent social and economic needs of a poor country. Science and technology could be harnessed to usher in material prosperity but without losing the ethical values embedded in India's cultural, philosophical and religious heritage. This was a revolutionary idea as is evident from the comment in the *Report of the Commission on Christian Higher Education in India and Burma*:

> Hinduism and the railway bridge were coming to terms with each other. This could be seen in the untiring efforts of Pt. Madan Mohan Malaviya that had led to the creation of a modern Hindu University, whose purpose among others is to stimulate studies in Hindu literature and culture, religion and philosophy. But what has it actually accomplished? The recognised and apparently outstanding achievement of the Hindu University was the creation of an efficient department of engineering.[17]

Therefore, the essence of Pandit Malaviya's vision was that if India had to be freed and made into a prosperous nation, it was necessary to impart holistic education that could enthuse a transformative process in India. For this, industrial and technical education was necessary.

His far-reaching vision also made him realise the importance of commercial education as a factor in national and international progress. It had been recognised in the leading countries of the West, that

> The leaders of commerce and business need to be scientifically trained just as a doctor or a barrister or professional man is...Modern experience shows us that business requires administrative capacity of the very highest type. It needs not merely technical knowledge, but also the power of dealing with new situations, of going forward at the right moment and of controlling labour.[18]

These are just the qualities, which universities have always claimed as being their special business to foster. Yet India's own cultural and spiritual heritage had to form the foundation of the educational vision because every nation had its own genius and could only grow according to it. The prospectus of the proposed Banaras Hindu University noted:

> ...mere industrial advancement cannot restore India to the position which she once occupied among the civilised countries of the world. And even industrial prosperity cannot be attained amongst all concerned, and these can only prevail and endure amongst those who are fair in all their dealings, strict in the observance of good faith and steadfast in their loyalty to truth. Such men cannot be found in sufficiently large numbers to keep a society in an organised, efficient and healthy condition, when the society to which they belong is not under the abiding influence of a great religion acting as a living force.[19]

The proposed university placed the formation of character in youth as one of its principal objects. Pandit Malaviya said:

> It will seek not merely to turn out men as engineers, scientists, doctors, merchants, theologians, but also as men of high character, probity and honour, whose conduct through life will show that they bear the hallmark of a great university. Such character can be most securely built upon the solid foundation of religion.
>
> Religion enjoins truthfulness, integrity, fortitude, self-help, self-respect, self-control, abstinence from injury, forgiveness, compassion; philanthropy, hospitality, unselfish action for public good, reverence for age and authority, discipline and devotion to duty, and above all the service of God through the service of man and friendliness to the whole creation. In short, all the virtues which elevate human character, support human society, and promote peace on earth and goodwill among men are inculcated by means of solemn injunctions, touching anecdotes and eloquent discourses. Hindu philosophy cooperates with Hindu religious literature in the task of leading man into the path of righteousness, in as much as it teaches him that every creature around him is his own self in another guise, and that he rises in the scale of being by doing good to those with whom he comes in contact and degrades himself by injuring his fellow creatures.[20]

Pandit Malaviya did not want to follow the India of 5,000 years ago. Dr S. Radhakrishnan said:

> He adjusted himself to the spirit of modern times and did his level best to inspire his countrymen with progressive impulses and utilise science for the service of the man. While preserving the imperishable treasures of our past, he moved forward with the times. He was responsible to an extent for the renaissance of our spiritual heritage. The renewal of

those ideals and their application to the needs of our country is an important lesson which we take from the life of Malaviyaji.[21]

The Banaras Hindu University Bill was introduced in the Imperial Legislative Council on March 22, 1915. In the discussion on the Bill, Malaviyaji answered the charge that he was creating a denominational institution that would encourage sectarianism and divisiveness:

> The University will be a denominational institution, but not a sectarian one. It will not promote narrow sectarianism but a broad liberation of mind and a religious spirit which will promote brotherly feeling between man and man...I believe instruction in the truth of religion, will tend to produce men who, if they are true to their religion, will be true to their God, their King and their country....Where the true religious spirit is inculcated there must be an elevating feeling of humility and where there is love of God there will be a greater love and less hatred of man....[22]

Thus, Pt. Madan Mohan Malaviya tried to bring together his vision of modern education most suited to India in the establishment of Banaras Hindu University that was to be the meeting ground of science, humanities, living indigenous knowledge systems and spiritual values.

References

1. Tara Chand, 1967, Reprint 1974, *History of the Freedom Movement in India*, Vol. II, Delhi: Publications Division, Ministry of Information and Broadcasting, p. 41.
2. *Ibid.*, p. 66.
3. *Ibid.*, p. 348.
4. Singh, Parmanand and Sunita Singh, 2012. "Malaviya as a Great Visionary for Higher Education: Celebrating his 150th Birthday", *International Journal of Scientific and Research Publications*, Vol. 2, Issue 3, March 2012, www.ijsrp.org
5. Bayly, Susan, 1999. Caste, Society and Politics in India from the Eighteenth Century to the Modern Age in *The New Cambridge History of India*, Vol. 4, Part 3, Cambridge: Cambridge University Press, pp. 97-232.
6. Bayly, C.A. 1971. "Local Control in Indian Towns – The Case of Allahabad 1880-1920," *Modern Asian Studies*, Vol. 5, Issue 4 (1971), pp. 282-298.
7. Cabral, Amilcar. "National Liberation and Culture," http://www.historyisa-weapon.com/defcon 1/cabralnlac.html
8. Sri Aurobindo, 1972. "A Preface on National Education," 1920, The Hour of God and other Writings, SABCL, Vol.17, Pondicherry.
9. Jha, Narmadeshwar. "Rabindranath Tagore, 1861-1941," ww.ibe.unesco.org/publications/thinkerspdf/tagore
10. *Ibid.*

11. Krishna Kumar, "Mohandas Karamchand Gandhi (1869-1948)", www.ibe.-unesco.org/publications/thinkerspdf/Gandhie
12. *Ibid.*
13. Maini, S.K.,Vishwanath Pandey and K. Chandramouli, *Visionary of Modern India: Madan Mohan Malaviya*, New Delhi: Roli Books, 2011 p. 116.
14. *Ibid.*
15. *Ibid.*, p. 112.
16. Singh, Parmanand and Sunita Singh, 2012. "Malaviya as a Great Visionary for Higher Education: Celebrating his 150th Birthday," *International Journal of Scientific and Research Publication*, Vol. 2, Issue 3, March 2012, www.ijsrp.org
17. Report of the Commission on Christian Higher Education in India. 1931. An Enquiry into the place of the Christian College in Modern India London: Oxford University Press, p. 31.
18. Maini, S.K., Vishwanath Pandey and K. Chandramouli, Op.cit. pp. 102-103.
19. *Ibid.*, p. 103.
20. *Ibid.*
21. *Ibid.*, pp. 103-104.
22. *Ibid.*, p. 107.

Index

B

C

J

T